Cultural and Environmental Change on Rapa Nui

Rapa Nui, one of the world's most isolated island societies and home to the *moai*, has been at the centre of a tense debate for the past decade. Some see it as the site of a dramatic cultural collapse occurring before Western contact, where a self-inflicted ecocide was brought on by the exhaustion of resources. Others argue that the introduction of Western pathogens and the slave raids of 1862 were to blame for the near extinction of the otherwise resilient Rapa Nui people.

Cultural and Environmental Change on Rapa Nui brings together the latest studies by prominent Rapa Nui researchers from all over the world to explore the island's past and present, from its discovery by Polynesians, through the first documented contact with Western culture in 1722, to the 20th century. The exiting new volume looks beyond the *moai* to examine such questions as: was there was a cultural collapse; how did the Rapa Nui react to Westerners; and what responses did the Rapa Nui develop to adjust to naturally – or humanly –induced environmental change?

This volume will appeal to scholars and professionals in the fields of history, archaeology and ecology, as well as anyone with an interest in the challenges of sustainable resource management, and the contentious history of Rapa Nui itself.

Sonia Haoa Cardinali is a Rapa Nui archaeologist with extensive experience – 41 years – in Rapa Nui archaeology. She began her work with Dr William Mulloy and the Orongo restoration project. She has worked with a multitude of international scholars in the management and direction of island excavations that include some of the largest and most impressive monuments on the island, and some 28,000 sites. She has directed the comprehensive island-wide survey of archaeological features and is also keenly interested in the prehistoric ecology of the island and has actively pursued a program of reforestation in conjunction with CONAF. Her abiding interest is in the way humans everywhere relate to the landscape and environment, and how to give back to the present the rich discoveries made in the past.

Kathleen B. Ingersoll, BA, MA, PhD. Her academic interests lie in anthropology, environmental and landscape archaeology, food/horticulture, historic preservation and museum studies, and the interpretation of landscapes, especially in the eastern US and Polynesia. Her latest work includes consulting on museum exhibits for The Mata Ki Te Rangi Foundation on Rapa Nui, both on the island of Rapa Nui and in Tenerife, Spain. She is also a Master Leave No Trace environmental educator and believes in the importance of understanding the relationship between humans, nature, and heritage on a global scale. In this vein, she successfully designed and implemented study tours to Rapa Nui that combined Leave No Trace training with archaeology.

Daniel W. Ingersoll, Jr. His interests include historical archaeology, experimental archaeology, American culture, symbolism, agriculture, and Rapa Nui culture. Ingersoll received his A.B. and Ph.D. in anthropology from Harvard College and Harvard University, respectively. Now professor emeritus, he taught at the University of Massachusetts, Amherst, and then St. Mary's College of Maryland for 37 years until retirement. Publications include *Experimental Archaeology*, with William K. Macdonald and John Yellen and *Mirror and Metaphor: Material and Social Constructions of Reality*, with Gordon Bronitsky. Ingersoll's interest in Rapa Nui studies began in 2006.

Christopher M. Stevenson received his doctorate from The Pennsylvania State University in 1984 for his work on the archaeology of Easter Island (Rapa Nui). Since that time he has worked within cultural resource management and academic contexts and continues to focus on Easter Island prehistory. Since 1988 he has led over 19 expeditions to Rapa Nui and works collaboratively with Rapa Nui/Chilean archaeologists. He has served as a Fulbright Specialist in Chile. His other interests include obsidian hydration dating, the Colonial archaeology of Virginia and Eastern United States prehistory. Currently he is an Assistant Professor Anthropology in the School of World Studies, Virginia Commonwealth University.

Routledge Studies in Archaeology

For more information on this series, please visit www.routledge.com/ Routledge-Studies-in-Archaeology/book-series/RSTARCH

23 **Exploring the Materiality of Food 'Stuffs'**
   Transformations, Symbolic Consumption and Embodiment(s)
   Edited by Louise Steel and Katharina Zinn

24 **Archaeologies of "Us" and "Them"**
   Debating History, Heritage and Indigeneity
   Edited by Charlotta Hillerdal, Anna Karlström and Carl-Gösta Ojala

25 **Balkan Dialogues**
   Negotiating Identity Between Prehistory And The Present
   Edited by Maja Gori and Maria Ivanova

26 **Material Worlds**
   Archaeology, Consumption, and the Road to Modernity
   Edited by Barbara J. Heath, Eleanor E. Breen, and Lori A. Lee

27 **An Archaeology of Skill**
   Metalworking Skill and Material Specialization in Early Bronze Age Central Europe
   Maikel H.G. Kuijpers

28 **Dwelling**
   Heidegger, Archaeology, Mortality
   Philip Tonner

29 **New Perspectives in Cultural Resource Management**
   Edited by Francis P. Mcmanamon

30 **Cultural and Environmental Change on Rapa Nui**
   Edited by Sonia Haoa Cardinali, Kathleen B. Ingersoll, Christopher M. Stevenson, and Daniel W. Ingersoll, Jr.

Cultural and Environmental Change on Rapa Nui

Edited by
Sonia Haoa Cardinali,
Kathleen B. Ingersoll,
Daniel W. Ingersoll, Jr., and
Christopher M. Stevenson

LONDON AND NEW YORK

First published 2018
by Routledge
2 Park Square, Milton Park, Abingdon, Oxon OX14 4RN

and by Routledge
711 Third Avenue, New York, NY 10017

Routledge is an imprint of the Taylor & Francis Group, an informa business

© 2018 selection and editorial matter, Sonia Haoa Cardinali, Kathleen B. Ingersoll, Daniel W. Ingersoll, Jr., and Christopher M. Stevenson; individual chapters, the contributors

The right of Sonia Haoa Cardinali, Kathleen B. Ingersoll, Daniel W. Ingersoll, Jr., and Christopher M. Stevenson to be identified as the authors of the editorial material, and of the authors for their individual chapters, has been asserted in accordance with sections 77 and 78 of the Copyright, Designs and Patents Act 1988.

All rights reserved. No part of this book may be reprinted or reproduced or utilised in any form or by any electronic, mechanical, or other means, now known or hereafter invented, including photocopying and recording, or in any information storage or retrieval system, without permission in writing from the publishers.

Trademark notice: Product or corporate names may be trademarks or registered trademarks, and are used only for identification and explanation without intent to infringe.

British Library Cataloguing-in-Publication Data
A catalogue record for this book is available from the British Library

Library of Congress Cataloging-in-Publication Data
A catalog record for this book has been requested

ISBN: 978-1-138-24001-8 (hbk)
ISBN: 978-1-315-29445-2 (ebk)

Typeset in Sabon
by Apex CoVantage, LLC

Printed and bound in Great Britain by
TJ International Ltd, Padstow, Cornwall

Contents

List of contributors ix

Introduction 1

1 Prehistoric settlement, ancient gardens and population dynamics on the Hiva Hiva lava flow, Rapa Nui, Chile 9
CHRISTOPHER M. STEVENSON, THEGN N. LADEFOGED AND OLIVER CHADWICK

2 A vanished landscape – phenomena and eco-cultural consequences of extensive deforestation in the prehistory of Rapa Nui 32
ANDREAS MIETH AND HANS-RUDOLF BORK

3 The potential for palm extinction on Rapa Nui by disease 59
KATHLEEN B. INGERSOLL AND DANIEL W. INGERSOLL, JR.

4 New interpretations of pollen data from Easter Island 74
JOHN FLENLEY AND KEVIN BUTLER

5 Subsistence strategies on Rapa Nui (Easter Island): prehistoric gardening practices on Rapa Nui and how they relate to current farming practices 87
JOAN A. WOZNIAK

6 By the Quebrada of Ava Ranga Uka A Toroke Hau – about landscape transformation and the significance of water and trees 113
BURKHARD VOGT AND ANNETTE KÜHLEM

7 Re-use of the sacred: late period petroglyphs applied to
red scoria topknots from Easter Island (Rapa Nui) 133
GEORGIA LEE, PAUL BAHN, PAUL HORLEY,
SONIA HAOA CARDINALI, LILIAN GONZÁLEZ NUALART,
AND NINOSKA CUADROS HUCKE

8 An earthly paradise? Easter Island (Rapa Nui) as seen by
the eighteenth-century European explorers 156
JAN J. BOERSEMA

9 The impact of the whalers and other foreign visitors
before 1862 179
RHYS RICHARDS

10 Healing a culture's reputation: challenging the cultural
labeling and libeling of the Rapanui 188
KATHLEEN B. INGERSOLL, DANIEL W. INGERSOLL AND
ANDREW BOVE

11 Reflections 203

Index 209

Contributors

Paul Bahn, M.A., Ph.D., F.S.A. is British archaeologist, freelance researcher, specializing in prehistoric art, especially that of the Ice Age, and also in Easter Island. Co-author with John Flenley of the widely read book entitled "Easter Island, Earth Island", 1992. An updated 4th edition of "Easter Island, Earth Island" will be published in 2017.

Jan J. Boersema (1947) is professor of Principles of Environmental Sciences at the Institute of Environmental Sciences (CML) at Leiden University. He studied biology at the University of Groningen, and at the same university gained his Ph.D. in theology with his thesis *The Torah and the Stoics on Humankind and Nature* (Brill, Leiden). He has been a lecturer at Groningen University, a professor at the Vrije Universiteit Amsterdam and is former secretary-general of the Council for the Environment at the Dutch Ministry of Housing, Spatial Planning and the Environment. He has published work on the environment, theology, history, philosophy and criminology in scientific publications, and has been editor of several academic volumes. In 2009–2010 he was a fellow of the University of Cambridge. His current research relates to the question: how green is progress? In this he examines the issues from a philosophical and historical perspective. Boersema was editor-in-chief of a Dutch textbook *Basisboek Milieukunde* (Boom, Amsterdam), of which more than 35,000 copies were sold between the years 1984 and 2000. He was editor of *Environmental Values*, and since 2002 has been editor-in-chief of the *Journal of Integrated Environmental Sciences* and the textbook *Principles of Environmental Sciences* (Springer, Berlin 2009). His most recent book is *The Survival of Easter Island. Dwindling Resources and Cultural Resilience* (Cambridge University Press, 2015).

Hans-Rudolf Bork is geographer, soil scientist and professor for Ecosystem Research at Kiel University, Germany. He is investigating the long-term impact of humans on the development of landscapes, namely on soils and sediments in Europe, on Easter Island, on Robinson Crusoe Island, in China and in Ethiopia.

x   *Contributors*

Andrew P. Bove was born and raised in Columbia, Maryland. He received his M.A. from the George Washington University, in Washington, D.C., and his B.A. from St. Mary's College of Maryland, in St. Mary's City, MD, where he developed his interests in cultural anthropology and folklife. He has lengthy experience with cultural documentation through oral history and has studied diverse topics including oyster aquaculture in the Chesapeake Bay, the history of tobacco barns in Southern Maryland, and the nexus of UNESCO, the environment and tourism in Rapa Nui, Chile. He currently lives and works in the Washington D.C. metro area.

Kevin Butler has spent a number of years in a research role at Massey University mostly using palynology to seek answers to questions in paleo research, particularly Pacific prehistory, but later dabbling in Paleo climate reconstructions. He has a deep interest in Easter Island but also holds a fascination for the Marquesas Island and Chatham Island off the east coast of New Zealand. His current role is more administration than research based.

Oliver Chadwick holds an M.S. from Cornell University and a Ph.D. from the University of Arizona in soil and water science. Chadwick is a professor in the Department of Geography, University of California, Santa Barbara. Chadwick has published over 120 papers on hydrology, soils, and soil chemistry. His interest areas include pedology, geomorphology, Quaternary geology and biogeochemistry.

John Flenley holds an honours B.A. in Natural Sciences (specialism Botany) from Cambridge University, a Ph.D. in Biogeography from ANU, Canberra, and an Sc.D. from Cambridge. He is a Fellow of the Royal Society of New Zealand. His specialty is palynology which he has applied to the understanding of Quaternary climatic change in New Guinea, Indonesia, and Easter Island. He is the author of *The Equatorial Rain Forest: A Geological History* (1979), *Easter Island, Earth Island* (with Paul Bahn, 1992), *The Enigmas of Easter Island* (with Paul Bahn 2003). He edited *The Quaternary in Britain* (with J.Neale, 1981) and *Tropical Rainforest Responses to Climatic Change* (with M. Bush, 2007). He has also been recently awarded the medal of the Geographical Society of New Zealand for Distinguished Research.

Paul Horley, Ph.D., started his research of Rapa Nui history and culture after visiting the Island in 2002. His scientific interests include rongo-rongo script or Easter Island, study of rock art and 3D computer modelling of archaeological sites.

Ninoska Cuadros Hucke attended the Colegio Ingles Religiosas Pasionistas, the Universidad de Valparaiso, and also studied management at Inacap Viña. She currently serves as the provincial director of CONAF (National Forest Corporation) on Rapa Nui.

Annette Kühlem is an archaeologist who has worked in Europe, Central and South America, Asia and the Pacific Region. In recent years her interests have been focused on the aspects of anthropogenic landscape transformations, especially the role of water and trees as parts of ritual landscape architecture. Currently she is conducting comparative research on holy trees in Polynesia. She has been a member of the German Expedition to Easter Island since 2010 and has a project in French Polynesia that is financed through a scholarship from the German Archaeological Institute.

Thegn Ladefoged is a Professor of Archaeology at the University of Auckland. He received his doctorate in 1993 from the University of Hawai'i for his study on socio-political change on Rotuma. His current research interests include Polynesian prehistory, the development of agricultural systems, socio-political transformations, landscape archaeology and the application of GIS technology to archaeological problems. Ladefoged's present projects include the analyses of changing Māori social networks, Hawaiian ecodynamics, and Rapa Nui terrestrial resource dynamics and societal change. Much of his research is inter-disciplinary in nature and has resulted in numerous authored and co-authored journal articles and book chapters.

Georgia Lee (1926–2016) received her Ph.D. from UCLA for her outstanding research and documentation of rock carvings and paintings of Easter Island. This research project embraced many years of intensive field work, culminating in publication of the "Rock Art of Easter Island: Symbols of Power, Prayers to the Gods", which became the landmark reference book in the field. Further, Dr Lee worked extensively in the Hawaiian Islands (publishing another prominent book "Spirit of Place: Petroglyphs of Hawai'i" in co-authorship with Edward Stasack) and continued on with important research of Chumash rock paintings in California. Georgia Lee established the *Rapa Nui Journal*, which for thirty years served as an important forum for academic discussions in Rapa Nui studies and Polynesian archaeology. She was also the founding member of the Easter Island Foundation that provides scholarships to the promising students of Rapanui heritage, helping to continue their education in leading colleges and universities. She lived in California until she passed away, July 9, 2016. She will be sorely missed.

Andreas Mieth studied Biology and Ecology. He works currently as science-coordinator at the Christian-Albrechts-University of Kiel. Foci of his research are interactions between environmental changes, human impacts and technical evolution, especially on islands. Research on Easter Island has been an important part of his work since 2002.

Lilian González Nualart is a cultural anthropologist with a degree from the Universidad de Chile. She is versed in anthropology, anthropological linguistics and archaeology. For many years she has worked on the Rapa

Nui island-wide archaeological survey. She currently serves as an anthropologist with the Mata Ki Te Rangi Foundation project staff working on Rapa Nui.

Rhys Richards, a former career diplomat, has published many books, mainly on Pacific maritime history before 1850. These include whaling and sealing, and shipping arrival and departure lists for the Bay of Islands, Tahiti, and Honolulu. Other books include re-viewing the first foreign visitors to southern New Zealand, the Chatham Islands, the Samoas, the Austral Islands, the Cook Islands and Easter Island. In the U.S. in 2000 he was awarded the prestigious L. Byre Waterman award "for maritime history". Since then he has writing mainly on Pacific Island arts and artefacts, especially in the Solomon and Austral Islands, New Zealand and elsewhere. He has also been a not-for-profit publisher of small print run books on the Pacific as the Paremata Press at mrhys@paradise.net.nz.

Joan A. Wozniak earned her M.A. and Ph.D. from the University of Oregon's Department of Anthropology. Her dissertation centred on the archaeological survey and series of excavations on the Northwest coast of Rapa Nui at Te Niu, where she studied the prehistoric agricultural process and the subsequent environmental changes that resulted within the Te Niu settlement. She continues to study subsistence practices on Rapa Nui and how they changed over time. Current research relates to the general subsistence practices on Rapanui – food production in the early 21st century. She also is involved in research of one of the major ahu complexes on the south coast, Ura Uranga te Mahina.

Introduction

Things are not always what they seem . . . the sentiment is an appropriate observation and one that scholars engaged in fieldwork on an unfamiliar landscape know all too well. Anthropologists, historians, geologists and archaeologists, in particular, delve into the past without a secret decoder ring, but instead with the hypotheses and physical remnants of the culture they wish to learn more about. They are mindful of the fluidity of time and space that seductively acts to bring particular objects – monumental or minute – into sharp relief, and that those objects may ultimately serve as the bedrock that supports theory. In the case of Rapa Nui, or as English-speaking Westerners refer to it, Easter Island, the monumental statues on their altars were so intriguing and mysterious that they stole the ink of interpretation at the very first European contact, a foundation for a legacy that has held sway for more than three hundred years.

To be certain, the *moai* and *ahu* are powerful, mysterious and grand in scale and design. They constitute awesome material statements of cultural meaning and chiefly legitimacy writ large on the landscape. As with monumental stonework around the world, they evoke speculation and awe, especially when they are located in a remote island setting more than two thousand miles away from any substantial body of land. The *moai* and their *ahu* have been romanticized and glorified by explorers and scholars in recent history, most notably by Thor Heyerdahl and Jared Diamond in the twentieth century. These two scholars, with extremely different research agendas, had one thing in common: the ability to write in a fashion that captivated the lay audience through either swashbuckling adventure or blanket theories of cultural disconnect and disruption. Both scholars used the *moai* as their linchpin, capitalizing on their sheer volume and construction to advance theories of migration that "prove" indigenous people incapable of achievement (Heyerdahl) or cost benefit analyses that show they exhausted their resources (Ponting, Diamond, and others).

Such actions demonstrate the dangers of the adage above – things are not always what they seem – and the limitations of lifting one element, especially the most obvious element, up to the light without explaining the larger overarching picture. Each scholar, with equal amounts of Barnum and Bailey aplomb and Madison Avenue salesmanship, sold a Rapa Nui story that was anchored in a current Western motif – exploration of the Pacific via an experimental sailing vessel or going to the ends of the earth to find the poster children for environmental degradation and cultural collapse. Both models were palatable and exciting for armchair explorers and the green machine looking for someone to blame for the end of the world as we know it. The advent of the Internet and its memes helped to spread these ideas around the world, and Rapa Nui became a hot ticket on the wealthy eco-travel express so nimby (not-in-my backyard) visitors could congratulate themselves as witnesses to cultural collapse.

While the controversies in the media progressed in the late twentieth century, promoting movies and books related to the island's negative components, a remarkable paradigm shift slowly took shape among Rapa Nui scholars. Scholars began to look at the landscape from a settlement pattern perspective that acknowledged the presence of the *moai* and *ahu* but only from their location within the larger domestic pattern. Any visitor to the island marvels, and maybe curses, the sheer volume of rock on the island that hampers easy access to sites and beaches. In fact, if you look around, you realize that you are often in a sea of rocks looking out to a limitless ocean from one vantage point or to the backbone of the island from the shore. One of us, Sonia Haoa Cardinali, a Rapanui archaeologist who worked and consulted with both Heyerdahl and Diamond on Rapa Nui, remembers talking to the island's elders about landscape patterns, especially as related to gardens and subsistence. The use of rocks as landscape resources was a recurring story. When coupled with the current tradition of using rocks for planting, a very different landscape story has slowly come to light thanks to the work of a cadre of international scholars. Far from a culture of collapse and doom, a snapshot of extreme innovation and resolve has emerged. As the most prolific resource on the island, rocks could be thought of as the medium or the currency for the creation of gardens, cooking ovens and boathouses that frequently align with a focal *ahu* and *moai*.

Archaeologists from around the world have worked for the last twenty years on projects not focused on the extraordinary *moai* and *ahu* but rather the more mundane domestic arrangements all cultures share as they go about their day-to-day lives. Advances in environmental sciences have granted new ways to look at stone tools, plant materials, and soil amendments. What has emerged is a story of a remarkable set of innovations that served to feed groups of people in a sustainable fashion that is emulated today with great success. In reality the Rapanui were a far cry from the resource sucking entity as defined by Diamond and others and any cultural collapse came at the hands of Europeans who enslaved the Rapanui and introduced disease.

The articles included in this text demonstrate the power of seeing things in a different light and help to explain how the smallest details can be more meaningful than the largest monuments in the creation of a sustainable and innovative world.

If you face inland, standing at the edge of the ocean where most of the *ahu* and *moai* are or were situated, what about the landscape that stretches from the shore up to the summit of the volcano cones? What did it look like? What was there? Was it occupied? How did that expanse from shore to crater relate to the total cultural and social world of the Rapanui at various points in time?

This volume addresses what you see if you look past the *moai*, inland. The pre-Western contact Rapa Nui landscape is addressed in Chapters 1 to 6, mostly with the tools of archaeology and palynology (pollen analysis), including archaeological survey and testing, mapping and laboratory analysis. Chapter 7 is a pivot point, dealing with petroglyphs both before and after Western contact. Chapters 8 through 11 explore the post-Western contact period and what happens to the landscape, using archaeology and historical documents.

How were settlements organized with respect to gardens? In Chapter 1, "Prehistoric settlement, ancient gardens and population dynamics on the Hiva Hiva lava flow, Rapa Nui, Chile" Christopher M. Stevenson, Thegn N. Ladefoged and Oliver Chadwick analyse settlement patterns on the Hiva-Hiva lava flow (western Rapa Nui, about half-way up the west coast), an area where volcanic activity may have occurred as recently as 10,000 years before the present. An earlier archaeological survey logged in over 2200 cultural features from which the present study defined two smaller survey areas within the Hiva Hiva lava flow. Encountered in the survey areas were remains of dwellings, stone walls and pavements, lithic workshops, extensive rock gardens, rock quarries and other features, all relocated or located with great precision on GIS (Geographic Information System) maps. Soil samples for nutrient analysis were taken, both from inside and outside of the ubiquitous stone gardens. From these soil samples, it was possible to relate the soils to the surface lava flow events and to evaluate the productivity potential of the soils. Carbon and obsidian samples were dated and a chronological framework was constructed that enabled the researchers to trace changes in settlement intensity in the two survey areas through time, and to derive an indirect measure of population density fluctuations there. The result: the researchers' melding of field survey, biogeochemistry, radiometric and obsidian hydration dating and GIS, generates for us a much sharper picture of evolving Rapanui life and community on a local scale.

In Chapter 2, Andreas Mieth and Hans-Rudolf Bork provide a context for how an emphasis on the control of water came about. In their contribution, "A vanished landscape – phenomena and eco-cultural consequences of extensive deforestation in the prehistory of Rapa Nui", the authors argue that the scale and rapidity of forest clearing was a remarkable, transformative event for the population of a small island. Upon arrival to the island, in their estimation perhaps as early as 700 AD (others researchers argue ca. 1200 AD), the Polynesians entered a pristine environment believed to be untouched by human hands. Initially, human modification to the environment was minimal as agricultural plantations were less intensive and intermingled with standing palms. However, this was short-lived and within 300 years the impacts of humans on the landscape is dramatic. They use zoological, palynological, and landscape investigations to show the rapidity of human forest clearance and its impacts. What motivated the residents of Rapa Nui to systematically clear the island? Was it the need to establish intensive agricultural fields to raise the staple crops of sweet potato and taro for an expanding population, or were there additional needs? Their observation that very little palm wood was used for fuel in the hearths and earthovens suggests the trees were felled for another reason. They postulate that the core of palm containing many litres of sap was one of the driving forces. The need for moisture again rears its head as a central concern of the Rapa Nui.

What caused the disappearance of the palm? This question is considered in Chapter 3, "The potential for palm extinction on Rapa Nui by disease" by Daniel and Kathleen Ingersoll. The chapter opens by examining some of the popular hypotheses and statements in the literature concerning the extinctions of the palms of Rapa Nui. The focal species is the *Jubaea chilensis*-like palm, or *Paschalococos disperta*. Overharvesting, climate change and predation by the introduced rats (*Rattus exulans*) currently represent the major proposed hypotheses. Alternative hypotheses deserve serious consideration including fungi, viruses, bacteria, nematodes, insects, birds and combinations such as insects transmitting fungi. Some examples of palm loss to these threats on other Pacific islands besides Rapa Nui are discussed.

Chapter 4 by John Flenley and Kevin Butler, "New interpretations of pollen data from Easter Island", builds upon Flenley's early investigations of pollen analysis in the Rano Kau fresh-water crater lake to sceptically address the questions of initial human settlement on Rapa Nui. Taking advantage of new AMS dating methods, and the ability to date the smallest of seeds, the pollen record for Rano Kau is re-dated and re-interpreted. With the former dating inversions in the profile removed, the environmental changes in the Holocene become readable, but the causes of ecological changes are sometimes difficult to interpret. This is especially true for the time period around 100 AD where they document a decline in palm abundance and increase in charcoal accumulation. The low probabilities associated with volcanism or lightning in the creation of repeated burning points at the intervention of man on the landscape during this early period, a full thousand years before recent reconstructions of Polynesian dispersal places humans on Rapa Nui (Wilmherst et al. 2011). Flenley and Butler argue for an earlier colonization, and possible abandonment of Rapa Nui, that may have been partially obliterated by sea level rise. Although additional evidence in the form of cultural material is absent, this signature for human environmental impact in the pollen record requires that we keep an open mind with respect to Polynesian human dynamics and dispersal.

What is a rock garden and why do they cover nearly half the landscape? Joan A. Wozniak in Chapter 5, "Subsistence strategies on Rapa Nui (Easter

Island): prehistoric gardening practices on Rapa Nui and how they relate to current farming practices", addresses the subsistence role of rock, stone or lithic mulch gardens, as they are variously called. A wide array of data sources including archaeological field work at *Ahu Te Niu* (located about two thirds of the way up the west coast) and laboratory analysis as well as the historical literature, ethnography and Rapanui oral tradition are synthesized to provide an understanding of the terminology, types, function, distribution and time depth of rock gardens. A review of comments on Rapa Nui's horticulture by eighteenth- and nineteenth-century western observers sets the scene. A consideration of ethnographic data and information gained from Wozniak's and others' informants helps shed light on how the landscape was gardened. Analysis of microfossils such as pollen, phytoliths and starch residues from Ahu Te Niu and other sites makes it possible to know which plants such as sweet potato, taro and banana were grown and where, and to discover salient characteristics about the make-up of the humanly-amended soils underlying the rock gardens. Wozniak advances the interesting postulate that some of the rocks for mulching the gardens may have come from piles of reused materials, employed in an earlier period for moving and erecting the *moai* – one of her informants suggested that *moai* were moved on small rocks that served as roller bearings. But perhaps the most important aspects of rock mulches that Wozniak reveals is their ability to buffer temperature changes, reduce wind and water erosion, offer shelter from the wind and conserve moisture and render horticulture practical and sustainable without fallowing.

The Rapanui transformed the landscape with rock, but that is not the only way. Burkhard Vogt and Annette Kühlem in Chapter 6, "By the Quebrada of Ava Ranga Uka A Toroke Hau – about landscape transformation and the significance of water and trees", describe a remarkable site located midway up the slopes of the main volcano, Maunga Terevaka, that focused upon the control of water. At this location two large earthen and rock dams were positioned below a small waterfall within the ravine to capture the seasonal rainfall from higher elevations. Behind the dams a series of superimposed pavements covering the valley floor give further evidence for a significant level of effort directed to creating an abundance of fresh water on an island largely devoid of surface streams. A carved basin of basalt blocks, decorated with petroglyphs, was constructed below the waterfall and water flow was directed through the basin to comfort the bather. The positioning of an *ahu* on the lip of the ravine suggest that access to the oasis was not for everyone, but likely restricted to the chiefly elite who could rest under the shade of maintained palm trees on an island that was nearly deforested. Clearly, this was a sacred place of central importance to the leadership of one island lineage.

In Chapter 7, Georgia Lee et al. look at another aspect of sacred behavior in the latter parts of prehistory. "Re-use of the sacred: late period petroglyphs applied to red scoria topknots from Easter Island (Rapa Nui)" documents the changing meaning of sacred objects. The body of Easter Island rock art, comprising several thousand images, is one of the most impressive in Oceania. A wide array of motifs were executed on a large variety of carving surfaces: cave entrances and ceilings, house entrances, the inner side of worked basalt house foundation slabs, stones in the vicinity of water sources, statue quarries at Rano Raraku and top knot quarries at Puna Pau, basalt boulders at the ceremonial center of 'Orongo, as well as countless carved flat lava panels scattered over the island. One of these images, a stylized boat with curved stern and prow, is disproportionally located on the red scoria topknots (*pukau*) that once adorned the yellow tuff statues (*moai*). Applied after the topknots had become separated from the head, an interpretation of the boat image meaning becomes problematical within a new interactive context where society is changing quickly in response to frequent European visits and the biological pathogens, such as small pox, left behind. The documentation of these motifs by 3D scanning, and their association with many of the European landing locations, provides some indication that the images document the arrival events of the post-contact period.

On 9th April, 1722, Dutch explorers, under the command of Jacob Roggeveen, were the first Europeans to set foot on Easter Island. They were later followed by explorers from Spain (1770), Great Britain (1774) and France (1786). Each of these expeditions produced accounts of their findings on this remote Polynesian isle including a variety of official logs, notes by crew members, reports by scientists and even "second hand" writings. Jan J. Boersema's Chapter 8, "An earthly paradise? Easter Island (Rapa Nui) as seen by the eighteenth-century European explorers" summarizes the main revelations of these accounts in respect to food production. What do the accounts tell us about the ecological and cultural situation at the time of these visits? Do they render reliable information on (over)population and/or (over)exploitation? How are the various reports to be interpreted in view of later scientific studies? The conclusion drawn is that the accounts do not confirm the reported collapse, suggested by Clive Ponting and Jared Diamond. Easter Island may not have been the "earthly paradise" that Jacob Roggeveen deemed possible, but rather appears to support the existence and continuation of a sustainable society in the pre-European period, even after deforestation.

Substantial literature concerning the first Western contacts beginning with Roggeveen (1722) is readily available including republished original accounts and interpretations of them. Earlier in this volume, Wozniak draws on some of the eighteenth-century visitors' records for valuable horticultural observations. Here in Chapter 9, "The impact of whalers and other foreign visitors before 1862", Rhyss Richards offers a unique contribution to Rapa Nui studies by pulling together all the known visitors' accounts from the late eighteenth century until 1862 when the slaving expeditions arrived. Richards identifies what it is the visitors sought – usually re-provisionings for ships' water, fruit and vegetables – and how the exchanges with the Rapanui were transacted. What emerges overall is a picture of a vigorous horticultural economy on a small island that produced sufficient surplus to supply ships with surprising quantities of sweet potatoes, bananas and sugar cane. While many of the encounters proceeded peacefully, some of the ships exhibited confrontational behaviour early on, which prompted the emergence of an offshore exchange protocol. Meeting offshore, Richards argues, limited possibilities for modes of cultural accommodation such as the presence of beachcombers, and may even have delayed gradual development of immunities to Western diseases.

Western explorers, anthropologists, archaeologists, historians, novelists, and filmmakers create captivating and enduring stereotypes of other cultures. Once established, some of the stereotypes emerge as conceptually dominant and especially resistant to modification. In Chapter 10, Daniel and Kathleen Ingersoll and Andrew Bove argue that the pre-European contact Rapanui (Easter Islanders) have been mislabelled and libelled since the initial encounters. Some of the prevalent stereotypes they examine follow: the *moai* were built, not by the Rapanui, but by people from North or South America who arrived first but were later replaced by the Rapanui; the late period pre-European contact Rapanui became a society immersed in civil discord ruled by blood thirsty warriors and cannibals; a massive cultural collapse occurred on Easter Island after the palms were harvested to extinction; Rapanui cultural practices led to ecocide. This chapter challenges the dominant Western cultural characterizations of the Rapanui and attempts to redress the situation.

We especially hope this book will help provide balance to a literature and media picture often dominated by an emphasis on a glorious distant past of *ahu* and *moai* followed by gloom and doom. We wanted to draw attention to the full, vibrant Rapanui world, past and near-present, following the Rapanui from their beginnings on the island through the nineteenth century. In this vein, we dedicate this book to the Rapanui people for their kindness and hospitality, and for the inspiration of their unquenchable human spirit.

References

We offer the readily available sources below as a means for our readers to explore topics we do not directly address or cover in detail such as general culture, art forms, *moai* and *ahu*.

Bahn, P. and J. Flenley. 1992. *Easter Island Earth Island*. New York: Thames and Hudson.
Bahn, P. and J. Flenley. 2011. *Easter Island, Earth Island*. Rapanui Press.
Boersema, J. J. 2015. *The Survival of Easter Island: Dwindling Resources and Cultural Resilience*. Translated by Diane Webb. New York: Cambridge University Press.
Diamond, J. 2005. "Twilight at Easter." In *Collapse: How Societies Choose to Fail or Succeed*, 79–119. New York: Viking.
Diamond, J. 2007. "Easter Island Revisited." *Science* 317: 1692–1694.
Drake, A. 1992. *Easter Island: The Ceremonial Center of Orongo*. Illustrations by Georgia Lee. El Cerrito, CA: Easter Island Foundation.

Englert, Father Sebastian. 1970. *Island at the Center of the World: New Light on Easter Island*. Translated and edited by William Mulloy. New York: Charles Scribner's Sons.

Fischer, S. R. 2005. *Island at the End of the World: The Turbulent History of Easter Island*. London: Reaktion Books, Ltd.

Flenley, J. and P. Bahn. 2002. *The Enigmas of Easter Island: Island on the Edge*. Oxford: Oxford University Press.

Heyerdahl, T. 1975. *The Art of Easter Island*. Garden City, NY: Doubleday.

Hunt, T. L. and C. P. Lipo. 2011. *The Statues That Walked: Unraveling the Mystery of Easter Island*. New York: Free Press.

Kjellgren, E., J. A. V. Tilburg, and A. L. Kaeppler. 2011. *Splendid Isolation: Art of Easter Island*. New York: Metropolitan Museum and Yale University Press, New Haven.

Kurze, J. S. 1997. *Ingrained Images: Wood Carvings from Easter Island*. Woodland, CA: The Easter Island Foundation and Cloud Mountain Press.

Lee, G. 1990. *An Uncommon Guide to Easter Island: Exploring the Archaeological Mysteries of Easter Island*. International Resources.

Lee, G. 2006. *Rapa Nui, Island of Memory*. Easter Island Foundation.

Loret, J. and J. T. Tanacredi, eds. 2003. *Easter Island: Scientific Exploration into the World's Environmental Problems*. New York: Kluwer Academic/Plenum Publishers.

McAnany, P. and N. Yoffee, eds. 2010. *Questioning Collapse: Human Resilience, Ecological Vulnerability, and the Aftermath of Empire*. New York: Cambridge University Press.

McCall, G. 1994. *Rapanui: Tradition and Survival on Easter Island*. Honolulu: University of Hawaii Press.

McLaughlin, S. 2004. *The Complete Guide to Easter Island*. Los Osos, CA: Easter Island Foundation.

Metraux, A. 1957. *Easter Island: A Stone-Age Civilization of the Pacific*. Translated from the French by Michael Bullock. New York: Oxford University Press.

Rapa Nui Journal. The Journal of the Easter Island Foundation. Published by the Easter Island Foundation. Full text available from 1986 to 2014 at http://island heritage.org. Computer searchable. A selection of books and research reports on Rapa Nui and Polynesia are also available from the foundation.

Routledge, K. 2007 [1919]. *The Mystery of Easter Island*. London: Sifton, Praed and Co. Ltd.

Sanger, K. K. 2011 and 2015. *Easter Island: The Essential Guide*. Los Osos, CA: The Easter Island Foundation.

Shepardson, B. 2013. *Moai: A New Look at Old Faces*. Rapanui Press.

Soza, F. 2008. *Easter Island: Rapa Nui*. Copyright Editorial S. & E. S. A., 2007, English version 2008. Santiago: NICEYE.

Thompson, W. J. (Paymaster). 1891. *Te Pito Te Henua, or Easter Island*. Report of the National Museum, 1888–1889, 447–552. Washington, DC: Government Printing Office.

Van Tilburg, J. A. 1994. *Easter Island: Archaeology, Ecology, and Culture*. Washington, DC: Smithsonian Institution Press.

Van Tilburg, J. A. 2003. *Among Stone Giants: The Life of Katherine Routledge and Her Remarkable Expedition to Easter Island*. New York: Scribner.

1 Prehistoric settlement, ancient gardens and population dynamics on the Hiva Hiva lava flow, Rapa Nui, Chile

*Christopher M. Stevenson,
Thegn N. Ladefoged and Oliver Chadwick*

Introduction

When colonialists arrived on Rapa Nui around AD 1100–1300 (Hunt and Lipo 2006; Wilmshurst et al. 2011; Mulrooney 2013) their double-hulled canoes were loaded with the plants and animals necessary to start a new life on a remote volcanic island. This pristine habitat mostly covered by a dense palm forest (Mieth and Bork 2005) and an understory of about a dozen shrubby species (Orliac 2000) was the home to nesting sea birds and possibly a small rail (Steadman et al. 1994). While this diminished biodiversity might have worried the Polynesians arriving during the initial discovery voyage, it was not sufficient to deter a later colonization effort. What could not be assessed at that time was the full range of ecological and geological constraints, the eventual human-generated environmental challenges, and technological changes that would eventually impact the Rapa Nui farmers in the years to come.

Recent research into prehistoric agriculture on Rapa Nui has demonstrated that its small size, low elevation, wind-driven evapotranspiration, cool temperatures, and lower rainfall restricted these farmers to dryland agriculture (Horrocks and Wozniak 2008; Stevenson et al. 2006; Wozniak 1999) and small-scale irrigation by rain-water capture techniques (Stevenson 1997). During the first few centuries of settlement, the surface vegetation may have served to buffer environmental stresses but with the rapid slash-and-burn process of deforestation that cleared the lower elevations of Rapa Nui by AD 1450 and the upper elevations by the early AD 1600s (Horrocks et al. 2015), the damage to agricultural productivity must have been soon recognized. In the face of this self-inflicted change in environmental conditions, the Rapa responded technologically by creating rock gardens and behaviourally by more direct supervision and management of agricultural production (Stevenson et al. 2005).

The Hiva Hiva lava flow (Figure 1.1) is one such place on Rapa Nui where pre- and post-deforestation agriculture would have been practiced. This geological substrate represents the most recent volcanic activity on Rapa Nui and its emplacement is dated to approximately 0.11 mya (Vezzolli and Acocella 2009). The recent age of the flow, in comparison to the

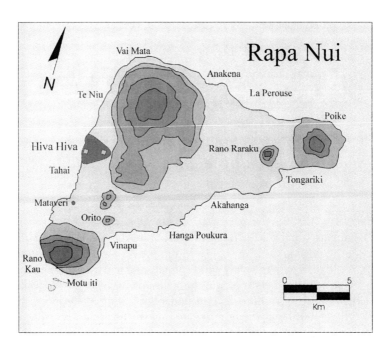

Figure 1.1 Island of Rapa Nui showing the location of Hiva Hiva

more extensive and older lava sheets (0.78–0.3mya) covering the remainder of Rapa Nui, means that the newly created ground surface has experienced much less weathering and rainfall leaching. As a result, the surface has the appearance of basalt rock outcrops covered by thin soils in convex positions that are interspersed with accumulated tephra- and/or volcanic loess-based soils in swales. These factors suggest that human use of the landscape would have required adaptations to a unique set of circumstances not found in many other parts of the island.

Archaeological survey and remote sensing within the last decade (Stevenson and Haoa 2008; Ladefoged et al. 2012) has identified the numerous rock gardens that cover much of the Rapa Nui landscape. These gardens consist of a variety of stone accumulations that can be characterized as boulder, veneer, or lithic mulch gardens (Stevenson et al. 1999). The Hiva Hiva terrain is covered by numerous prehistoric rock gardens. It is also well suited for farming on a treeless and windy terrain because the ground surface is undulating and has many swales and protected areas created by elevated lava exposures. In addition, the large quantity of basalt surface rock provides ample raw material for the construction of rock gardens and walled enclosures.

The success of ancient farming also depended upon the quality of the soil. In many other parts of Rapa Nui the soils have been characterized as nutrient poor (Louwagie et al. 2006; Ladefoged et al. 2005; Vitousek et al. 2014) as reflected by low levels of available plant phosphorus (P). This is clearly the situation at higher elevations on Maunga Teravaka (300m+) where orographic generated rainfall over hundreds of thousands of years have resulted in excessively leached soil nutrient profiles (Stevenson et al. 2015). On more recent substrates such as Hiva Hiva, we would expect the soils to be more nutrient rich, but it is also possible that available nutrient levels are limited since mineral weathering of the substrate has not been extensive (Lincoln et al. 2014). A second possibility is that soils in the swales could be composed of eroded material that has been re-deposited by wind. A third possibility is that the soils overlie older volcanics below the Hiva Hiva flows and could have been incorporated into less fertile *in situ* soils through farming.

In this work we present the results of systematic pedestrian field survey within the Hiva Hiva flow which has documented the rock gardens and stone domestic features that cover the landscape. We use soil chemical analyses to assess the nutrient status of gardens, their formation processes, and the strategies of enrichment. Radiocarbon dating and obsidian hydration dating is used to track the intensity and duration of landscape use.

Archaeological investigation of Hiva Hiva

A comprehensive archaeological survey of Quadrangle 15, which contains the Hiva Hiva lava flow, was completed in 2007 and the effort recorded over 2200 cultural features (Haoa n.d.). These data were integrated into a comprehensive GIS data base. From this large data set, we selected cultural features within two 500m × 500m survey areas as a sample of the larger flow. Survey Area 1 was placed near the west coast and Survey Area 2 was located inland near the eastern margin of the flow which contained the cinder cone named Hiva Hiva (Figure 1.1; Figure 1.2).

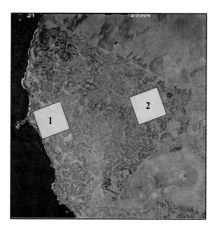

Figure 1.2 The Hiva Hiva lava flow showing the location of Survey Areas 1 and 2

The objective of the field investigation was to re-survey the two sample areas at an intensive level to record the distribution and boundaries of the prehistoric rock gardens not captured in the original survey. Once identified and mapped with GPS, a sample of the gardens were tested with 50cm^2 shovel tests to confirm if an anthropogenic soil, or Ap-horizon, was present beneath the surface rock layer. Obsidian artefacts and charcoal samples were recovered when present. Soil samples were also taken for a nutrient assessment of garden fertility. Approximately 150 grams of earth were recovered from the shovel test profiles at a depth of 20–25 cm. Shovel tests were also placed outside of gardens to obtain soil samples from equivalent depths in non-cultivated contexts. A total of 38 gardens and 31 non-gardens were tested (Figure 1.3).

Each previously recorded cultural feature was relocated using GIS maps and a list of UTM coordinates. These features included above ground structural remains such as houses and alignments, as well as modified natural

Figure 1.3 Garden and test unit locations for Survey Area 1 (top) and Survey Area 2 (bottom)

Prehistoric settlement 13

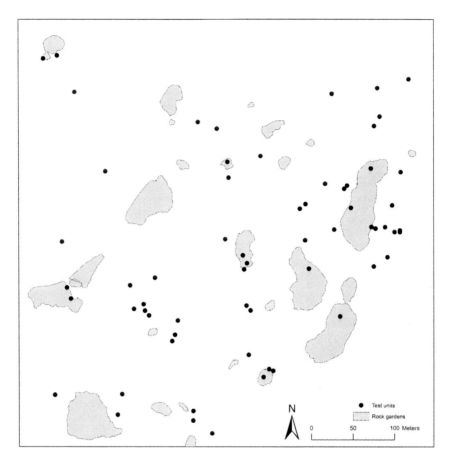

Figure 1.3 Continued

features such as caves. Shovel testing was also conducted adjacent to these remains to assess the depth of deposits and to recover obsidian and carbon for chronometric dating. A total of 251 sites were relocated and 70 were tested (Figure 1.3; Figure 1.4).

Prehistoric landscape settlement

Survey area 1

The terrain in Survey Area 1 consists of low hills and ridges separated by small valleys that gradually decline in elevation from East to West. Archaeological surface remains are numerous and a total of 91 features were documented in the initial survey (Haoa n.d.). The major categories of features included beach

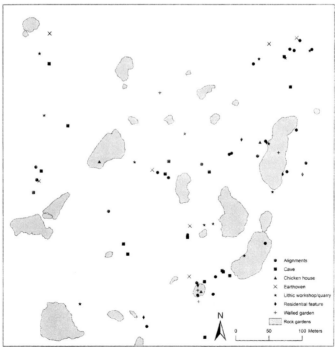

Figure 1.4 Feature locations in Survey Area 1 (top) and Survey Area 2 (bottom)

cobbles (*poro*), stone mounds, stone walls, lithic workshops, walled gardens (*manavai*), and worked stone (*paenga*). Prehistoric settlement remains were not evenly distributed and formed clusters of features in the northwest, northeast, and southeast quadrants of the survey area (Figure 1.4). The regions between the clusters exhibit few indications of prehistoric settlement.

The northwest cluster contains two domestic habitation areas defined by beach cobbles and a pavement that are indicative of former houses. Two walled gardens are near the houses, and stone walls and small stone mounds are located at the periphery of the cluster and near the adjacent rock gardens. These are likely agricultural windbreaks located within or at the margins of gardens. A single basalt stone quarry for the production of garden boulders was also present.

The northeast cluster consists of numerous surface features within a large garden complex (Figure 1.4). Amidst the gardens is an association of domestic features that suggests a permanent settlement. These features consist of a large chicken house (*hare moa*), a house pavement, an activity area defined by core-filled walls (*muro vakaure*), numerous walled gardens, and various low stone mounds. These domestic features and the associated gardens suggest that the feature cluster represents an agricultural hamlet.

The southeast cluster exhibits a different association of stone surface features. Several beach cobbles suggest that a dwelling was once present. Positioned close to them were a set of four low-density obsidian workshops and a water hole. On the eastern edge of the cluster five caves, a water hole, and a basalt stone quarry were spatially associated. Gardens were few in this part of the survey area and indicate that farming may not have been the primary activity. Obsidian reduction for flake tools may have been the principal task.

Survey area 2

The central terrain feature of Survey Area 2 is the volcanic cinder cone called Hiva Hiva. The cone is approximately 40 m high and occupies about a third of the survey area. On top of, and surrounding the cone, are 160 cultural features. At the summit of the cone are a set of two large depressions created to extract basalt blocks that were modified into finished rectangular blocks (*paenga*) which served as building materials for religious platforms (*ahu*) or elite houses. Large exposures of basalt in this area were also exploited for suitable raw material and numerous unfinished blocks surround the cone at the base (Figure 1.4). Also located on top of the cinder cone, but at a lower elevation to the east, is a tight clustering of features that forms a well-defined living area. A level living terrace contains an alignment of worked stone, inferred to represent a substantial house. It overlooks a collapsed lava bubble that has been converted into a rock garden that is 30m in diameter. At the margin of the garden were an activity terrace, a small cave, a water hole, and two additional walled gardens. A shovel test placed on the activity terrace revealed that the surface was formed by compacted basalt particles 1–2 mm in diameter. These particles were the byproducts of *paenga* manufacture and were likely imported from the nearby quarry. This physical link suggests that the quarry labourers probably resided at this location.

Additional habitation sites defined by beach cobble pavements surrounded the base of the cinder cone and are associated with the numerous gardens in this area. On the south side of the cinder cone, a well-articulated elite house is present and other isolated worked stones (*paenga*) indicate that additional houses of this type may have once been in the area. This suggests that an elite managerial presence was associated with the quarrying activity on top of the Hiva Hiva cinder cone.

The northeast portion of the survey block contains two areas of intensive occupation. The first is located around the margin of a very large rock garden contained within a collapsed lava tube. House pavements, an elite house, stone alignments, obsidian concentrations, a chicken house, and stone walls overlook the garden that is located 10m below. This rock garden and the others in the immediate area, in all likelihood, helped support the quarry labourers and elite managers at Hiva Hiva. The second area is positioned immediately north of the garden and consists of an elite house associated with obsidian lithic scatters or workshops, a cave with an image of the Birdman on the exterior, and numerous water holes. Adjacent household gardens were absent from this cluster of surface features

The distribution of geological features, rock gardens, and surface cultural remains on the Hiva Hiva landscape reflect distinct types of activity occurring at separate locations. The Hiva Hiva cinder cone (Survey Area 2) was a focal point for the production of worked stone blocks used in elite construction projects. The presence of numerous unfinished blocks within and surrounding the quarry depressions supports this interpretation. Habitation areas, with many closely associated domestic features, indicated that quarry workmen lived on-site and were likely supported by foods derived from the surrounding rock gardens. All of these activities appear to have been managed by members of the chiefly class that resided in formal houses. In contrast, the settlement near the coast (Survey Area 1) lacks a well-defined elite presence. Elite houses are absent and the simpler cobble house patios constituted the dwellings, which along with chicken houses, walls, and stone mounds, were found in association with a large rock garden complex. Subsistence farming activities appear to have dominated.

Rock garden survey and testing

Pedestrian survey of Survey Areas 1 and 2 mapped the number and extent of ancient rock gardens. Using a Trimble GeoXT, the boundaries of all gardens were recorded by walking around the garden margins (Figure 1.3). Survey Area 1 contained 51 discreet rock gardens that were of variable types and dimensions. Boulder gardens were the most frequent followed by boulder/ veneer and boulder/mulch. The total area under cultivation in Survey Area 1 was 17,137m². Simple boulder gardens constituted 62% of the total cultivated area followed by nearly equal amounts for boulder/veneer gardens (18%) and boulder/mulch planting areas (16%). Other garden forms accounted for about 4% of the cultivated area.

Survey Area 2 has approximately the same amount of land under cultivation (16,545m²) but the configuration of gardens is slightly different. As in Survey Area 1, boulder and boulder mulch gardens account for most of the land under cultivation. However, boulder/veneer pavements are absent and simpler veneer gardens have taken their place. It is not immediately obvious why the boulders have been omitted but it may be due to the fact that more wind protected areas were present around the base of the Hiva Hiva cinder cone. Walled garden enclosures (*manavai*) and very dense rock gardens (*pu*) occurred in low numbers while lithic mulch gardens are slightly more frequent in Survey Area 2.

The size of rock gardens varies considerably within each survey block. In Survey Area 1 the vast majority of gardens are less than 500m² and may be as small as 30m² (Figure 1.5). A small number of gardens (n = 6) are substantially larger and range up to 2,248m². The same pattern holds for

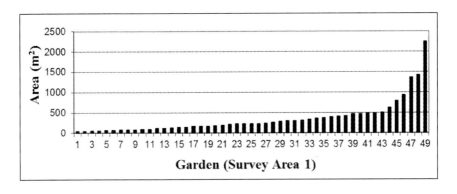

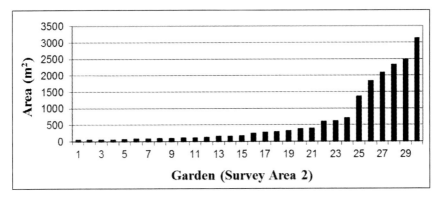

Figure 1.5 Surface area in meters of all rock gardens in Survey Area 1 (top) and Survey Area 2 (bottom)

18 Stevenson, Ladefoged, Chadwick

Survey Area 2 where small gardens have a maximum area of 700m² after which there exists a limited number of larger gardens that range in size from 1,357–3,118m² (Figure 1.5). It is possible that the set of small gardens represent those associated with individual or extended family households while the larger gardens are a product of larger community gardening efforts.

If the garden sizes are sorted and plotted according to garden type it is clear that in Survey Area 1 (Figure 1.6) the largest gardens are confined to the simple boulder garden and that boulder/mulch and boulder/veneer forms

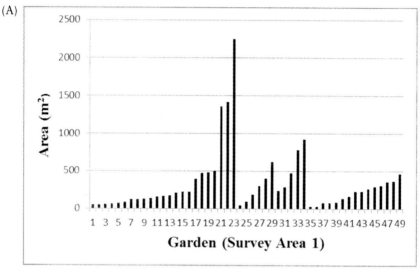

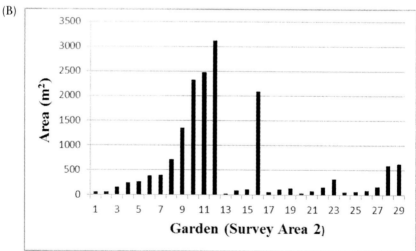

Figure 1.6 SA1: Boulder (1–23), Boulder/Mulch (24–29), Boulder/Veneer (30–34), Veneer (35–49). SA2: Boulder (1–12), Boulder/Mulch (13–16), Lithic Mulch (20–23), Veneer (24–29). Surface area in meters of rock gardens by type in Survey Area 1(A) and Survey Area 2(B)

are all smaller than 1000m². This pattern holds in Survey Area 2 (Figure 1.6) with one exception where a boulder/mulch garden is 2,088m² in size (SA2: Garden 30). Boulder/veneer, lithic mulch, and scree gardens are all less than 625m² in area. These distributions suggest that the cost of garden creation is energetically expensive and that the largest gardens simply use dispersed boulders. The other garden forms use larger amounts of small and large field stone and this may have required more effort to accumulate and place the rock in a suitable growing pattern.

Soil nutrient analysis

We sampled two stratigraphic soil profiles within swales in Survey Area 1 to evaluate their development and stratigraphic properties. We then collected a large number of spatially distributed samples to evaluate whether there were systematic differences in soil nutrients inside and outside of garden areas in Survey Area 1 (coastal) and Survey Area 2 (inland). Thirty-eight samples were excavated within rock gardens to bedrock or to within the B-horizon. Soil samples were taken at a standard depth of 20 to 25cm below ground surface. A further 31 samples were excavated in zones surrounding the gardens that showed no surface, or subsurface, indications of farming activity. These 31 samples acted as controls for the 38 garden samples. Soils were analysed for cation exchange capacity and base saturation; total and exchangeable Ca, Mg, Na, and K; resin-extract and total P; and total Si, Al, Fe, Zr, and Nb pools. These analyses include determinations of biologically available nutrient pools (exchangeable cations, resin P) as well as total pools of multiple elements that facilitate understanding of the long-term dynamics of soils. Measurements were carried out in biogeochemistry analytical labs at UC Santa Barbara and Stanford University and analytical methods are described in Chadwick et al. (2003) and Vitousek et al. (2004, 2014).

The two deep soil profiles in the swales revealed different stratigraphies above the bedrock. In unit HHGU2, we went to 78cm before hitting unweathered rock whereas in HHPO1, we went to 200cm before encountering rock. HHGU2 was a relatively simple soil profile composed of a thin A horizon, a transitional AB horizon, and four Bw horizons (Figure 1.7). By contrast, HHPO1 was composed of a surface soil similar to HHGU2, but it was superimposed on a buried soil that contained palm root casts.

The chemical composition of soil samples was analysed to understand the extent of soil profile development and the nutrient status of each horizon. One way to evaluate the extent of soil development is to compare the chemical composition of samples to the composition of the volcanic ejecta from which they formed (Chadwick et al. 1990). Here we evaluate the change in four elements relative to their concentrations in the Hiva Hiva lavas. These elements cover a range of solubility and therefore allow us to further parse the extent of weathering and soil depletion. The results suggest that the soils are strongly weathered. In HHGU2, about 95% of the Ca and 80% of the

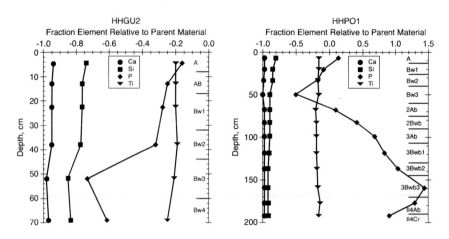

Figure 1.7 Soil depth profiles from swales in Survey Area 1

Soil horizons are noted on the right of each graph. The depth graphs are the mass fraction of each element listed that has been leached from the soil during weathering. The graphed data are the total element within each profile corrected for volume change by using the "immobile element" niobium (Chadwick et al. 1990; Bern et al. 2015).

Si has been lost from the soils. By contrast, only about 20% of the Ti has been leached, which makes sense because it is usually quite immobile in soil environments (though not as immobile as niobium (Nb), which is used here as an immobile reference element for our calculations (Chadwick et al. 1990). A similar pattern exists for Ca, Si, and Ti in the HHPO1 soil although in each case the elemental losses appear to be somewhat greater. In both soils, weathering losses are substantial and greater than what we might expect from weathering of volcanic ejecta as young as the Hiva Hiva lavas (Lincoln et al. 2014; Chadwick et al. 2003).

The results strongly suggest that the larger swales in the Hiva Hiva lavas are actually windows into an underlying soil surface that pre-dated the Hiva Hiva flow – this is particularly true for the profile excavated at HHPO1. The depth pattern for P shows much more structure than the other elements. In HHGU2 and the surface soil of HHPO1 (top 60cm), the loss of P relative to lava declines toward the surface and in HHPO1 P shows a slight gain in the surface horizon. This pattern is indicative of root uptake of P at depth and its subsequent deposition in dead vegetation at the surface, a process that has been interpreted elsewhere as a significant contributor to soil nutrient availability for Polynesian agriculture (Vitousek et al. 2004; Vitousek and Chadwick 2013). The depth pattern for P in HHPO1 indicates that P levels were greater in the past than they are today at the surface. It is possible that P near the surface was more enriched in the past and that the Rapanui depleted it through agricultural extraction.

The elemental measurements and calculated loss/gain profiles highlighted above are meant to help us understand soil history. Another way to understand soil properties is to index plant availability of nutrients, which help us interpret present soil productivity (Louwagie et al. 2006; Chadwick et al. 2003). Here we evaluate plant available P, Ca, and % base saturation, which is an index of how strongly soils have been leached of their nutrient cations (see Vitousek et al. 2014 for a discussion of these measures with respect to Polynesian agriculture in Hawaii). In contrast to the fraction of P lost from the profile, the depth pattern for resin P shows lower concentrations near the surface relative to the subsurface (Figure 1.8). In a similar fashion exchangeable Ca and base saturation exhibit lower values at the surface compared to the subsurface.

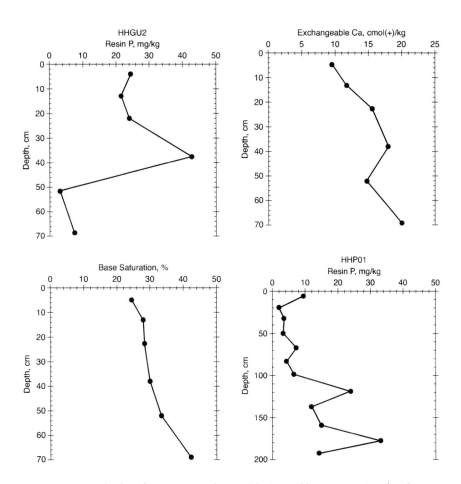

Figure 1.8 Depth plots for resin P, exchangeable Ca and base saturation for the two swale soils excavated in Survey Area 1

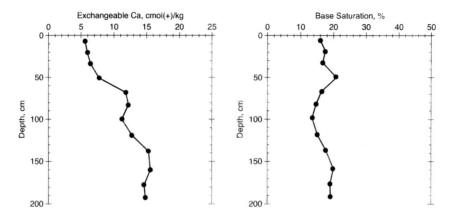

Figure 1.8 Continued

To interpret the agricultural implications of these numbers, we use analyses from ancient agricultural systems in Hawaii to evaluate the relative fertility of the Hiva Hiva soils. The Hawaiians did not find it effective to intensify their agriculture when resin P values fell below about 50 mg/kg, when exchangeable Ca fell below about 10 cmol(+)/kg, and when base saturation dropped below about 30% (Vitousek et al. 2004; Vitousek et al. 2014). In Figure 1.8, we note that resin P is far below the fertility cutoff determined from our work in Hawaii – especially so for HHPO1 – and the exchangeable Ca and base saturation are also low in the near-surface horizons. These measurements suggest that at Hiva Hiva nutrient management would have been very important, particularly within Survey Area 1.

We also conducted a spatial analysis that compared soil properties inside and outside of identifiable gardens in Survey Area 1 and Survey Area 2. To avoid post-European contact disturbance we collected samples from 20–25cm depth. In Table 1.1 we show the average mass fraction lost or gained for the same elements we considered in Figure 1.7. In Survey Area 1, the weathering sensitive elements, Ca and Si, show somewhat less elemental loss inside the garden boundaries than outside, which could indicate that the garden areas are more mixed due to cultivation and hence some deeper, less weathered material has been brought into the sampling zone or that vegetative and rock mulching has increased element concentrations (and hence lowered the loss term). By contrast we do not see any garden-based difference for the relatively weathering insensitive element Ti. Phosphorus shows meaningful gains of 60% and 34% for the garden and non-garden areas in Survey Area 1.

Table 1.1 Mass fraction lost or gained relative to Hiva Hiva lava. Samples were taken from 20–25cm depth and represent a four way comparison among Survey Area 1 (coastal) and Survey Area 2 (inland) and inside and outside of identifiable garden features.

Location	Garden Status	τTi mean/s.d.	τSi mean/s.d.	τCa mean/s.d.	τP mean/s.d.	n
Coastal	in	−0.15/0.048	−0.71/0.11	−0.94/0.032	0.60/0.59	22
Coastal	out	−0.14/0.035	−0.80/0.069	−0.98/0.11	0.38/0.35	22
Inland	in	−0.066/0.059	−0.76/0.10	−0.95/0.037	0.011/0.23	15
Inland	out	−0.11/0.035	−0.76/0.031	−0.95/0.012	−0.049/0.029	12

Table 1.2 Measures of plant available phosphorus and exchangeable cations. Samples were taken from 20–25cm depth and represent a four way comparison among Survey Area 1 (coastal) and Survey Area 2 (inland) and inside and outside of identifiable garden features.

Location	Garden Status	Resin P mean/s.d. mg/kg	Ca_x mean/s.d. cmol(+)/kg	Base Saturation mean/s.d. %	n
Coastal	in	6.50/6.86	8.14/4.56	14.02/7.31	22
Coastal	out	5.84/5.30	3.37/1.67	9.01/3.91	22
Inland	in	6.28/5.49	7.58/5.09	15.54/11.80	15
Inland	out	10.48/2.54	8.75/2.40	16.59/4.19	12

Similar to Ca and Si, it appears that P has been augmented by mulching in the garden areas.

In Survey Area 2, there are virtually no differences in the mass fraction losses of Ti, Si, and Ca between samples taken in the gardens and outside them (Table 1.1). Also, there are no differences between the inland and coastal sites. There is, however, much lower mass fraction change for P in the inland sites compared to the coastal ones; however the inland garden and non-garden sites show no difference in P change.

Comparisons of resin P, exchangeable Ca, and base saturation in the spatial sampling provide a less clear picture because there is considerable variability in the data as indicated by the standard deviation values in Table 1.2 – there are no statistically significant relationships using an ANOVA analysis. The resin P values are low everywhere and are quite similar to the similar depths of the HHPO1 profile shown in Figure 1.7. Exchangeable Ca and base saturation are also low and similar to the HHPO1 profile. From an agricultural perspective plant available P is 5 to 10 times lower than optimal, exchangeable Ca is 60–70% of optimal, and base saturation is about 50% less than optimal (see Vitousek et al. 2014).

In summary, significant losses of Ca, Si, and even some loss of Ti indicate that the Hiva Hiva soils are highly weathered and hence appear to be considerably older than the approximately 0.11mya age of surface lava flows. Therefore, it is likely that the soils were developed on an older underlying flow that was incompletely covered by the Hiva Hiva lavas. This is a relatively common feature on islands that have had recent volcanism. Although the soils show losses of Ca, Si, and Ti everywhere, the pattern for P shows an enhancement near the surface which could be due to natural biocycling of P over many millennia or could be interpreted to mean that P was augmented by mulching near the surface. Even though there is evidence for surface augmentation, it does not provide a significant pool of plant-available P (or exchangeable Ca and other base cations), which suggests that any agricultural efforts in Hiva Hiva would have had limited productive potential and would have been highly dependent on vegetative mulching from external sources.

Occupational chronology

Chronological dating was conducted on samples of carbon and obsidian from test units placed adjacent to archaeological features. The samples were not selected randomly but depended upon the discovery of carbon and obsidian in a suitable context as well as the overall quantity of obsidian. Despite this sampling limitation, the chronological data is informative about the use of the region.

Eight AMS dates were conducted on small carbon fragments removed from the agricultural horizons, or anthropogenic zones, within rock gardens. Because of the mixed nature of the deposits, larger identifiable carbonized wood fragments were rarely preserved. One AMS date was on a more durable palm nut endocarp (*Jubea sp.*) fragment found in a test unit placed adjacent to an isolated house beach cobble (*poro*) and three samples were on small toromiro fragments from an earthen planting pit at Site 15–233h (Table 1.3). One sample (Beta 237458) returned a C^{14} age of less than fifty years and reflects recent contamination. The remaining dates show a presence of human activity in Hiva Hiva beginning in the AD 1100s (Beta 237459) that is followed by age estimates in the 14th and 15th centuries. Two age determinations are later than this time period. Beta 238063 (210+/−40) has a two sigma calibrated age range of AD 1640 to 1950 but has the highest probability of dating to AD 1725–1814. Similarly, Beta 237461 (150+/−40) returned a calibrated age range of AD1660–1960 but most likely dates to AD 1666–1784.

Table 1.3 AMS dates from sites in the Hiva Hiva project area.

Test Unit	Site	Beta No.	C^{14} Date	Calibrated 2 Sigma	Comments
52	15–90	237457	460+/–40	AD 1410 to 1470	Carbon from TU Level 1 profile
98	15–182	237458	<50 years	Modern	Carbon from TU fill
105	Rock Garden 15–68	237459	840+/–40	AD 1060 to 1270	Carbon Sample #1: Level 2
105	Rock Garden 15–68	237460	440+/–40	AD 1420 to 1490	Carbon Sample #2: Level 2
107	Midden	238582	490+/–40	AD 1400 to 1450	Coconut shell, TU fill
137	Rock Garden 16	238061	300+/–40	AD 1470 to 1660	Carbon from TU fill
145	Rock Garden 22	237464	560+/–40	AD 1310 to 1440	Carbon from TU fill
148	Rock Garden 25	238063	210+/–40	AD 1640 to 1950	Carbon from TU fill
141	Rock Garden 20	238062	570+/–40	AD 1300 to 1430	Carbon from TU W. profile
TU2	15–233h	254389	160+/–40	AD1663–1953	Toromiro, TU 2, L3
TU2	15–233h	254390	290+/–40	AD1483–1795	Toromiro TU 2, L4
TU2	15–233h	254391	100+/–40	AD1680–1954	Toromiro, TU 2, L6

Obsidian hydration dates were run from 23 test units in the Hiva Hiva region. Seventy-three samples were processed from Survey Area 1 and Survey Area 2 using the procedures for infrared obsidian hydration (Stevenson et al. 2013). The summed probabilities for the obsidian hydration dates were calculated to develop a frequency distribution for each area. These distributions can be treated a proxy for the intensity of land use in the area.

The obsidian dates show occupation beginning in the 13th century and activity continuing until the first half of the 19th century (Figure 1.9). However, the graph shows a very rapid growth in population which peaks around AD 1450 and then abruptly declines. Not all of the inhabitants leave Hiva Hiva and a small population is present in the survey areas between AD 1640–1750.

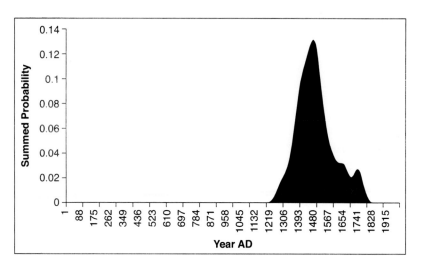

Figure 1.9 Obsidian hydration dates summed probabilities for Survey Area 1 and Survey Area 2, Hiva Hiva

Discussion

In the 11–12th century, the first recognizable human activity is identifiable in the archaeological record from Hiva Hiva. Within the next two centuries the resident population increases swiftly and created a complex archaeological record. In Survey Area 1, located near the western coast of the island, the cultural features form dispersed clusters that have been interpreted to represent small farming hamlets or workshop areas. The distribution of surface features in Survey Area 2 indicated that the Hiva Hiva cinder cone was a specialized quarry for the production of large crafted stone slabs or *paenga* for use on religious platforms or elite houses. Concentrated feature complexes and several elliptical elite houses (*hare paenga*) suggested that a specialized workforce was present and/or that chiefly managers may have had a role in the coordination of production. Surrounding the cinder cone were a number of large rock gardens within collapsed lava tubes or on the open terrain that provided food for the task groups.

The rock gardens in the Hiva Hiva region consisted mostly of boulder or boulder/veneer gardens. These gardens were used in areas where higher wind velocities imposed a burden on plants since they created turbulence that reduced overall wind speeds close to the ground surface. The lower frequencies of lithic mulch gardens suggests that soil moisture retention was less of a problem in many parts of Hiva Hiva compared to other parts of the island where a deep lithic mulch was used to retain moisture, especially on shallow soils where the basalt bedrock was near the surface.

Farming in the Hiva Hiva area was not without difficulty. An analysis of the soil properties from two deep test units within Survey Area 1, and a comparison of garden with non-garden soils, indicated that the most recent Hiva Hiva lava flow did not entirely cover the pre-eruptive surface and that the older and weathered substrates were utilized for food production. Low overall base saturation, exchangeable Ca, and plant available P meant that intensification of agricultural practices by dense annual plantings could not be sustained by the existing soil nutrients. It is likely that Rapa Nui agricultural fields in Hiva Hiva represented an extensive type of agriculture where plants were widely spaced. Nutrient inputs to these plants would have needed to be in the form of vegetative mulch or household waste brought into the planting areas.

Low intensity farming and stone quarrying within Hiva Hiva persisted over many centuries. Obsidian hydration dates have indicated usage of the area that reaches a population peak in AD 1450–1500. Usage then dropped severely and remained at a low level in AD 1600s–1700s before experiencing a final decline that ended in the middle 19th century. This pronounced decline in this part of the island begins nearly 200 years before the arrival of Dutch navigators in AD 1722.

The question now becomes what initiated the decline in usage of the area in AD 1450–1500 and why was there no recovery? The decline coincides with a period of nearly complete deforestation that had been in process for two centuries prior to this period. Faced with a nearly barren landscape, wind damaged and water stressed crops, it is hypothesized that garden yields were on the decline and exacerbated by a declining fertility of the already heavily weathered soils. An elevated regional usage of the area could not be sustained and most people left.

We propose this pressure on productivity could have been alleviated by the invention of the rock garden in its various forms which may have occurred in the 15th century as excavations at nearby Maunga Orito have suggested (Stevenson et al. 2006). This new form of environmental buffering may have eased direct stress but it was not a quick nutrient fix for the occupants of Hiva Hiva. Possibly introduced at this time were fertilization measures that had not been seen as necessary as long as ash and carbon producing slash-and-burn horticulture was the normative practice. Both of these new measures had the potential to generate a higher annual yield and support a greater number of people.

Yet at the same time, the costs of agriculture had become much higher. The rock gardens themselves consisted of accumulations of thousands, to tens of thousands, of stones of varying size (5–80cm in diameter) that were amassed within a limited space. The level of effort to accumulate these stones was significant, especially for larger stones, or small boulders, that were 50 to 80cm in diameter and weighed up to 50 kilos. As the larger loose boulders became utilized, new boulders were created by prying apart the basalt outcrops and moving the materials downhill into gardening areas. Even after the garden infrastructure was fully in place their use still demanded an extra effort. This was especially true for veneer and lithic mulch garden forms where the small surface rock had to be removed from the tops of planting pits prior to the planting and harvesting events. These efforts, repeated thousands of times, consumed many more calories than agricultural activities conducted in areas of minimal surface rock.

Rock gardens may have ameliorated evapotranspiration and improved growing conditions but two issues remained. Soil organic amendments were likely limited in supply and may have come from burning grasses within the fields or through household earthoven debris (Stevenson and Haoa 2008). Prehistoric agricultural soil horizons are defined by the presence of carbon flecking but their presence within the scores of garden test excavations was low and many times barely perceptible. We are of the opinion that the soil amendments of the Rapa Nui were, in the case of Hiva Hiva, not sufficient to sustain long term production. The fact that the abandoned soils sampled in this analysis show P and Ca depletion supports this interpretation.

Therefore, it is likely that the people of Hiva Hiva experienced the constraints of farming around AD 1500 and relocated to areas with more nutrient rich soils. The number of persons present in the Hiva Hiva lava flow quickly diminished. The population stabilized at a low level in the 17th–18th centuries until it converged with an island-wide loss in population caused by pathogens introduced by Europeans in the AD 1860s.

Conclusion

The domestic archaeological record of Rapa Nui with its use of stacked field stone is highly generic in form and difficult to partition into temporally discreet human behavioural events. A strategy taken here has been to look at landscape soils and their substrates, gardens, and artefacts contained within them to examine landscape use in prehistory. We have shown through archaeological survey in Hiva Hiva that the landscape was exploited for its stone building materials and extensively farmed. However, this farming was challenging because of the low available nutrients. It has been pointed out before that the soils on Rapa Nui were nutrient poor (Louwagie et al. 2006; Ladefoged et al. 2005; Vitousek et al. 2014; Stevenson et al. 2015) and this work confirms those earlier observations.

This investigation has demonstrated how soil biogeochemical studies can shed light on the volcanic formation processes of landscapes and how this has structured human usage. The deep testing and soils analysis conducted here indicates that the young Hiva Hiva lava flow only partially covered the older volcanic substrate and created an interspersed set of swales that were used by Rapa Nui agriculturalists. Soils within these settings were not derived from the young, mineral rich, lava flow but were the old, weathered, and nutrient poor soils from many millennia earlier. The concentration of phosphorus and calcium was low and at levels, considered by other Polynesian farmers on other islands, to be too low for intensification. Therefore, the extensive rock gardens on Rapa Nui likely generated consistently low yields even with the addition of organic soil amendments. The invention of the rock garden within this context counteracted the detrimental human-induced environmental changes of lower soil moisture and greater evapotranspiration, but it did not greatly enhance the nutrient status of the soil.

Obsidian hydration dating of a large sample of artefacts taken from domestic sites was used as a proxy for the intensity of land usage over time. Here we have been able to put land usage on a continuum and look at its fluctuation over nearly the entire period of human settlement on Rapa Nui. This metric has shown a significant variation in the intensity of use of Hiva Hiva. We have proposed that declines in the occupation of the area stemmed from two factors: that of deforestation and the inability of people to provide sufficient soil amendments. The trends noted for Hiva Hiva may be not be representative of island wide processes but exemplifies the complexity of landscape usage in Rapa Nui prehistory.

Acknowledgments

This work was completed under funding from the National Geographic Society and the National Science Foundation (Award BCS-0911056). We extend our appreciation to the National Council of Monuments of Chile and the Council of Monuments, Rapa Nui, for permits to conduct archaeological research.

References

Bern, C.R., A. Thompson, and O. A. Chadwick. 2015. "Quantification of colloidal and aqueous element transfer in soils: The dual-phase mass balance model." *Geochimica et Cosmochimica Acta* 151: 1–18.

Chadwick, O. A., G. H. Brimhall, and D. M. Hendricks. 1990. "From a Black Box to a Grey Box: A Mass Balance Interpretation of Pedogenesis." *Geomorphology* 3: 369–390.

Chadwick, O. A., R. T. Gavenda, E. F. Kelly, K. Ziegler, C. G. Olson, W. C. Elliott, and D. M. Hendricks. 2003. "The Impact of Climate on the Biogeochemical Functioning of Volcanic Soils." *Chemical Geology* 202: 195–223.

Haoa, Sonia. n.d. Archaeological survey of the Quandrangle 15, Rapa Nui. GIS data on file, Hanga Roa, Rapa Nui.

Horrocks, M. and J. Wozniak. 2008. "Plant Microfossil Analysis Reveals Disturbed Forest and a Mixed-Crop, Dry Land Production System at Te Niu, Easter Island." *Journal of Archaeological Science* 35: 126–142.

Horrocks, M., W. T. Baisden, M. A. Harper, M. Marra, J. Flenley, D. Feek, S. Haoa-Cardinali, E. D. Keller, L. Gonzalez Nualart, and T. Edmonds Gormon. 2015. "A Plant Microfossil Record of Late Quaternary Environments and Human Activity from Rano Aroi and Surroundings, Easter Island." *Journal of Paleolimnology* 54: 279–303.

Hunt, T. L. and C. P. Lipo. 2006. "Late Colonization of Easter Island." *Science* 311: 1603–1606.

Ladefoged, T. N., C. M. Stevenson, P. Vitousek, and O. A. Chadwick. 2005. "Soil Nutrient Depletion and the Collapse of Rapa Nui Society." *Rapa Nui Journal* 19(2): 100–105.

Ladefoged, T. N., A. Flaws, and C. M. Stevenson. 2012. "The Distribution of Rock Gardens on Rapa Nui (Easter Island) as Determined by Satellite Imagery." *Journal of Archaeological Science* 40(7): 3021–3030.

Lincoln, N. K., O. A. Chadwick, and P. M. Vitousek. 2014. "Patterns of Soil Fertility and Indicators of Precontact Agriculture in Kona Hawaii." *Ecosphere* 5: 1–15.

Louwagie, G., C. M. Stevenson, and R. Langohr. 2006. "Impact of Moderate to Marginal Land Suitability on Prehistoric Agricultural Production and Models of Adaptive Strategies for Easter Island (Rapa Nui), Chile." *Journal of Anthropological Archaeology* 25: 290–317.

Mieth, A. and H.-R. Bork. 2005. "Traces in the Soils: Interaction between Environmental Change, Land Use, and Culture in the (Pre)history of Rapa Nui (Easter Island)." In *The Renaca Papers: VI International Conference on Easter Island and the Pacific*, edited by C. M. Stevenson, J. M. Ramirez, F. J. Morin, and N. Barbacci, 55–66. Los Osos, CA: Easter Island Foundation.

Mulrooney, M. A. 2013. "An Island-Wide Assessment of the Chronology of Settlement and Land Use on Rapa Nui (Easter Island) Based on Radiocarbon Data." *Journal of Archaeological Science* 40(12): 4377–4399.

Orliac, C. 2000. "The Woody Vegetation of Easter Island between the Early 14th and the Mid-17th Centuries AD." In *Easter Island Archaeology, Research on Early Rapa Nui Culture*, edited by C. M. Stevenson and W. E. Ayres, 211–220. Los Osos, CA: Easter Island Foundation and Bearsville Press.

Steadman, D., P. Vargas, and C. Cristino. 1994. "Stratigraphy, Chronology, and Cultural Context of an Early Faunal Assemblage from Easter Island." *Asian Perspectives* 33(1): 79–96.

Stevenson, C. M. 1997. *Archaeological Investigations at Maunga Tari: An Upland Agricultural Complex*. Los Osos, CA: The Easter Island Foundation and Bearsville/Cloud Mountain Press.

Stevenson, C. M., J. Wozniak, and S. Haoa. 1999. "Prehistoric Agricultural Production on Easter Island (Rapa Nui)." *Antiquity* 73: 801–812.

Stevenson, C. M., T. N. Ladefoged, S. Haoa, and A. Guerra Terra. 2005. "Managed Agricultural Production in the Vaitea Region, Rapa Nui." In *The Renaca Papers: VI International Conference on Easter Island and the Pacific*, edited by C. M. Stevenson, J. M. Ramirez, F. J. Morin, and N. Barbacci, 125–136. Los Osos, CA: Easter Island Foundation.

Stevenson, C. M., T. Jackson, A. Mieth, H.-R. Bork, and T. N. Ladefoged. 2006. "Prehistoric-Early Historic Agriculture at Maunga Orito, Easter Island (Rapa Nui), Chile." *Antiquity* 80: 919–936.

Stevenson, C. M. and S. Haoa. 2008. *Prehistoric Rapa Nui*. Los Osos, CA: Easter Island Foundation and Bearsville Press.

Stevenson, C., T. N. Ladefoged, and S. W. Novak. 2013. "Prehistoric Settlement on Rapa Nui, Chile: Obsidian Hydration Dating Using Infrared Photoacoustic Spectroscopy." *Journal of Archaeological Science* 40: 3021–3030.

Stevenson, C. M., C. Puleston, P. M. Vitousek, O. A. Chadwick, S. Haoa, and T. N. Ladefoged. 2015. "Variation in Rapa Nui (Easter Island) Land Use Indicates

Production and Population Peaks Prior to European Contact." *Proceedings of the National Academy of Sciences* 112: 1025–1030.

Vezzolli, L. and V. Acocella. 2009. "Easter Island, SE Pacific: An End-Member Type of Hotspot Volcanism." *Geological Society of America Bulletin* 121(5/6): 869–886.

Vitousek, P. M., T. N. Ladefoged, P. V. Kirch, A. S. Hartshorn, M. W. Graves, S. C. Hotchkiss, S. Tuljapurkar, and O. A. Chadwick. 2004. "Agriculture, Soils, and Society in Precontact Hawai'i." *Science* 304: 1665–1669.

Vitousek, P. M. and O. A. Chadwick. 2013. "Pedogenic Thresholds and Soil Process Domains in Basalt-Derived Soils." *Ecosystems* 16: 1379–1395.

Vitousek, P. M., O. A. Chadwick, S. C. Hotchkiss, T. N. Ladefoged, and C. M. Stevenson. 2014. "Farming the Rock: A Biogeochemical Perspective on Intensive Agriculture in Polynesia." *Journal of Pacific Archaeology* 5(2): 51–61.

Wozniak, J. A. 1999. "Prehistoric Horticultural Practices on Easter Island: Lithic Mulched Gardens and Field Systems." *Rapa Nui Journal* 13(4): 95–99.

Wilmshurst, J. M., T. L. Hunt, C. P. Lipo, and A. J. Anderson. 2011. "High-Precision Radiocarbon Dating Shows Recent and Rapid Human Colonization of East Polynesia." *Proceedings of the National Academy of Sciences* 108(5): 1815–1820.

2 A vanished landscape – phenomena and eco-cultural consequences of extensive deforestation in the prehistory of Rapa Nui

Andreas Mieth and Hans-Rudolf Bork

Introduction

The complete deforestation of the widespread palm woodland on the mere 164 km² large Easter Island (Rapa Nui) is among the worldwide most dramatic examples of anthropogenic environmental changes and its effects on a prehistoric human society. Soils and sediments on Easter Island provide a rich geo-bio-archive, from which the authors were able to gain new insights into the development of the landscape as well as into the history of humans and environment on Easter Island. The geo-archaeological investigations reveal that Easter Island was almost completely covered by woodland at the time of its discovery by the Polynesians and that its vegetation was probably dominated by an endemic, now extinct palm species.

Beginning around AD 1250, the inhabitants of Easter Island cleared the woodland extensively. Stumps and other residue remaining on open areas were burned down. Vast layers rich in charred remains, burnt stumps and hearths found in the geo-archives are proof of this massive anthropogenic intervention. The deforestation had severe consequences for land-use, sacred culture and everyday life in many areas of Easter Island. Exposed to weather conditions, fertile soils eroded from the slopes of the volcanoes. Settlements, sacred sites and fertile garden soils were buried under sediments. The population and utilisation of certain regions was relinquished entirely. Other areas remained populated but the type and intensity of land use changed; for example, horticulture ended in some parts of Rapa Nui completely. In these areas, the old fertile garden soils are to this day preserved under thick covers of fine-layered sediments. The loss of palm trees was a dramatic loss of resources for the island's inhabitants, even though this occurred gradually over hundreds of years. Recent research findings rebut more and more the theory that the deforestation caused a "collapse" on Easter Island. It is becoming clear that the Rapa Nui found effective responses to the dramatic environmental changes that they brought on themselves, which made it possible for their culture to survive up to the time of European contact. Also, this is indicated by preserved fertile garden soils in the geo-archives, in this case hidden under stone mulch covers from the last extensive land use era.

The landscape of long ago and today

Most radiocarbon data seem to suggest that Rapa Nui remained untouched by humans until AD 1100 to 1300 (Mulrooney 2013). Older radiocarbon data are scarce, but some data from newer investigations indicate human activities centuries before an assumed "late" colonization (Rull 2016; Vargas et al. 2006). Also the large number of 1100 to 1300 dates spread over the entire island compiled in Mulrooney 2013 are an argument for an earlier colonization. How else could an island-wide intensive use of landscape in this time be explained than by a high population number after centuries of population growth and an island-wide distribution and migration of people over many generations? This chapter will show the phenomenon of an island-wide woodland clearance as an important part of land use, which started in the 13th century AD. This fact is not explainable with a small "just arrived" population of some hundred people or less at the same time.

A colonisation around AD 700/800/900 or even earlier is supported by additional findings of our own investigations. In the geo-archives below the soils with charcoal we found in many areas of Rapa Nui, older garden soils with proof of extensive anthropogenic land use in the form of planting pits. These planting pits number in the millions, spread over the island and belonging to the first phase of woodland gardening, a technique which was relatively lacking in burning practices and thus not leaving much behind in the way of charcoal remains. This first phase of land-use will be described later in this chapter.

As Polynesian discoverers stepped onto the island of Rapa Nui at around AD 800/900 or earlier, the island must have looked like paradise to them. A dense, subtropical woodland dominated by palm trees, such as they had never seen before, lined the beach. Deciduous trees and shrubs grew in-between. The woodland canopy provided pleasant shade but without complete darkness. The forest floor was covered with fruit from the palm trees. They looked, in fact, quite similar to small coconuts and tasted just as delicious. There was more than enough wood for use, since the woodland stretched as far as the eye could see. The palm trees grew densely even on the cliffs (Figure 2.1) and where even these highly adaptive palm trees could not grow flourished a new and unknown flora. The woodland was filled with the sounds of bird songs. Squawking parrots fluttered though the treetops. Flightless, trusting rail scurried over the forest floor. Great colonies of sea birds showed themselves on the small rocks that edged the island: terns, different types of boobies and frigate birds. They clearly profited from the great abundance of fish. Meat would be plentiful. Fruit would also grow well on the island. The arrivals were sure to find drinking water. It was a paradise worth staying for.

Figure 2.1 Palm trees once covered most areas of Easter Island
(Graphic: Gerd Klose, Source: Mieth and Bork 2004).

The landscape of Easter Island looks completely different today. There, we generally encounter a dry, yellowish grassland only temporarily taking on a bright green colour after periods of rainfall (Figure 2.2).

The bleak silhouettes of volcanic craters and the millions of stones on the surface of the island intensify the impression of a barren landscape. This impression is emphasized even more by areas of strong, partly extreme, soil erosion. Farming and horticulture are rarely found. It is hard to imagine that people could have lived here and provided for their needs. How could they have fed themselves? Where could they have found firewood? From what could they have made houses and boots? Visitors to Easter Island today can easily see that there are some forested areas on the island, but upon closer inspection, one can tell that the trees growing here are not native ones. Eucalyptus (*Eucalyptus spp.*), Robinia (*Robinia pseudoacacia*), Chinaberry (*Melia azederach*) and Monterey pine (*Pinus radiata*) are trees that all originate from Australia, Asia and North America and were imported onto the island in the past century. Eucalyptus trees were planted on a large scale as early as 1920. This was repeated once again, more intensively, in the mid-20th century, in order to systematically provide sources of energy from plantation wood, however, this project has not been implemented. The coconut

Figure 2.2 Easter Island's present grassy landscape with some eucalyptus trees from the 20th century
(Photograph by Andreas Mieth).

trees around the bay of Anakena that create an idyllic picture were planted there in the 1960s. These are not the same palm species that the Polynesian discoverers once found so plentiful. The coconut trees that commonly grow on the tropical island of the South Pacific today never grew on Easter Island. Instead, a different palm species which was better adapted to the cooler subtropical climate of Easter Island flourished. This palm tree is extinct today. If it weren't for the clear relics and traces of the woody vegetation in the geo-archives, it would be hard to believe it existed at all.

The paleoecological reconstruction

Relics of several plant and animal species have been preserved in soils and sediments, in hearths and burnt layers, and in cooking and waste pits. The zooarchaeologist David Steadman for example, systematically searched for the bones of vertebrate animals on Rapa Nui. He found remains of at least six species of land birds, probably woodland inhabitants, which died out after losing their habitat. The bone findings also prove that there was once a greater variety of seabirds than today. Thirteen species of seabirds that once lived on Rapa Nui can no longer be found on the main island or the surrounding islets. Finally, the bone remains record the import of domestic fowl and Pacific rats (Steadman et al. 1994).

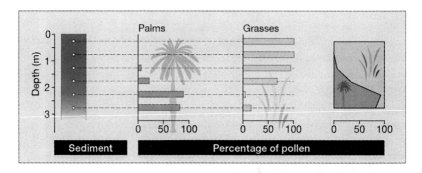

Figure 2.3 Simpliified pollen profile from the lake sediments of *Rano Kau*
(Diagram from the data of Flenley 1996, Graphic: Doris Kramer.)

Pollen is an important class of data for paleobotanical research. In particular, these can be found in the sediments of the lakes in the volcanic craters of *Rano Raraku*, *Rano Kau* and *Rano Aroi*. The New Zealand scientist John Flenley has carried out pioneering work in the investigation of Easter Island's pollen archives (Flenley 1993; Flenley et al. 1991; Flenley and King 1984). The pollen spectrum gives insight to the species composition of trees, shrubs and grasses of different eras. The analysis clearly shows the change from woodland to grassland during the period of human habitation (Figure 2.3). In the crater sediments of Rapa Nui, Flenley and his colleagues also found pollen from the extinct palm tree that once covered the island. They named this newly discovered species *Paschalococos disperta* (Dransfield et al. 1984). However, certain indices (pollen and endocarp morphology, pattern of roots) plead for a classification to the genus *Jubaea* and, as such, a close relationship to the recent Chilean Wine Palm (*Jubaea chilensis*). The *Jubaea chilensis* can reach an age of more than 750 years, a height of up to 30 meters and a diameter of more than 2 meters (Grau 2004). Pictures from regions in central Chile where the Chilean Wine Palm naturally grows probably convey a quite realistic picture of how the vegetation on Easter Island must once have looked (Figure 2.4). Grau (2005, 1996) believes that fruit from continental palm trees in Chile (from *Jubaea chilensis*) found their way by rivers and sea currents to Easter Island long ago, where they ensured the establishment of this species. It is possible that a species specific for this island or a subspecies of the *Jubaea* palm tree developed in this way after thousands of years.

As we will show in this chapter, the woodlands of Easter Island were dominated by this palm species. Nevertheless, anthracological investigations show that Rapa Nui's vegetation consisted of mixed woodland. The French botanists Catherine and Michel Orliac have gathered tens of thousands of

A vanished landscape 37

Figure 2.4 Chilean Wine Palms (*Jubaea chilensis*) in their natural habitat near La Campana, Chile
(Photograph by Andreas Mieth.)

charcoal samples from hearths and have compared these wood structures to trees and shrubs throughout Polynesia. The scientists were able to verify more than 20 (now extinct) tree and shrub species on Rapa Nui (Orliac and Orliac 2005, Orliac 2003, Figure 2.5). Further, charcoal samples which have not yet been identified indicate that the actual number of species was even higher. Sometimes plants left phytoliths in the soil: microscopically small silica which was once part of the living cells. Due to the structural characteristics of phytoliths, it is sometimes possible to conduct a taxonomic identification of the associated plant. Also the structure of phytoliths of the Easter Island palm tree suggests a close relationship to continental *Jubaea* palm trees. Recent studies found variability in the phytoliths of the palm trees, leading the French botanist Claire Delhon to the conclusion that there may have been even more than one palm species growing on Rapa Nui (Delhon and Orliac 2010; Gossen 2011; see also Gossen 2007).

However, sometimes the analyses of pollen, charcoal structures and phytoliths allow only a rough taxonomic identification to the level of plant family. One reason is that species-related reference material is absent,

Figure 2.5 The endemic Toromiro shrub was once native to the woodlands of Easter Island. Very few cultivated specimens exist today. All of them are descendants from the last individual, which survived at Rano Kao up to the 20th century

(Photograph by Oscar Fernandez.)

precisely because many species, even on other Pacific islands, have vanished completely. The reconstruction of past species' compositions also remains incomplete because many animal and plant species leave no determinable relics behind. Even when the taxonomical determination of a relic species is possible, this only reveals a limited amount of information about the biocoenotic association of, the abundance of and the spatial distribution of plants or animals. For example, the remains of wood found in the hearths had been collected in different ways and had been burnt to different degrees, thus furnishing only an imperfect representation of the former vegetation. Likewise, the pollen found in the sediments of crater lakes conveys a partial and a more qualitative than quantitative picture of the flora, as some pollen are carried easier and farther than others. Thus, not all pollen had the same chance of landing in the craters. Despite these limitations, the analysis of micro and macro plant remains over the past years has contributed considerably to the reconstruction of the former ecosystem and its change.

The traces of the palm trees

More than just micro and macro plant remnants from the once most dominant plant on Rapa Nui, the *Jubaea-* (or *Paschalococus-*) palm have been discovered: its traces in rocks and soils. The imprints of their stems in petrified lava are conclusive evidence of their existence (Figure 2.6). The lava of volcanic eruption flowed through woodland areas, snapped and buried trees tens of thousands of years ago. Embedded in lava, the stems burned. To this day, they leave long, open tubes the same diameter as the stems as proof. The interior walls of the tubes often clearly show the typical bark structure of palms. Several beautiful exemplars of these imprints can be found in the lava rock in the northwest section of Anakena bay.

By far, the most widespread evidence of palms is the imprints of their roots in the soil (Figure 2.7), which no other tree or shrub species has provided with such intensity. These traces are clearly visible at stepped erosion surfaces, on embankments and at the edges of gullies, even without archaeological excavations. They are more or less dark grey, 5–7 mm thick, round hollow tubes in cross section passing through the ground without branching out. They often extend deep into the weathered volcanic rock, found at a depth of more than 10 meters below the surface. The root tubes are in contrast to the typical yellow-brownish soils as their inner surfaces are often lined in black-greyish, primarily inorganic coverings of iron and manganese oxides and seldom encountered with organic coverings of charred root

Figure 2.6 Imprints of palm stems in an old stream of lava near Anakena
(Photograph by Andreas Mieth.)

Figure 2.7 Typical root imprints made by the extinct Easter Island palm tree in a soil profile at Maunga Orito
(Photograph by Andreas Mieth.)

material. The soil particles at the border of the root tubes are sealed together, stabilizing and preserving the tube structure. The arrangement of the root tubes is characteristic. They are arranged relatively parallel to each other far below the surface but merge conically near the (former) soil surface, where the roots once set off from the stem (Figure 2.8, Figure 2.9). Quite often there are also relics of the bottom part of the palm trunks: charred stumps, evidence of the burning and clearing of woods by humans (see below). The various diameters of the root cones and stumps in the soil profiles represent the different ages and sizes of the palms. The largest stem diameter the authors found was approximately 1.5 meters.

The majority of Easter Island was covered with woodland at the time of colonisation, presumably AD 700/800/900 or earlier. In our excavations, we found traces of palm roots on three-fourths of the island's surface. We found palm root imprints to a height of 300 meters above sea level on the Poike peninsula and at Maunga Terevaka. We were able to precisely match root imprints to singular tree individuals in numerous soil profiles and, hence, we could reconstruct the in situ density of trees in the woods. Using the analysed mean of 2.6 meters growth distance between the individual palm and based on the area verified to be populated by palm trees, we initially calculated (Mieth and Bork 2003, 2004) that approximately 16 million palm trees existed on Rapa Nui at the time of the arrival of the first Polynesians; later, revised estimates with new data approached 19.7 million palms (Mieth and Bork 2015).

Figure 2.8 Root bases at the trunk of a recent *Jubaea* palm near La Campana, Chile
(Photograph by Andreas Mieth.)

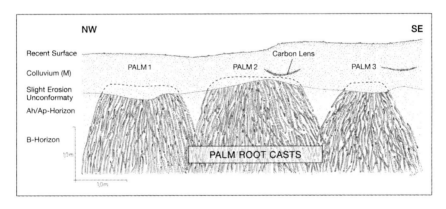

Figure 2.9 Individual, assignable example of the Easter Island palm roots in a soil profile at Maunga Orito
(Graphic: Doris Kramer, Source: Stevenson et al. 2006.)

This was an enormous and precious resource for the discoverers.based on the area verified to be populated by palm trees, we initially calculated (Mieth and Bork 2003, 2004) that approximately 16 million palm trees existed on Rapa Nui at the time of the arrival of the first Polynesians; later, revised estimates with new data approached 19.7 million palms (Mieth and Bork 2015). This was an enormous and precious resource for the discoverers.

Horticulture in the former palm woodland

The palm woodland was the most important area for living, protection and culture during the earliest centuries. Woodland clearance potentially played a local role; for example, smaller areas might have been opened up to build settlements and ceremonial sites and horticulture was carefully integrated into the palm woods (Figure 2.10). Evidence of soil cultivation between palm trees is clearly visible in soil explorations; it is characterized, on the one hand, by the loose substrate structure and, on the other hand, by the considerably great humus content of the soil, recognizable by the strong dark grey-brown colouring. Sometimes single planting holes with a depth of

Figure 2.10 Early horticulture took place under the protecting canopy of the palm trees

(Graphic: Gerd Klose, Source: Mieth and Bork 2004.)

30 to 70 cm can be identified. They were once made by using digging sticks to grow crops such as taro, yams, bananas or sugar cane.

These holes are not always individually evident in the soil cultivation horizons. In general, the cultural soil layers have been completely homogenized by mechanical processing over the course of decades and centuries. In that case, larger plant holes can be identified as downwards, u-shaped indentation in the lower processing boundary. The high humus content of the garden soils (anthrosols) may indicate that organic plant residue had been worked into the soils extensively in a recycling process, and in turn, the absence of soil degradation and soil erosion indicates that the early cultures exercised a sustainable use of the soil. The areas between palms were frequently completely used for soil cultivation. Relics of soil cultivation almost reach laterally close to the tree trunks and the corresponding root cones, whereas the roots, or rather their imprints, remain intact – evidence for the compatible coexistence of woodland and early horticulture and the meticulous method of soil cultivation which was gentle to the palms.

Initially, the palm trees were not in competition with horticulture. On the contrary, the horticulture profited from the climatic advantages and protection of the woodland. The canopy protected the delicate crops from bright sunlight, from desiccation as well as from heavy winds and rainfall. In this way, soil erosion could be fully avoided in spite of intensive soil cultivation. Harvesting the tasty and nutritious palm nuts was a nice addition to the horticulture and was another gentle method of woodland utilization. The woodland's function as protection from hot and windy climatic extremes was quite beneficial to humans as well. There in the light shade of the trees they found substantially better living and working conditions than they would under the relatively treeless landscape of Easter Island today.

Woodland clearance and the end to woodland-dependent horticulture

From the mid-13th century on, there was a profound change in landscape on Easter Island which resulted in the end of living and working under the protection of the palm woodland. The inhabitants began to clear the island's woodland bit by bit. Within just a few centuries, entire regions were turned into open landscape. Woodland clearance required extraordinary manpower. In a model calculation, we estimated that a mean of 300 to 500 labourers must have worked daily during the time of woodland clearance in order to chop down, transport and process the numerous palm trees (Bork and Mieth 2003).

The useless remains of palms and the accompanying vegetation in the cleared area were set on fire. Considerable evidence of the clearings and burnings can be found in soil exposures: layers of ash and charcoal cover the earlier layers of soil cultivation and relics of palm roots (Mieth et al. 2002; Mieth and Bork 2003). These layers of burnt material are often several millimetres thick and extend over several thousand square meters.

Figure 2.11 Charred nutshells of the Easter Island palm
(Photograph by Doris Kramer.)

They commonly include charred nutshells of the *Jubaea* palm (Figure 2.11). Great bundles of charcoal above the root cones of the palms in the exposures clearly trace the charred tree stumps that were left after clearing (Figure 2.12). These stumps were apparently burned down intentionally because it would have been difficult, even for very strong men, to dig up these deep and sometimes very thick stumps. However, even burning the stumps required a great deal of effort; the palm wood did not catch fire easily. Thus, thin twigs and dry grass were heaped onto the stumps in order to help set them on fire. We found charred remains of thin twigs and dry grass particularly massed near the relics of stumps (Mieth and Bork 2003).

In many of the charred palm stumps, we found traces of cooking sites: anthropogenic mixtures of charcoal and the leftovers of meals, for example, bones, molluscs and nut shells. We also found that the roots burned together with the stumps. It was apparently the profound heat that caused the soil particles near the roots to harden and stabilize the root tubes. This is how the root imprints of the *last* cleared and charred palm generation has been preserved island-wide in the geo-archives and is how these can be identified so clearly and individually. The sustainable preservation of the traces of roots over centuries was due to the fact that Easter Island has very few soil-dwelling organisms which could have destroyed these structures by means of their digging activities (bioturbation).

Radiocarbon dating of the charred palm relics from different locations on Easter Island, in particular the dating of charred palm nuts, enables spatiotemporal reconstruction of the woodland clearance (Figure 2.13).

Figure 2.12 Relic of a charred palm stump
(Photograph by Wibke Markgraf.)

This process advanced in phases over a period of approximately 400 years, from circa AD 1250 to circa AD 1650. Our own data is to a great extent consistent with the data of other authors (compare to Mulrooney 2013; Delhon and Orliac 2010; Wozniak and Horrocks 2010; Hunt and Lipo 2006; Cauwe et al. 2006; Mieth and Bork 2003, 2004, 2006).

Thus clearing of woodland spanned over a period of 300–400 years, which might correlate with 15 to 20 generations of humans. Therefore, one single generation probably did not comprehend how dramatic the change in landscape really would be at the end. Each generation registered that there was a bit less woodland coverage than the generation before. This "effect of familiarization" over a period of hundreds of years could be the reason that the Rapa Nui mentally, spiritually, ecologically or economically permitted or even supported such a dramatic decimation of woodland resources and why they eventually allowed the last tree to be chopped down. Our cultures today have similar experiences. Without examining archives or scientific data, few of us can understand or even imagine how much nature, how many animals and plants, how many species have disappeared in our own regions in the past centuries. We would only be consciously and maybe even emotionally aware of the losses that occurred during our own lifespan.

Rats or climatic disaster?

The extinction of the palm trees on Easter Island has triggered an intensive discussion about the underlying causes, about the chronology of landscape

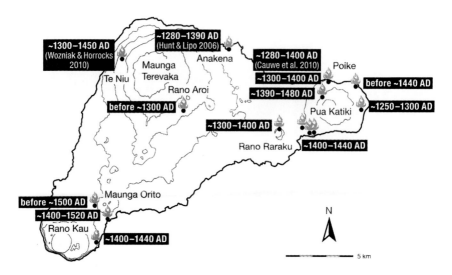

Figure 2.13 Chronology of the woodland clearance as documented by radiocarbon dating

(Graphic: Doris Kramer, Source: Mieth and Bork 2015)

change and about the ecological and cultural effects that have been summarized by Rull et al. (2010). Despite all the findings that provide strong proof of man-made deforestation, some scholars argue that a climatic disaster might possibly be the cause of the forest depletion on Easter Island (Hunter-Anderson 1998; Orliac and Orliac 1998; Orliac 2010). However, there is no direct evidence of an abrupt climatic change that would account for such dramatic consequences for the forests on Easter Island. On the contrary, pollen analyses from the sediments of crater lakes prove that the palm trees had existed continuously on the island the previous 35,000 years up to the time of forest clearance. This implies that the palm population must have successfully survived the very different climate of the last glacial period as well as years of extreme weather conditions repeatedly (Prebble and Dowe 2008; Flenley et al. 1991). Even a drought period of several months could hardly have destroyed the old palm mixed forest. Furthermore, there is no paleoclimatic evidence of such extreme weather conditions and these are highly improbable according to model calculations (see Junk and Claussen 2011; Mann et al. 2008; MacIntyre 2001).

The American scientist Terry Hunt (2007) had a different suspect in mind: the Pacific rat (*Rattus exulans*) that once came to Easter Island with the Polynesians. Hunt's hypothesis is that the rats multiplied phenomenally soon after their arrival on Easter Island and, by eating the trees' fruit, prohibited new palms from growing. However, some facts contradict this theory. On the one hand, there are the distinct anthropogenic traces of forest clearance and layers of burnt material as described above, and on the other hand, there is the fact that very few nuts (Figure 2.11) found in these burnt layers have gnawing marks (Mieth and Bork 2010). Correspondingly, well-preserved nutshells from a deposit found at Ava Ranga Uka o Toroke Hau on the southern side of Maunga Terevaka also show no gnawing marks from rats (Vogt and Moser 2010). However, the nutshells which Hunt (2007: 496) documented and Orliac (2003: 195) mentioned that have rat gnawing marks play a special role. These nuts do not originate from geo-archives, but from cave deposits that were probably accessible to rats over hundreds of years and, thus, very likely to have been consumed by the rats at some point during this time. Therefore, this finding does not reflect the "normal" environmental situation in the open landscape. Aside from the hypothetical assumption that consumption by rats caused significant fruit decimation, the further question arises as to how the rats could have damaged fully grown palms. Many of the great, long-living trees most certainly would have survived a plague of rats, at least up to historic times, if men had left the trees alone. There is also no evidence that the rat population of the time expanded excessively; after all, the rats were a valued source of nutrition (Métraux 1940) and were apparently not as abundant as one might assume. And finally, we found evidence at the northeast slope of Rano Raraku demonstrating that new palm trees were established by natural regeneration at least for a short time after the main period of deforestation, even though rats had long been living on the island at that time. The root imprints of a new generation of palms can be made out in the colluvia deposited near Rano Raraku after the first forest clearing (Mieth and Bork 2010).

It is also important to mention that while the number of palm trees decreased, many other types of trees and shrubs on Easter Island dwindled and then disappeared altogether as well. This has been documented in the hearths, as mentioned above: the change in fuel from wood to grass. This is additional proof of human intervention, as it is almost impossible that all of these different tree and shrub species, all with different regeneration strategies, should equally fall victim to rats.

Why was the forest cleared?

One very popular proposition is that the Rapa Nui cleared the forest in order to have enough wood to transport the large stone sculptures. However, there is no evidence to prove this; the exact means of transportation is still unknown. Even if the tree trunks were utilised as poles, rollers or rafts, only a small proportion of the roughly 19.7 million palm trees would have been necessary to move only several hundred stone statues, which we find today at the *ahu* and along the *moai* roads.

From geo-archaeological research, for example, on the Poike peninsula, we know that settlements and ceremonial sites were built on the cleared area immediately after the trees had been chopped down, as their foundations lie directly on the burnt layers (Cauwe et al. 2006, Mieth et al. 2002). Other studies imply that the cleared areas were used for intensified horticulture (see, for example, Wozniak and Horrocks 2010; Horrocks and Wozniak 2008). The nutrient-rich ash from the fires could have served as fertilizer for the soil, at least for a short period of time. For example, we found planting holes with a high concentration of charcoal and ash on Poike peninsula (Mieth et al. 2002). Nevertheless, were the installation of new gardens, settlements or sacred buildings the main reason for the forest clearance, or were they more likely the secondary benefits?

And what happened to the wood of the palms? The most obvious explanation, that it was used as firewood, has not yet been proven correct. Charcoal from many different types of trees has been found in the hearths on the island, but with only a small amount of charred palm wood. The current findings from the extinct palm trees consist almost entirely of charred nuts and leaf stalk fragments, aside from the charred palm stumps as macro remains (Delhon and Orliac 2010; Orliac and Orliac 2005; Orliac 2003). Could it not be possible that the sweet sap in the palm trunks was the desired target and not the wood itself? When chopping down the first palm trees, the Rapa Nui must have noticed that a sweet and nutritious liquid ran from the cuts in the trunks. Even the current use of *Jubaea chilensis* in central Chile shows that a felled palm is capable of yielding more than 400 litres of sweet sap over a period of 1 to 1.5 years. Did the Rapa Nui use the sap as a source of nutrient-rich drinking liquid from the 13th century onwards (Figure 2.14)?

After all, all other water sources available on Easter Island were of inferior quality: both the ferrous-rich water from the volcanic lakes (Figure 2.15) and the fresh water sources on the coast which were contaminated by salty sea spray. Many families had only limited access to these few water sources either due to the long distances or possibly due to clan boundaries and taboos. It was even difficult to collect rainwater since rainfall quickly seeped away on the island's porous volcanic rock. In contrast, it seems much easier to chop down a palm and collect several litres of delicious liquid per day for weeks, just by continuously replenishing the cut surface by cutting thin slices of the trunk. Collecting of palm sap may also be the purpose of the many stone basins found on Rapa Nui, whose function has not yet been determined. One to two palm trees would have supplied enough liquid for the needs of one person for an entire year while also providing a high-calorie, nutritional supplement. Assuming that the total population was between 5,000 and 10,000 people, the exploitation of more than 19.7 million palm trees for palm sap harvest would also fit mathematically (Bork and Mieth 2003). Occasionally, the sweet potato (*kumara*) has been referred to as the "propellant" of the labour-intensive megalithic culture on Easter Island. In this sense, perhaps the sap of the *Jubaea* palms played an equally important, if not greater, role. The decomposition of the relics of the palms that were

Figure 2.14 Were the palms chopped down in order to extract sap from the trunks?
(Graphic: Gerd Klose.)

Figure 2.15 The few volcanic crater lakes (here the lake at Rano Raraku) provided drinking water of inferior quality

(Photograph by Andreas Mieth.)

cut for sap extraction and not burned would explain why primarily only the charred stumps and nuts could be found in the geo-archives, but hardly any charred palm wood.

The search for evidence supporting these or other theories concerning the forest clearing is certainly one of the most exciting challenges of Easter Island research. Another ongoing question is why the people of Easter Island suddenly began chopping down the palms after they had been practicing sustainable woodland utilization for hundreds of years. Were there other factors, maybe new impulses from outside?

The consequences of deforestation

The social and environmental impacts of the deforestation were dramatic. Not only did the palm trees become extinct, but many other tree and shrub species as well as most of the endemic forest fauna disappeared. Within about 400 years after the beginning of extensive deforestation in the 1300s the Rapa Nui lost all resources linked to the former woodlands. They were then missing the delicious sap and the nutritious nuts of palm trees. Firewood became scarce, which is documented by charred remains of thin branches and grass instead of charred wood being found in the hearths used after the mid-17th century (Orliac 2010, 2000, Figure 2.16). The people also ran short on building materials. The leaves and twigs of palms and other trees could no longer be used as roofing material for houses. There was insufficient wood appropriate for building the canoes needed for fishing or, more importantly, for the construction of sea-worthy boats with which they could have left the island. The micro-climate changed dramatically as well. Where people once farmed in the shade of the trees, the scorching sun now burned plants and dried up soil. Storms and wind shear could now damage entire crops at exposed locations.

Although information about the loss of animal and plant species caused by deforestation is incomplete, we have detailed information about the spatial and temporal changes of the soils. After thousands of years of soil development, erosion was triggered as a result of the forest clearings on slopes. Left unprotected, the grounds eroded extensively under the effects of temporary droughts, interspersed with heavy rainfalls and storms. Erosion initially began at the lower mid-slopes and later, over the course of centuries, spread to the higher slope regions. For example, it did not reach the summit of the 370 meter high Poike volcano Pua Katiki until the beginning of the 20th century. Radiocarbon dating provides proof of these long-term consequences of prehistoric deforestation (Mieth et al. 2005). The eroded soil was deposited in hundreds of fine layers at slightly concave or straight sections of the slope a few meters to tens of meters below the erosion areas (Figure 2.17). The stratigraphic analyses provide evidence that some colluvial deposits reached a thickness of one meter or greater in the course of just a few decades (Mieth and Bork 2003, 2004; Stevenson et al. 2006). Whereas

Figure 2.16 The change in charcoal provenance in the hearths of Easter Island (According to Orliac 2010, graphic: Doris Kramer.)

the lower sections of the colluvial deposits consist of eroded garden soils from the slopes, the upper sections consist of less fertile vulcanite because of inverse deposition. At the erosion sites, horticulture became impossible for the Rapanui because of the loss of fertile anthrosols and, at the deposit sites, because of the poor colluvia at the surface. Furthermore, settlements and ceremonial sites that were founded after forest clearing were buried under the colluvial soil. As with several other areas in Rapa Nui, the Poike peninsula lost its importance as a settlement and cultural location due to the consequences of deforestation and subsequent deposition of sediments by soil erosion (Mieth and Bork 2003). Humans had no chance of survival at locations where buildings and gardens were buried under sediments in

Figure 2.17 Fine layer of sediments at a lower mid-slope on *Poike* peninsula which originate from the extensive erosion further up-slope that took place after deforestation

(Photograph by Andreas Mieth.)

mere decades, so they migrated to other parts of the island. This may have resulted in problematic social consequences as the land and its resources were carefully distributed between the separate clans.

Water became an even more precious commodity after the loss of the palm forests and the related drying effects of wind and sun on the exposed soils, while heavy rainfalls locally and temporarily unfurled catastrophic impacts. Researchers of the German Archaeological Institute, Bonn, Germany, recently found great post-deforestation terrace complexes with an imbedded channel system as well as a water basin fashioned out of stone in a valley below the crater outlet at Rano Aroi that only temporarily carried water (see the chapter by Vogt and Kühlem in this volume; Vogt and Moser 2010, Figure 2.18). The entire complex may have served a ritual water cult under the more difficult land use conditions after the clearance of the palm trees; the monumental constructions have remarkable references to the palms of Easter Island. Undecomposed palm nuts and other plant material were found in a layer of mud in an anthropogenic deposit under the water basin (Vogt and Moser 2010). Furthermore, we recently discovered planting pits with palm root imprints that were integrated into stone pavements at ceremonial sites. This indicates that the palms were planted there in a spiritual, sacred context (Figure 2.19) and is the first proof for Easter Island that

Figure 2.18 A water basin made of stone slabs in Quebrada Vaipu at the southern slope of Rano Aroi. The basin is apparently part of a water cult that was established after deforestation

(Photograph by Burkhard Vogt. Source: Vogt and Moser 2010)

Figure 2.19 *Ahu* from the post-clearing period at Ava Ranga Uka A Toroke Hau. The arrow indicates a planting pit with palm root casts integrated in the stone pavement in front of the ahu

(Photograph by Andreas Mieth.)

palm trees were specifically planted. So far nothing is known about further strategies of wood or forest management (arboriculture) on Easter Island.

Was there a social collapse after the forest clearing?

A frequently asked question is aimed at the reason for the end of the *moai* culture, which ceased almost simultaneously with the main phase of deforestation. Was the end of the *moai* culture an expression of a cultural collapse? Regardless, there was a cultural change and this change was expressed by an increasing importance of the "birdman" cult (Rull 2016). In all probability, this change may be interpreted as a consequence of the anthropogenic change in landscape and a newly arisen environmental pressure, an argument also supported by Rull (2016). The sum effect of many degradative phenomena must have exerted significant pressure on the Rapa Nui society: the loss of palm trees as an exceedingly valuable source of material, nutrition and drinking water; the loss of fruitful soils and areas suitable for horticulture; the forced abandonment of settlements and sacred sites; the usage-related changes in local climatic conditions; bad harvests and a considerable increase in the amount of work needed for the change in horticulture.

New environmental conditions might have prohibited the Rapa Nui from putting effort into the *moai* culture but resulted in other labour-intensive activities elsewhere. It is certainly appropriate to speak of a decline in resources and of extremely difficult general conditions as Bahn and Flenley (2011) have done in their new edition of *Easter Island- Earth Island*. Nevertheless, was there a social collapse on Easter Island (see, for example, Rainbird 2002; Diamond 2005; Nagarajan 2006)? No, according to our research there is no evidence that there was a general cultural collapse after deforestation. On the contrary, there are numerous signs that an advanced culture remained on Easter Island after the forest coverage was lost completely (Figure 2.20). Even after deforestation, the island's population was able to accomplish exceptional work, such as: stone mulching and other stone-based techniques of horticulture (Bork et al. 2004; Baer et al. 2008; Stevenson and Haoa 2008); building monumental structures (Vogt and Moser 2010); and industrial-like production of colour pigments (Mieth and Bork 2015).

Even in the cultural phases which directly followed the extensive forest clearings, there was a sufficiently large population on Easter Island to recruit the man-power needed for exceptional cultural accomplishments. The workers, in turn, could have only performed this enormous amount of work with adequate nutrition. The invention of the lithic mulching technique for horticulture (see Wozniak, Chapter 5) moderated the negative ecological and economical consequences of deforestation with the result that, for much of the island, the soil fertility was sufficient for producing adequate nutrition (Bork et al. 2004). To this day, many soils under the lithic mulch cover show a relatively high fertility (Ladefoged et al. 2010). Nutrition physiological

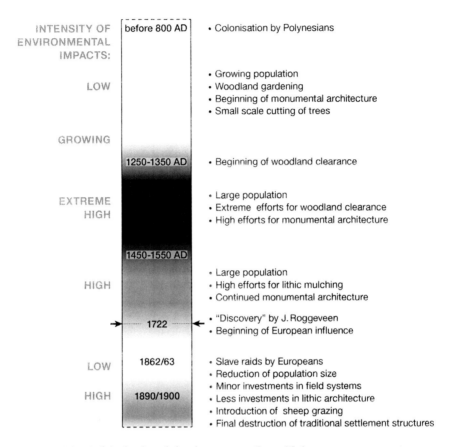

Figure 2.20 Model of cultural development on Rapa Nui
(From Mieth and Bork 2015. Graphic: Doris Kramer)

proxy data do not suggest that the population of the late prehistoric phase suffered from malnutrition. On the contrary, studies of the micro surface structure of preserved teeth verifies that they had a consistently sufficient and even diverse supply of animal and plant foods (Polet 2011).

However, what initially triggered the extensive forest clearing remains unanswered. Was it the technical, cultural development of a society under the special conditions of extreme isolation or was it the import of technology that caused a paradigm shift after hundreds of years of self-sustaining subsistence farming? This is a question that cannot (yet) be answered. It should not be so surprising that even the last palm tree on Easter Island was felled "with eyes wide open" in prehistoric times – today there are numerous analogue examples worldwide of human consumption and exhaustion of irreplaceable resources.

References

Bahn, P. and J. R. Flenley. 2011. *Easter Island: Earth Island*. Santiago: Rapa Nui Press.

Baer, A., T. N. Ladefoged, C. M. Stevenson, and S. Haoa. 2008. "The Surface Rock Gardens of Prehistoric Rapa Nui." *Rapa Nui Journal* 22(2): 102–109.

Bork, H.-R. and A. Mieth. 2003. "The Key Role of *Jubaea* Palm Trees in the History of Rapa Nui: A Provocative Interpretation." *Rapa Nui Journal* 17(2): 119–122.

Bork, H.-R., A. Mieth, and B. Tschochner. 2004. "Nothing but Stones? A Review of the Extent and Technical Efforts of Prehistoric Stone Mulching on Rapa Nui." *Rapa Nui Journal* 18(1): 10–14.

Cauwe, N., D. Huyge, J. de Meulemeester, M. de Dapper, D. Coupé, W. Claes, and A. de Poorter. 2006. "New Data from Poike (Rapa Nui-Easter Island): Dynamic Architecture of a Series of Ahu." *Rapa Nui Journal* 20(1): 31–36.

Diamond, J. 2005. *Collapse: How Societies Choose to Fail or Succeed*. New York: Viking.

Delhon, C. and C. Orliac. 2010. "The Vanished Palm Trees of Easter Island: New Radiocarbon and Phytolith Data." In *The Gotland Papers: Selected Papers from the VII International Conference on Easter Island and the Pacific: Migration, Identity, and Cultural Heritage* edited by P. Wallin and H. Martinsson-Wallin, 97–110. Visby: Gotland University Press.

Dransfield, J., J. R. Flenley, S. M. King, D. D. Harkness, and S. Rapu. 1984. "A Recently Extinct Palm from Easter Island." *Nature* 312: 750–752.

Flenley, J. R. 1993. "The Palaeoecology of Rapa Nui, and Its Ecological Disaster." In *Easter Island Studies: Contributions to the History of Rapanui in Memory of William T. Mulloy*, edited by S. R. Fischer, 27–45. Oxford: Oxford Books.

Flenley, J. R. 1996. "Further Evidence of Vegetational Change on Easter Island." *South Pacific Study* 16(2): 135–141.

Flenley, J. R. and S. M. King. 1984. "Late Quaternary Pollen Records from Easter Island." *Nature* 307: 47–50.

Flenley, J. R., S. M. King, J. Jackson, and C. Chew. 1991. "The Late Quaternary Vegetational and Climatic History of Easter Island." *Journal of Quaternary Science* 6(2): 85–115.

Gossen, C. L. 2007. "Report: The Mystery Lies in the Scirpus." *Rapa Nui Journal* 21(2): 105–110.

Gossen, C. L. 2011. *Deforestation, Drought, and Humans: New Discoveries of the Late Quaternary Paleoenvironment of Rapa Nui (Easter Island)*. Dissertation at Portland State University.

Grau, J. 1996. "Jubaea, the Palm of Chile and Easter Island." *Rapa Nui Journal* 10(2): 37–40.

Grau, J. 2004. *Palmeras de Chile*. Santiago: Ediciones Oikos Ltda.

Grau, J. 2005. "Prehistoric Presence of the Chilean Palm in Easter Island." In *The Reñaca Papers: VI International Conference on Rapa Nui and the Pacific*, edited by C. M. Stevenson, J. M. Ramírez, F. J. Morin, and N. Barbacci, 29–34. Los Osos, CA: Easter Island Foundation.

Horrocks, M. and J. A. Wozniak. 2008. "Plant Microfossil Analysis Reveals Disturbed Forest and a Mixed-Crop, Dryland Production System at Te Niu, Easter Island." *Journal of Archaeological Science* 35: 126–142.

Hunt, T. L. 2007. "Rethinking Easter Island's Ecological Catastrophe." *Journal of Archaeological Science* 34: 485–502.

Hunt, T. L. and C. P. Lipo. 2006. "Late Colonization of Easter Island." *Science* 311: 1603–1606.

Hunter-Anderson, R. 1998. "Human vs Climatic Impacts at Rapa Nui: Did the People Really Cut Down All Those Trees?" In *Easter Island in Pacific Context South Seas Symposium: Proceedings of the Fourth International; Conference on Easter Island and East Polynesia*, edited by C. M. Stevenson, G. Lee, and F. J. Morin, 85–99. Los Osos, CA: Easter Island Foundation.

Junk, C. and M. Claussen, M. 2011. "Simulated Climate Variability in the Region of Rapa Nui During the Last Millennium." *Climate of the Past* 7: 579–586.

Ladefoged, T., C. M. Stevenson, S. Haoa, M. Mulrooney, C. Puleston, P. M. Vitousek, and O. A. Chadwick. 2010. "Soil Nutrient Analysis of Rapa Nui Gardening." *Archaeology in Oceania* 45: 80–85.

MacIntyre, F. 2001. "ENSO, Climate Variability, and the Rapanui. Part II: Oceanography and Rapa Nui." *Rapa Nui Journal* 15(2): 83–94.

Mann, D., J. Edwards, J. Chase, W. Beck, R. Reanier, M. Mass, B. Finney and J. Loret. 2008. "Drought, Vegetation Change, and Human History on Rapa Nui (Isla de Pascua, Easter Island)." *Quaternary Research* 69: 16–28.

Métraux, A. 1940. *Ethnology of Easter Island*. Honolulu: Bernice Bishop Bulletin 160.

Mieth, A., H.-R. Bork, and I. Feeser. 2002. "Prehistoric and Recent Land Use Effects on Poike Peninsula, Easter Island (Rapa Nui)." *Rapa Nui Journal* 16(2): 89–95.

Mieth, A. and H.-R. Bork. 2003. "Diminution and Degradation of Environmental Resources by Prehistoric Land Use on Poike Peninsula, Easter Island (Rapa Nui)." *Rapa Nui Journal* 17(1): 34–42.

Mieth, A. and H.-R. Bork. 2004. *Easter Island-Rapa Nui: Scientific Pathways to Secrets of the Past*. Kiel: Christian-Albrechts-Universität zu Kiel, Ökologie-Zentrum.

Mieth, A. and H.-R. Bork. 2005. "History, Origin and Extent of Soil Erosion on Easter Island (Rapa Nui)." *Catena* 63: 244–260.

Mieth, A. and H.-R. Bork. 2006. "The Dynamics of Soil, Landscape and Culture on Easter Island (Chile)." In *Soils and Societies*, edited by J. R. Mc Neill and V. Winiwarter. Isle of Harris: The White Horse Press.

Mieth, A. and H.-R. Bork. 2010. "Humans, Climate or Introduced Rats: Which is to Blame for the Woodland Destruction on Prehistoric Rapa Nui (Easter Island)?" *Journal of Archaeological Science* 37: 417–426.

Mieth, A. and H.-R. Bork. 2015. Degradation of Resources and Successful Land Use Management on Prehistoric Rapa Nui: Two Sides of the Same Coin. Proceedings of the Royal Academy for Overseas Sciences, Brussels.

Mieth, A., Bork, H.-R. and Vogt, B. 2015. "New research results on palaeo-ecology and palaeo-land use on Rapa Nui." Paper presented on the 9th *International Conference on Easter Island and the Pacific*, June 21st – 26th 2015, Berlin.

Mulrooney, M. A. 2013. "An Island-Wide Assessment of the Chronology of Settlement and Land Use on Rapa Nui (Easter Island) Based on Radiocarbon Data." *Journal of Archaeological Science* 40: 4377–4399.

Nagarajan, P. 2006. "Collapse of Easter Island: Lessons for Sustainability of Small Islands." *Journal of Developing Societies* 22(3): 287–301.

Orliac, C. 2000. "The Woody Vegetation of Easter Island between the Early 14th and the Mid-17th Centuries AD." In *Easter Island Archaeology: Research on Early Rapa Nui Culture*, edited by C. M. Stevenson and W. S. Ayres, 211–220. Los Osos, CA: Easter Island Foundation.

Orliac, C. 2003. "Ligneux et Palmiers de L'île de Pâques du XIème au XVIIème Siècle de Notre Ère." In *Archéologie en Océanie Insulaire: Peuplement, Sociétés et Paysages*, edited by C. Orliac, 184–199. Paris: Éditions Artcom.

Orliac, M. 2010. "Why Would They Have Cut Down All Their Trees?" In *Easter Island: An Epic Voyage*, edited by Montréal Museum of Archaeology and History, 92–97. Montréal: Pointe-à-Callière, Montréal Museum of Archaeology and History.

Orliac, C. and M. Orliac. 1998. "The Disappearance of Easter Island's Forest: Over-Exploitation or Climatic Catastrophe?" In *Easter Island in Pacific Context: South Seas Symposium: Proceedings of the 4th International Conference on Easter Island and East Polynesia* edited by C. M. Stevenson, G. Lee, and F. J. Morin, 129–134. Los Osos, CA: Easter Island Foundation.

Orliac, C. and M. Orliac. 2005. "La Flore Disparue de l'île de Pâques." *Les Nouvelles de l'Archéologie* 102(4): 29–33.

Polet, C. 2011. "Health and Diet of Ancient Easter Islanders: Contribution of Paleopathology, Dental Microwear and S Isotopes." Paper presented at the meeting of the Section of Natural and Medical Sciences.

Prebble, M. and J. L. Dowe. 2008. "The Late Quaternary Decline and Extinction of Palms on Oceanic Pacific Islands." *Quaternary Science Reviews* 27: 2546–2567.

Rainbird, P. 2002. "A Message for the Future? The Rapa Nui (Easter Island) Ecodisaster and Pacific Island Environments." *World Archaeology* 33(3): 436–451.

Rull, V., N. Cañellas-Boltà, A. Sáez, S. Giralt, S. Pla, and O. Margalef. 2010. "Paleoecology of Easter Island: Evidence and Uncertainties." *Earth-Science Reviews* 99: 50–60.

Steadman, D. W., C. P. Vargas, and C. C. Ferrando. 1994. "Stratigraphy, Chronology and Cultural Context of an Early Faunal Assemblage from Easter Island." *Asian Perspectives* 33: 79–96.

Stevenson, C. M., T. L. Jackson, A. Mieth, H.-R. Bork, and T. N. Ladefoged. 2006. "Prehistoric and Early Historic Agriculture at Maunga Orito, Easter Island (Rapa Nui), Chile." *Antiquity* 80: 919–936.

Stevenson, C. M. and S. Haoa. 2008. *Prehistoric Rapa Nui: Landscape and Settlement Archaeology at Hanga Ho'onu*. Los Osos, CA: Easter Island Foundation.

Vogt, B. and J. Moser, J. 2010. "Ancient Rapanui Water Management: German Archaeological Investigations in Ava Ranga Uka A Toroke Hau, 2008–2010." *Rapa Nui Journal* 24(2): 18–26.

Wozniak, J. A. and M. Horrocks. 2010. "Plant Microfossil Analysis of Deposits from Te Niu, Rapa Nui, Demonstrates Forest Disruption c. AD 1300 and Subsequent Dryland Multi-Cropping." In *The Gotland Papers: Selected Papers from the VII International Conference on Easter Island and the Pacific: Migration, Identity, and Cultural Heritage*, edited by P. Wallin and H. Martinsson-Wallin, 111–124. Visby: Gotland University Press.

3 The potential for palm extinction on Rapa Nui by disease

*Kathleen B. Ingersoll and
Daniel W. Ingersoll, Jr.*

Introduction

What led to the disappearance of the *Jubaea chilensis*-like palm, *Paschalococos disperta* on Rapa Nui? The main causes mentioned in the literature argue for overharvesting, climate change (cold periods or drought) (Orliac and Orliac 1998), and the consumption of nuts and young plants by rats (*Rattus exulans*) that may have arrived with the Polynesian colonizers. To avoid that anathema in science – pre-mature closure – we think alternative hypotheses deserve serious consideration. For that reason, we have surveyed a wide range of threats to various palm genera to establish a general field of future enquiry; in this chapter, we will focus mainly on disease. Documented extinction/extirpation threats for palms including fungi, viruses, bacteria, phytoplasma, nematodes, and combinations such as insects and nematodes transmitting pathogens are considered for various parts of the world. We have discovered only one instance where pathogens have been suggested: concerning a paper by Maurice Arnold, Michel Orliac, and Hélène Valladas, entitled "Donnees Novelles sur la Disparition du Palmier," in a volume edited by Heide-Margaret Essen-Bauer (1990), and reviewed by Alison Smith. Smith writes about this paper: "They suggest that some destructive parasite or climatic condition may have killed the palms as they find it hard to believe that people would knowingly destroy all their palm trees" (1991: 39). A parasite!

Tongareva palm blight

We begin by relating an event that would have horrific implications for the Rapanui and thousands of other Polynesians, and in a way, it all began by the chance arrival of a barque, the *Adalente*, on an atoll in the Cooks – Tongareva (aka Penrhyn or Mangarongaro) – where the coconut palms were, as Maude states, "suffering from a devastating disease, most of them were dead, and the rest only produced a few shriveled nuts" (Maude 1981: 5). Tongareva's tiny *land* (vs. lagoon) area is about 9.8 square km (3.8 square miles), about 6% of the area of Rapa Nui. In desperation, the starving inhabitants of Tongareva were more than willing to relocate; they had already been assisted by the Aitutaki, about 320 km (200 miles) away, who had brought them life-sustaining coconuts. The *Adalante* had departed Callao in June of 1862, with Joseph Charles Byrne on board as agent for the firm Ugarte y Santiago, and the barque had previously put in at Nukuhiva (Marquesas) in July to take on supplies. The *Adalante* then headed to Tongareva to investigate the possibility of obtaining *bêch-de-mer* and pearl shell from its lagoon. Instead, and this is the "by chance part," the barque ended up taking 253 consenting recruits to Callao, Peru, where they were sold for the cost of passage to be domestics and agricultural laborers. Just days before the *Adalante* arrived, a French Protectorate schooner, *Latouche-Treville*, had set local precedent by transporting 130 Togarevans to Tahiti to work two year contracts on Tahiti plantations.

Within weeks, the enormous profitability of the *Adalante*'s sale of human cargo in Callao inspired other ships to rapidly fit out for the labor trade in Polynesia – much closer than the opportunities in Melanesia. Within weeks, other ships were headed for Polynesian islands to obtain labor. Peru had abolished slavery in 1854; following abolition, plantation owners were pressed for means to secure inexpensive replacement labor. To address this situation, new legislation to promote the introduction of colonists from Asia and Polynesia was passed by the Peruvian Congress in March 1861 (Maude 1981: 1–4).

Among those ships racing out into the Pacific were the ones that raided Easter Island beginning in December 1862: "the Spanish barque *Rosa y Carmen*; the smaller Peruvian barques *Rosa Patricia* and *Carolina*; two Peruvian brigs, the *Guillermo* and *Micaela Miranda*, and three Peruvian schooners, the *Jose Castro*, *Hermosa Delores*, and *Cora*" (Maude 1981: 15). The *Adalante*'s Christianized recruits from Tongareva most likely were voluntary and perhaps the recruits from ships taking on Rapanui in October of 1862 were voluntary, but the "December Raiders" used trickery, force of arms, and chains to capture hundreds of Rapanui and transport them to Callao labor markets. The very few Rapanui who were repatriated brought back smallpox and other diseases with them. Along with further removals to plantations on other Polynesian islands, these events led to the near extinction of Rapa Nui's population. Altogether, an estimated 6000 Polynesians died, "directly or indirectly from the Peruvian recruiting venture" (Maude 1981: 182). And the horror all began with the diseased and dying palms of Tongareva.

Palmerston palm blight

The next example is that of Palmerston, an island in an atoll in the Cooks of about 2.6 square km (1 square mile) land area. In 1777, Cook stopped at the then uninhabited Palmerston, a place he had encountered on an earlier voyage for refreshments – scurvy grass, coconuts, and pandanus palms. There Cook saw "sea birds, land crabs, lizards, and a few rats" and pieces of a canoe and paddles (Langdon 1995: 77; Beaglehole 1967: 94–95). Fifteen years later, remains of a derelict double canoe were reported by Captain Edwards of HMS Pandora (Langdon 1995: 77).

Nearly a century later, in the 1850s, Palmerston came to be occupied or reoccupied, this time by individuals of European extraction:

> In the 1850s, Englishman Jeffrey Strickland, by right of sole occupancy, claimed "ownership" of the entire atoll which then still lay outside the dominion of any nation. He soon sold his "rights" to Palmerston atoll to a Captain Bowles who, in turn, in the early 1860s sold this to the powerful British-born plantation owner John Brander of Tahiti. (This was the same John Brander who, nearly ten years later, would establish Rapa Nui's infamous sheep ranch.) In 1863 Brander sent his personal man-ship's carpenter and cooper William Masters, who allegedly came from Gloucestershire, England to Palmerston Island with instructions to supervise a handful of indentured "Tahitian" laborers in the planting of coconut palms and the production of copra.
>
> (Fischer 1998: 40)

Interestingly, Martienssen (2013: np), a filmmaker and BBC journalist at the time, was told on Palmerston that William Marsters was not born until about 1830, long after Cook had died in Hawaii.

Master or Marsters, working under the Brander aegis, settled there with his two Tongaraven (Penrhyn), later three, Tongaraven wives, eventually planted 200,000 additional coconut trees (Fischer 1998: 41), with a Brander ship coming in every six months or so to pick up the copra (for coconut oil). Marsters acted to claim Palmerston, and succeeded – Brander died 1877 – in 1888 with the designation of Protectorate by Great Britain. However, according to Martienssen in his BBC report, Marsters "died of malnutrition in 1899 after his coconut trees were destroyed by blight."

Note that Fischer (1998) does not mention this blight in his Rapa Nui Journal article, "Palmerston Island: End of the 'British Ariki'."

But for Tongareva and Palmerston, whatever the horrible disease or blight was, the palms have since recovered. Current photographs of Tongareva show prospering palms, and Fischer reports that "[m]ost of the few families who today remain on Palmerston tend arrowroot plots as well as double rows of tall coconut palms which (with *puka* trees [*Meryta sinclairi*]) also serve to mark family land boundaries" (1998: 40). The current human populations of Tongareva and Palmerston are about 213 and 62, respectively, down significantly from their earlier highs. What our first two Pacific examples show is how disease – apparently with no deliberate or indirect human agency implicated – can cripple or destroy a palm population. The Tongareva and Palmerston cases cited above, involve coconut palm (*Cocos nucifera*), but as related members of the Tribe Cocoeae, it is within the realm of possibility that *Jubaea* could have suffered a similar fate, especially with the high population densities that have been estimated, ranging from 600,000–1.5 million (Love 2004: 133) to 16 million (Mieth and Bork 2004: 51) and recently, even higher—19.7 million (Mieth and Bork 2015, and see the preceding chapter by Mieth and Bork).

Rapa Nui virus, larvae?

For the third example, we visit Rapa Nui, where a number of species of palm have been established, and can be admired along the streets and in the gardens of Hanga Roa, at CONAF, as well as in the occasional *manavai*, and at Anakena. In 1989, this report was published in the *Rapa Nui Journal* under "What's New in Hanga Roa:" "Botanic experts associated with CONAF (National Parks of Chile) are expected to arrive soon to the island to study the problem of the dying palm trees at Anakena, which seemingly are being attacked by a virus." Fortunately, this scenic grove recovered, but the potential for loss of palms by disease on Rapa Nui, is demonstrated. In 1987, published in *Rapa Nui Notes* under "Development Underway," this appeared:

> Beginning in September, 2000 palms will be planted around the airport and the village to provide a more tropical effect for incoming tourists. Some concern was expressed for the palms now on the island that seem to be under attack from larvae. Any palm tree specialists out there amongst our readers?
>
> (p.10)

In 1987, under "What's New in Polynesia" in the *Rapa Nui Journal*, it was reported that 100 *Jubaea chilensis* "shoots" were brought to Rapa Nui from Hacienda Cocalan in Chile; of these, 30 survived. Incidentally, Grau later reported in his *Jubaea* census, a population for Cocalan, Chile, of 35,000 *Jubaea* palms (Grau 1996: 38). According to Charola (1991: 65), "CONAF (National Parks of Chile) has recently planted some palms at Ovahe's beach. The conifers planted at Vai Atare a few years ago are doing well, as are the eucalyptus seedlings at Vaitea." When the movie *Rapa Nui* (released 1994) was being filmed, islanders were selling palms from their patios of Hanga Roa for the movie sets at $300–$720 each; these were dug up with power equipment and moved to Rano Aroi (Lee 1993: 7; Liller 1993: 36). But Hanga Roa and its environs happily recovered from this dramatic drain on its late 20th century palm resources.

Additional palms were sent to Rapa Nui from Tahiti; 500 coconut palm shoots of a projected 2000 from Tahiti were reported in 1997 in "What's New in Hangaroa." Later, in 1998 under the heading "Palm Tree Controversy," it was stated that 400 *Jubaea chilensis* palms were to be brought to Vaitea via the Chilean Air Force, including four large ones, for a new botanical garden. This was problematical for some islanders who pointed to a loss of prime agricultural land. In "What's New in Hanga Roa" (1998) of the subsequent issue of the *Rapa Nui Journal*, the cancellation of the new botanical garden at Vaitea was reported. In "What's New in Hanga Roa" (1999): "At the end of March, palm trees from Tahiti will be brought to the island to replace those in bad condition." (p. 59) No mention is made of what is ailing the palms, but this time, no palms were being dug up for Hollywood props.

Palm classification and characteristics

Before moving on to documented palm disease examples, we offer a quick note on classification, drawn from Dransfield and Uhl (1986). In this system, Subfamilies are divided into Tribes, then Subtribes, then Genera. The taxonomic relationship between *Cocos nucifera* and *Jubaea chilensis* is traced in the following way. Beginning with the Subfamily *Arecoideae* (one of 6), followed by the Tribe *Cocoeae* (one of 5), then the Subtribes (6), among them *Butiinae* with 9 Genera, including among others *Butia* (pindo or jelly palm), *Cocos*, *Syagrus* (queen palm), and *Jubaea*. To illustrate genetic compatability or relatedness, we would point to crosses that have been recorded or achieved between these palms: *Butia capitata* × *Jubaea chilensis* (both directions in regard to gender), *Jubaea chilensis* × *Syagrus romanzoffiana*, and *Cocos* × *Butia* (The Desert Northwest, www.desertnorthwest.com/articles/cocoid_hybrids.html; Kembrey 2012; Riffle and Craft 2003: 59, 281). The reason for including this quick introduction to classification is to show that *Jubaea/Paschalococos* likely share characteristics, genetic material, and pathogen risks in general and in parallel ways with other palms, especially cocoid palms such as *Butia*, *Syagrus*, and *Cocos*. As with traditional classification schema, the literature on palm genomics also indicates close genetic relatedness in the palms relevant here, again, especially with cocoid palms like *Attalea*, *Butia*, and *Cocos* (see for example Arunachalam 2012; Meerow et al. 2009, especially their cladograms in Figures 3.1 and 3.2).

A very quick sketch of palm characteristics: palms are monocots that differ in many ways from what Westerners usually think of when they think of trees. Unlike oaks, birches, or pines (*Quercus*, *Betula*, *Pinus*), palms trunk interiors consist largely of living, actively transporting, vascular bundles rather than dead sequestered cellulose and lignin. The vascular bundles contain both xylem and phloem. Unlike dicot trees, palm interiors in that sense are alive, top to bottom. There are no annular growth rings; instead there are rather flexible straw-like tubes that continue down to become un-branching tube-like roots. Unlike trees, palm trunk density increases almost imperceptibly from the innermost cortex to the outermost epidermis or "pseudo-bark" (Hodel 2009, 2015 web; see also Jones 1995; Lack and Baker 2011; Tomlinson 1990, 2006, and Tomlinson et al. 2011).

Examples of palm threats

The purpose here is a brief general exploration of a range of extinctions and extirpation threats to palms. Threats would include pathogens such as fungi, protista, viruses, bacteria, and helminthes and macro-threats such as insects (beetles, ants, termites), and birds. We have collected extensive data along these lines but here there is space here for only a few examples.

Fungi: bayoud

According to Fisher et al, "Web of Science literature searches and compilation of previous meta-analyses of infection-related species extinction and regional extirpation events show that fungi comprise the highest threat for both animal host (72%) and plant-host (64%) species" (2012: 188). Some symbiotic fungi assist in palm growth (Esmaeilifar 2013, addressing date palm), and can even be employed as biocontrol agents as in the case of the rhinoceros beetle, a serious threat to coconut palms (Shine et al. 2003: 171). Other fungi, however, can be disastrous, as in the case of bayoud, an affliction that causes the fronds to appear white. The cause of bayouds is a microscopic fungus, *Fusarium oxysporum forma specialis albedinis*, as described by Zaid et al:

> This disease was first reported in 1870 in Zagora-Morocco. By 1940, it had already affected several date plantations and after one century, the disease has practically affected all Moroccan palm groves, as well as those of the western and central Algerian Sahara.
> (Zaid et al. 2002: Section 2.1.)

Bayoud disease causes considerable damage that can sometimes take on spectacular proportions when the disease presents its violent epidemic aspect. In one century, Bayoud has destroyed more than twelve million palms in Morocco and three million in Algeria. Bayoud destroyed the world's most renowned varieties that are susceptible to the disease and particularly those which produce high quality and quantity fruit (Medjool, Deglet Nour, BouFegouss). It also accelerated the phenomenon of desertification (Figures 90a and b). The result is an influx of farmers who have abandoned their land and moved to large urban centers.

The continued spread of bayoud highlights the problem threatening the important plantations of Deglet Nour and Ghars in Oued Rhir, Zibans in Algeria and even in Tunisia, which is presently free of the disease, but has 70 % to 80 % of the date palm areas under varieties susceptible to it. The disease continues to advance relentlessly to the east, despite prophylactic measures and regular attempts at eradication undertaken in Algeria (Zaid et al. 2002: Section 2.1). It is evident, therefore, that Bayoud constitutes a plague to Saharan agriculture and at the present expansion rate, it will certainly pose serious problems of human, social, and economic nature to other date-producing areas of the world (Zaid et al. 2002, Chapter XII, section 2, Fungal Diseases of Date Palm, not paginated).

In the Canary Islands, the date palms, *Phoenix canariensis*, have recently been stricken by *Fusarium oxysporum f. sp. Canariensis*. *Jubaea chilensis* as well as the "true" date palm, *Phoenix dactylifer*, seem to be resistant (Flora Grubb Gardens web site 2013). However, this fungus is quite adept and capable of evolving incessantly. Other strains of this genus and species afflict plants as diverse as coconut palms (Siriwardhana et al. 2009: 67), tomatoes, melons, squash, pumpkins, taro, and bananas. Minor mutations in the plasmids could have changed, or could rapidly change the palm/fungus relationship, at any time, past, present, or future, for the genera *Jubaea* or *Paschalococos*.

We have considered only one fungus here – to represent a class of threats – but for *Cocos nucifera* alone, some 70 genera and species of deleterious fungi have been discovered and identified (Ploetz et al. 1999 [2017]).

Nematodes: red ring, Bursaphelenchus cocophilus

The next threat we would examine is nematodes. As with fungi, some benefit palms but others afflict them. Some nematodes infesting palms do so via the soil, as with *Meloidogyne* spp (Onkendi et al. 2014), but others infest palms from above ground, as is the case in our example, the nematode *Bursaphelenchus cocophilus*:

> *Bursaphelenchus cocophilus* causes the red ring disease of palms. Symptoms of red ring disease were first described on Trinidad coconut palms in 1905. Red ring disease can appear in several species of tropical palms, including date, Canary Island date, and Cuban royal, but is most common in oil and coconut palms. The red ring nematode parasitizes the palm weevil *Rhynchophorus palmarum* L., which is attracted to fresh trunk wounds and acts as a vector for *B. cocophilus* to uninfected trees.
>
> (Brammer and Crow 2002: np)

The nematodes appear anywhere in the parenchymatous tissue, and even in the roots and surrounding soil, though initial entry seems to be by means of the palm weevil. Other vectors may be implicated, such as ants, termites, and spiders, but palm weevils are able to travel impressive distances in a short time frame and multiply rates of infection. Note the range of palms impacted – one source states "over 17 species in the *Palmae* family" (Sullivan 2013: 6). The disease has been widely reported: Mexico, Central America, South America, and the Caribbean but not yet in Hawaii or the Continental United States, although specialists are on the alert because the disease can be very costly as this quote from Sullivan demonstrates:

> In Trinidad, red ring disease can kill 35% of young coconut trees. In Venezuela, 35% of oil palms (*Elaeis* spp.) were killed by red ring disease

over a 10-year period (Brammer and Crow 2002). Chinchilla (1991) states that losses of 5 to 15% in oil and coconut palm plantations as a result of *B. cocophilus* is common in several countries in Central and South America.

(Sullivan 2013: 6)

Today there are counters to reduce these losses, including insecticides to control the weevil vectors and infested tree removal – but imagine what the losses might be without modern treatments.

Phytoplasma: Phytoplasma palmae

Our third case example is lethal yellowing, a phytoplasmal disease (*Phytoplasma palmae*), one of about 15 known phytoplasmal diseases afflicting coconut palms alone. Phytoplasma, formerly known as mycoplasma-like organisms, are now usually classified as prokaryotic bacteria that lack cell walls (having a multilayered cell membrane instead) and a membrane-defined nucleus (a nucleoid, instead, containing limited DNA in a single cyclical double strand), that reside in phloem plant tissue and that require vectors for transmission. Insects such as planthopper *Myndus crudus* have been identified as vectors. The lethal yellowing disease affects not only coconut palms but also some 30 other palm species (Bourdeix et al); the disease has been reported in Florida, the Caribbean, Mexico, and Africa. Bourdeix et al.report:

It is quite difficult to get a precise evaluation of the losses caused by LY diseases. In Jamaica, the Coconut Industry Board's records show that out of the 6 million susceptible Jamaica Tall coconut palms in 1961, 90 % had been killed by LY by 1981. In Ghana, about one million coconut palms were killed during the last 30 years. In Togo, by 1964, about 60,000 palms, or 50 % of the coconut groves, were destroyed by the so-called 'Kaincopé disease'. In Florida, by 1973, at least 20,000 coconut palms (about 6 % of the total) were affected by the disease. In Mexico and Tanzania, thousands of hectares were also destroyed but no precise evaluation is available.

(Bourdeix et al. 1998–2006: np)

Insect: rhinoceros beetle, Oryctes rhinoceros

Our fourth case is an insect. Termites such as *Neotermes rainbowi* reported on Tuvalu, can "topple" palm trees (Shine et al. 2003: 177). Beetles can spread rapidly and do serious damage to palms. For example, the coconut leaf hispa or coconut hispine beetle, *Brontispa longissima*, "attacks and eventually kills palms and coconut trees. Its spread began in the 1960s from New Caledonia to all of the Society Islands, on to Nuku Hiva by 1970, to Tubai by 1981 and Rurutu by 1983, both in the Australs and Rangiroa in the Tuamotus" (Shine et al. 2003: 26). But here our focus is on another beetle, which evoked this headline in the *LA Times*, January 27, 2015: "Hawaii hopes to fend off invasion by coconut rhinoceros beetle," illustrated with a photo of this large palmivore. The rhinoceros beetle (*Oryctes rhinoceros Linné*), mentioned above, discovered in Hawaii in December 2014, likes palms, but apparently also potentially, bananas, papayas, sugar cane, if all available palms are destroyed (Lin 2015). The quote below from Zaid et al. describes the invasion process in oil palms:

> only the adult beetles are responsible for causing damage to the palms. The pest has been found to be more destructive to young plants. They remain hidden during the daytime and become active at night, when they fly about and reach the tops of date palms. They drill large holes close to the base of the growing heart-leaf and enter the stem. They feed on the softer tissues of the growing heart-leaf and cut right through it, with the result that further growth stops and the palm ultimately dies. The beetle also causes damage by boring into tender fronds, chewing tissues and throwing them out as a fibrous dry mass (Figure 122). Fronds may hence break and if the growing point is bored the plant dies off. Most of the damage occurs during the rainy season.
> (Zaid et al. 2002: Section 6.5)

The rhinoceros beetle is quite capable of killing coconut, oil, and other palms all by itself, but in addition, its burrowing opens up opportunities for infection by pathogens such as fungi. It has been a serious pest in the South Pacific since the early 20th century.

Conclusion

The first part of the paper concerned two Pacific island locations, Tongareva and Palmerston, where lethal diseases of palm created dire survival conditions for humans, and where without outside intervention, cultural collapse or near collapse could have occurred. Rapa Nui, the third location, recently experienced disease challenges to its introduced palms on which the human population thankfully did not depend. Fortunately, an unidentified disease (a virus?) and an insect infestation did not eliminate the Rapa Nui palms, but perhaps with extremely high population densities of palms, the outcome could have been more serious. In all three cases, we would emphasize that no human agency has been suspected or identified.

In the second part of the paper, we picked four examples from an extensive database we have accumulated on palms diseases and macro-parasites.

The examples illustrate how millions of palms may be lost through no direct human agency; without human intervention with insecticides, plant selection, gene manipulation, and culling, some of the afflicted palms might well have become extinct. Although our present examples do not currently include *Paschalococos* (not really possible) or *Jubaea*, we would point out that many of the palm diseases and parasites infect or attack a wide range of palm species and even other plants, and that with a few minor genetic changes, the possibility of pathogens and parasites jumping to new species arises.

Indeed, humans may speed up the diffusion process of diseases and parasites – with colonization, monoculture, ships, trains, and airplanes – but many means of purely natural transport exist. Winds loft spores and insects thousands of miles; sea currents move flotsam and jetsam hosting potential novel colonists; birds transport bacteria, viruses, and nematodes in the soils clinging to their feet. Massive conglomerations of debris following landslides, earthquakes, and volcanoes can convey rocks, soils, and living organisms across oceans as in the instance of the Krakatoa eruption in 1883 that generated enormous pumice rafts incorporating organic debris including human, simian (monkeys), and feline (tigers) corpses that reached distant Zanzibar (Winchester 2004: 7, 294–297). The Tōhoku tsunami of 2011 swept debris from Japan to distant North American shores (Gewin 2013). All of the Pacific islands that interest us here were populated with a varying range of life-forms before any human occupation, including extinctions and extirpation as a regular, ongoing ecological processes.

No island – actually, no landmass of any description – ever exits in equilibrium in regard to species, diseases, geology, climate, or sea level, with or without humans in the picture. Ultimately each volcanic island, unless part of a migrating rising/sinking chain, begins its life-form career as a *tabula rasa*. After emergence, you might argue that the life-form succession of an island becomes and remains a history and future of never-ending invasives, with or without human presence. Once upon a time, *Paschalococos disperta*, by one means or another, reached Rapa Nui shores, colonized it at some expense to other species, and eventually disappeared.

How *Paschalococos disperta* disappeared may have entailed direct or indirect human cultural agency – or maybe not. We still regard the Rapa Nui palm extinction as an unresolved question. Before seeking closure, in the mode of "the Rapa Nui mystery solved" approach, other lines of evidence merit consideration. What might be the means of exploring these other lines of evidence? Looking for fungal and bacterial spores, insect egg cases, and insect exoskeletal material in archaeological soil samples – a sort of forensic pathology – would be a start. Or examining charcoal fragments for signs of pathogen or insect damage, such as tunnels of palm-boring beetles. There is the possibility that *Paschalococos disperta*, with its densely crowded population suffered massive losses (see Figure 3.1).

Potential for palm extinction 69

Figure 3.1 What the millions of palms on Rapa Nui might have looked like terminally infected by a disease like phytoplasmal disease or red ring. If the fronds are gone, there is no possibility of recovery. Ahu Tongariki is in the foreground with the Poike rising in the background

(Drawing by F. A. Meatyard.)

Today on Molokai, the cherished Kapuaiwa Coconut Grove (*Cocos nucifera*) appears to be in critical condition (see Figure 3.2). In a *Molokai Dispatch* article, Uechi reported (2015: np):

> Last December, the Molokai/Maui Invasive Species Committee (MoMISC) gathered fruit and leaf samples from the grove for testing, according to Lori Buchanan, field outreach coordinator for MoMISC. The Department of Agriculture (DOA) and UH College of Tropical Agriculture tested the samples and identified multiple pests and diseases.
>
> "Besides the coconut mite, there are other pests adding to the overall decline of the trees," Buchanan said via email. "The following was also detected: coconut scale, a weevil, white flies and other hard scales. Also suspected is some type of fungus."

Figure 3.2 The Kapuaiwa Coconut Grove on Molokai, showing severe losses of its coconut palms

(Photograph by the authors, March 27, 2015.)

Tests of today's cultivated soils on Rapa Nui might disclose previously unrecognized nematodes or fungi still influencing the success potential of a range of plants, such as palms, taro, sugar cane, toromiro, and paper mulberry. Here is a case in point, although not for palms, but for the toromiro on Rapa Nui:

> There is no longer any need to underline what the *Sophora toromiro* represents for the inhabitants of Easter Island. This small – almost mythical – legendary tree, said to be created by the gods but of which the pollen has been dated to 35,000 years, left the land of its ancestors more than 30 years ago. The descendants of the last *Sophora toromiro*, taken by the team of Thor Heyerdahl in 1956 at 300 meters inside Rano Kau, are grown today in Sweden and inside greenhouses of a few botanical gardens. The Pascuans still remember the recent attempts to reintroduce the *Sophora toromiro* by Bjorn Alden in 1988. Unfortunately this effort resulted in a failure due to a root nematode which killed the plants.
>
> (Orliac 1993: 28)

A root nematode: such an organisim could have been brought in on dirt on the hooves of European livestock such as sheep, cattle, and horses. Efforts to reintroduce toromiro on Rapa Nui have been frustrating to say the least, as it often dies or grows very slowly.

This paper is part of a broader research project. We have been building a database on palm characteristics, pest and disease threats, and palm economics. This is a work in progress that we invite others to join in and contribute to.

Acknowledgments

We appreciate the many discussions and email exchanges with Sonia Haoa Cardinali, Christopher Stevenson, Andreas Mieth, and Burkhard Vogt on this topic. Thanks to Jon Smith and his students at Molokai High for help studying palm characteristics on Molokai.

References

Arunachalam, V. 2012. *Genomics of Cultivated Palms*. Amsterdam and Boston: Elsevier.

Beaglehole, J. C., ed. 1967. *The Journals of Captain James Cook on His Voyages of Discovery: The Voyage of the 'Resolution' and 'Discovery', 1772–1775*. Cambridge: Hakluyt Society.

Bourdeix, R., K. Allou, and J. L. Konan Konan. 1998–2006. Lethal Yellowing Diseases of the Coconut Palm: An Overview. Palm Diseases, Chapter 8. Palm and Cycad Societies of Florida, Inc. www.plantapalm.com/vpe/pestsndiseases/vpe_ly_coconut.htm.

Brammer, A. S. and W. T. Crow. 2002. Featured Creatures: Entomology and Nematology Publication number EENY-236, University of Florida. http://entnemdept.ufl.edu/creatures/nematode/red_ring_nematode.htm.

Charola, A. E. 1991. "Preservation Project." *Rapa Nui Journal* 5(4): 65.

"Development Underway." 1987. *Rapa Nui Notes* 4: 2.

Dransfield, J. and N. W. Uhl. 1986. "An Outline of a Classification of Palms." *Principes* 30(1): 3–11.

Esmaeilifar, A. 2013. "Study on Mycorhizal Symbiosis with Date Palm on Stability and Vegetative Growth Traits." *International Journal of Agriculture and Crop Sciences* 5(2): 160–167.

Essen-Bauer, H.-M. 1990. *State and Perspectives of Scientific Research in Easter Island Culture*. Frankfurt am Main: Courier Forschungsinstitut Senckenberg 125.

Fisher, M. C., D. A. Henk, C. J. Briggs, J. S. Brownstein, L. C. Madoff, S. L. McCraw, and S. J. Gurr. 2012. "Emerging Fungal Threats to Animal, Plant, and Ecosystem Health." *Nature* 484: 186–194.

Fischer, S. R. 1998. "Palmerston Island: End of the 'British Ariki?'." *Rapa Nui Journal* 12(2): 40–44.

Gewin, V. 2013. "Tsunami Triggers Invasion Concerns." *Nature* 495(7439): 13–14. www.nature.com/news/tsunami-triggers-invasion-concerns-1.12538.

Grau, J. 1996. "Jubaea, The Palm of Chile and Easter Island?" *Rapa Nui Journal* 10(2): 37–40.

Hodel, D. R. 2009. "Biology of Palms and Implications for Management in the Landscape." *HortTechnology*, October-December 19(4): 676–681. The American Society for Horticultural Science. See also http://horttech.ashspublications.org/content/19/4/676, 2015.

Jones, D. 1995. *Palms Throughout the World*. Washington, DC: Smithsonian Institution Press.

Kembrey, N. 2012. "Dr. Frankenstein Palms: Cold Hardy Hybrids." Chamaerops No. 46, published online March 18, 2003, accessed January 6, 2012 at www.palmsociety.org/members/english/chamaerops/046/046-09.shtml.

Lack, H. W. and W. J. Baker, eds. 2011. *Die Welt der Palmen/The World of Palms*. Berlin: Botanisches Museum Berlin-Dahlem.

Langdon, R. 1995. "Some Iconoclastic Thoughts about Those Polynesian Rat Bones at Anakena." *Rapa Nui Journal* 9(3): 77–80.

Lee, G. 1993. "There's No Biz Like Showbiz: Hollywood Comes to Rapa Nui." *Rapa Nui Journal* 7(1): 6–8.

Liller, W. 1993. "Ecocide: From Dr. Juan Grau, Secretary General of the Institute of Ecology in Chile, Comes the Following Item, Titled 'Ecocide in Rapa Nui' *(El Mercurio)*." Translation by Liller. *Rapa Nui Journal* 7(2): 36–37.

Lin, S. 2015. "Hawaii Hopes to Fend Off Invasion by Coconut Rhinoceros Beetle." *LA Times*, January 27. https://caps.ceris.purdue.edu/dmm/2137.

Love, C. 2004. "Quoted in Getting to Know You." *Rapa Nui Journal* 18(2): 132–134.

Martienssen, T. 2013. "Palmerston: The Island at the End of the Earth." *BBC News*, Palmerston, Cook Islands. December 29, 2013. www.bbc.co.uk/news/magazine-25430383.

Maude, H. E. 1981. *Slavers in Paradise: The Peruvian Labor Trade in Polynesia, 1862–1864*. Canberra: Australian University Press.

Meerow, A. W., L. N. James, W. Borrone, T. L. P. Couvreur, M. Mauro-Herrera, W. J. Hahn, D. N. Kuhn, K. Nakamura, N. H. Oleas, and R. J. Schnell. S. Jolly, ed. 2009. "Phylogenetic Analysis of Seven WRKY Genes across the Palm Subtribe Attaleinae (Arecaceae) Identifies *Syagrus* as Sister Group of the Coconut." *PLoS One*, 4(10): e7353. www.ncbi.nlm.nih.gov/pmc/articles/PMC2752195/.

Mieth, A. and H.-R. Bork. 2004. *Easter Island: Rapa Nui: Scientific Pathways to Secrets of the Past*. Man and Environment 1. Kiel: Schmidt and Klaunig.

Mieth, A., H.-R. Bork, and I. Feeser. 2002. "Prehistoric Land Use on Poike Penninsiula, Easter Island, Rapa Nui." *Rapa Nui Journal* 16(2): 89–95.

Mieth, A., Bork, H.-R. and Vogt, B. (2015). "New research results on palaeo-ecology and palaeo-land use on Rapa Nui." Paper presented on the 9th International Conference on Easter Island and the Pacific, June 21st–26th 2015, Berlin.

Onkendi, E. M., G. M. Kariuki, M. Marais, and L. N. Moleleki. 2014. "The Threat of Root-Knot Nematodes (Meloidogyne spp.) in Africa: A Review." In *Plant Pathology*. 2014: 1–11. Doi:10.1111/ppa.12202

Orliac, C. 1993. "A *Sophora tormiro* in the Exotic Botanoical Garden of Menton (France)." *Rapa Nui Journal* 7(2): 28–29.

Orliac, C. and M. Orliac. 1998. "The Disappearance of Easter Island's Forest: Over-Exploitation or Climatic Catastrophe?" In *Easter Island in Pacific Context South Seas Symposium: Proceedings of the Fourth International Conference on Easter*

Island and East Polynesia, edited by C. M. Stevenson, G. Lee, and F. J. Morin, 129–134. Los Osos, CA: The Easter Island Foundation.

"Palm Tree Controversy." 1998. *Rapa Nui Journal* 12(3): 93.

Ploetz, R., N. Harrison, and P. Jones. 1999 [2017]. "Common Names of Plant Diseases: Diseases of Coconut Palm." *American Phytopathological Society*. www.apsnet.org/online/common/names/coconut.asp (current link copyright 2017).

Rapa Nui. 1994. Film distributed by Warner Bros. Film directed by Kevin Reynolds, produced by Kevin Costner and Jim Wilson. Written by Kevin Reynolds and Tim Rose Price.

Riffle, R. L. and P. Craft. 2003. *An Encyclopedia of Palms*. Portland, Oregon: Timber Press.

Shine, C., J. K. Reaser, and A. T. Gutierrez, eds. 2003. *Invasive Alien Species in the Austral-Pacific Region*. National Report and Directory of Resources. The Global Invasive Species Programme.

Siriwardhana, P. H. A. P., L. C. P. Frenando, and J. M. M. A. Jayasundara. 2009. "Toxins Produced by Fusarium Species in Leaf Scorch Decline Affected Coconut Palms (Cocos nucifera L.): Quantitative Analysis of Fusaric Acid, Zearalenone and T-2." *Cord* 25(1): 69.

Smith, A. 1991. "Review of State and Perspectives of Scientific Research in Easter Island Culture, Heide-Margaret Essen-Baur, ed. Courier Forschungsinstitut Senckenberg 125. Frankfurt am Main. 1930." *Rapa Nui Journal* 5(3): 37–40.

Sullivan, M. 2013. CPHST Pest Datasheet for *Bursaphelenchus cocophilus*. USDA-APHIS-PPQ-CPHST. https://caps.ceris.purdue.edu/dmm/2137.

Tomlinson, P. B. 1990. *The Structural Biology of Palms*. Oxford: Clarendon Press.

Tomlinson, P. B. 2006. "The Uniqueness of Palms." *Botanical Journal of the Linnean Society* 151: 5–14.

Tomlinson, P. B., J. W. Horn, and J. B. Fisher. 2011. *The Anatomy of Palms: Arecaceae-Palmae*. Oxford: Oxford University Press.

Uechi, C. 2015. "Concerns Grow over Coconut Grove." Wednesday, June 3, 2015. https://themolokaidispatch.com/concerns-grow-over-coconut-grove/.

"What's New in Hanga Roa." 1989. *Rapa Nui Journal* 3(1): 10.

"What's New in Polynesia." 1993. *Rapa Nui Journal* 7(2): 36.

"What New in Hanga Roa." 1997. *Rapa Nui Journal* 11(2): 95.

"What's New in Hanga Roa." 1998. *Rapa Nui Journal* 12(4): 122.

"What's New in Hanga Roa." 1999. *Rapa Nui Journal* 13(2): 59.

Winchester, S. 2004. *Krakatoa: The Day the World Exploded, August 27, 1883*. New York: HarperCollins.

Zaid, A., P. F. de Wet, M. Djerbi, and A. Oihabi. 2002. Diseases and Pests of Date Palm. Chapter XII in Date Palm Cultivation, edited and compiled by Abdelouahhab Zaid. FAO Plant Production and Protection Paper 156, Rev. 1. Rome: Food and Agricultural Organization of the United Nations. www.fao.org/docrep/006/Y4360E/y4360e0g.htm.

4 New interpretations of pollen data from Easter Island

John R. Flenley and Kevin Butler

Introduction

Prehistory is an observational science. That is to say, it is based on the assembly of observations from a variety of sources. These include archaeology as a principal source, providing observations by the excavation of previous locations of human dwellings or other activity. There are, however, other sources such as glottochronology, in which the study of languages provides important clues, and many kinds of environmental history, which tell us not only about the environment in which people lived, but how they modified that environment. Did they, for instance, clear forests to create agricultural land?

Palynology (pollen analysis), among the sciences contributing to prehistory, has held pride of place in environmental reconstructions for a long time, especially since aided by radiocarbon dating. The beauty of pollen is that, unlike archaeology, the story it tells is not restricted to a tiny area. Pollen, especially from wind-pollinated plants, spreads some distance through the air, and is thus able to give a regional as well as a local picture. But it does not usually travel a very long way, and we know whether the story we are getting is local or regional by the distance which the pollen is likely to have travelled. For instance, a small pond in a forested area usually gives a very local picture, whereas samples from the middle of a large lake or swamp usually give a regional picture (Jacobson and Bradshaw 1981). The other great advantage of palynology is that the pollen is normally preserved in organic materials such as lake muds and peats, which make carbon dating somewhat easier. One has, however, as always, to be very careful about the origin of the materials dated; deposits may be contaminated by older (e.g., redeposited) material or by younger material such as roots growing down from above.

When I (JRF) first visited Rapa Nui in 1977, I was immediately astounded by the potential for palynology offered by three sites: Rano Kau, Rano Raraku and Rano Aroi. Their locations are shown in Figure 4.1. Cores from all three sites provided exciting results as recorded by Flenley et al. (1991). But there were complications. Rano Raraku looked the most promising in view of its proximity to the statue quarries, but dates suggested there was a

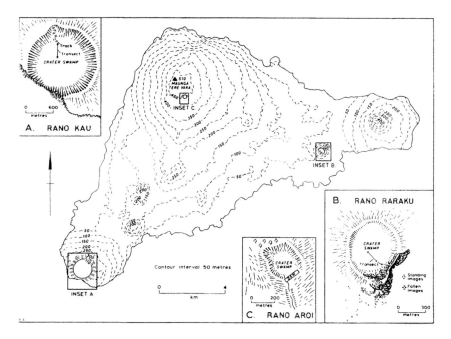

Figure 4.1 Map of Easter Island showing palynological sites

hiatus in deposition, giving an incomplete story. Subsequent studies (Mann et al. 2008) confirmed this, and make conclusions about human activity very difficult and inconclusive. Rano Aroi, it turned out, had been interfered with by people using teams of bullocks to scrape out sediment to the edges in an attempt to make a water conservation site in the 1920s.

That left Rano Kau: large, deep, dangerous, unique. The diameter of approximately 1 km for the swamp gave it a better chance of catching pollen from the entire island, compared with the smaller sites. The swamp appeared to be deep and dangerous to work in, but suggested a continuous record covering a long period of time. The height of the crater walls created a wind-free environment (van Steenis 1935). That feature and the reliable supply of fresh water must surely have been extremely attractive to people arriving with tropical crops from elsewhere in Polynesia. In fact, terracing had already been reported inside the crater (Ferdon 1961). All these features were unique on the island. The site was probably the finest site in Polynesia for palynology.

During my first visit to the island in 1977, I (JRF) collected a core (KAO 1) only 27 meters out from the NNW edge and bottoming on hard rock at 10 meters depth. Radiocarbon dates based on bulk sediment gave dates back to 1360 BP. These dates are all measured back from AD 1950, when radiocarbon dating was invented (BP = before present, i.e., before AD 1950). On a later trip in 1983 with Jim Teller and volunteers, we collected another core (KAO 2) ca. 300 meters out from the NNE edge that was fairly near the middle of the floating swamp which covers most of the crater. It was described by Flenley et al. (1991), which also included the pollen analysis of KAO 1. It showed the former existence of a palm forest, which went into decline around 1200 BP.

When we had core KAO2 carbon dated, we initially used bulk dating, which was usual at the time. The results were disappointing, as there were several inversions, but in general they showed that the core dated back to the Late Pleistocene, and probably covered the entire Holocene. Palynology took some time, and I enlisted the help of Kevin Butler. We eventually published the results in a conference proceeding (Butler and Flenley 2001), but they were difficult to interpret because of the date inversions. It was clear, however, that a sub-tropical rainforest had existed on the island, and that this had disappeared progressively during the last 2000 years or so. The dominant tree had been a palm, which was now extinct on the island.

This chapter is about the subsequent re-dating and interpretation of the Rano Kau 2 core, which has proved extremely rewarding. It was especially appropriate because it covered all likely settlement dates for the island. It became clear in the 1990s that people were getting much more consistent dates from swamp cores by dating individually selected macrofossils rather than bulk sediment. By choosing items such as fruits or seeds, one could be reasonably sure that one was dating the actual layer in which these items were found. This had become possible as the dating techniques required less material than before, using AMS dating. When we began to apply these techniques to the core samples, we found it was nearly always possible to extract the small one-seeded fruits of the reed *Scirpus californicus* from a sample by inspection under a low-power binocular microscope. *S. californicus* grows almost all over the Rano Kau swamp. It flowers each year, and the fruits fall to the surface of the mud that formed in the year of the flowering. These fruits were submitted for dating and produced a much more self-consistent set of results, with only a single inversion. That was near the surface of the floating mat, where human disturbance could well have been possible. These dates were published (Butler and Flenley 2010), and we were encouraged that Candace Gossen, having taken a similar core from the swamp, and applied the same techniques, obtained a perfect set of dates with no inversions (Gossen 2007).

Kevin Butler took the opportunity of the wait for the carbon dates to carry out further pollen analyses on intermediate samples from the core. Also, he had developed a special interest in the identification of charcoal particles in lake muds (Butler 2008), and this was applied carefully in the core, with very interesting results. Eventually we republished the entire pollen diagram, with the new and old dates and the charcoal data (Butler and Flenley 2010). Here I present a summary pollen diagram showing all significant data (Figure 4.2).

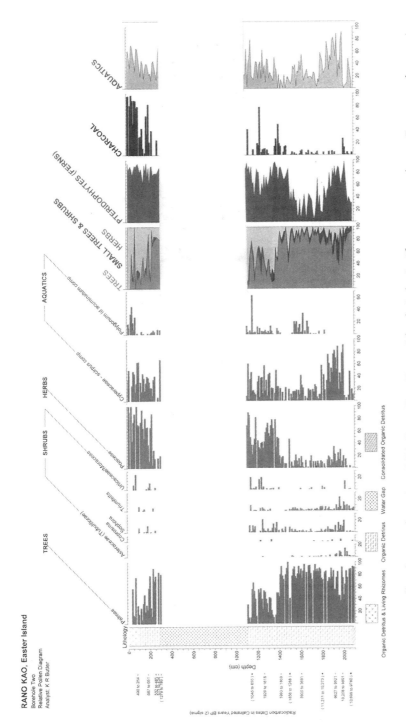

Figure 4.2 Summary pollen diagram from Core RK2, Rano Kau, Easter Island. Only significant taxa are shown. For a complete version, see Butler and Flenley (2010). Radiocarbon dates in brackets are bulk sediment dates that are now regarded as less reliable than others

Results of the coring

The diagram has been divided into zones to make discussion easier. This zonation was based on general ecological principles, e.g., that trees can shade out grasses, since there is no surviving natural vegetation on the island.

The zones are as follows (taken from Butler and Flenley 2010).

Zone RK2–1, 21 m – 20.3 m, c.10500 to 10000 BP

High percentages (some >80%) of palm pollen, *Poaceae* almost absent. Charcoal is at background levels.

Zone RK2–2, 20.3 m – 19 m, c.10000 to 9600 BP

Reduced palm pollen (one <40%) and temporary peaks of shrubby taxa such as *Asteraceae* (*Tubuliflorae*), *Coprosma*, *Sophora* (toromiro) and *Triumfetta* (hau-hau). There is also a multiple peak of *Poaceae* and a single peak of charcoal. Wetland taxa are common.

Zone RK2–3, 19 m – 14 m c.9600 to 1900 BP

High palm percentages (80–90%), low shrub percentages, low *Poaceae* (10–20%), low values for ferns, and charcoal at background levels.

Zone RK2–4, 14 m – 13 m, c.1900 to 1850 BP

Palm pollen drastically reduced (4 values <20%), *Poaceae* rises to 70%, there is a charcoal peak, *Sophora* has peak values. Ferns also peak.

Zone RK2–5, 13 m – 11 m, c.1850 to 1000 BP

Palm pollen recovers, but only once to previous levels, and fluctuates. *Poaceae* fluctuates between 40% and 90%. Shrub values fluctuate, with peaks for *Urticaceae/Moraceae*. Charcoal also has frequent peaks, as do ferns and wetland taxa.

Water Gap, 11 m – 3 m, c.1000 BP or later

At the end of zone RK2–5 there appears to have been a significant rise of water in the caldera. At the time of coring this rise amounted to a water depth of 8 meters. This rise in the water seems to have caused the surface of the swamp, probably the mass held together by the *Scirpus* rhizomes and root structure, to split off from the detritus beneath, and to form the floating mats of today. The exact date of this event is unknown. It could have been a single event or a progressive one.

Zone RK2–6, 3 m – 2 m, c.1000 to 600 BP

Palm pollen values recover to 80% at times, *Poaceae* values fall to around 20%. Shrubs are rather low. Ferns are consistently high. Charcoal fluctuates with some high values.

Zone RK2–7, 2 m – 0.5 m, c.600 to 150 BP

Palm pollen values generally decline, as do *Sophora* and *Triumfetta*. *Urticaceae/Moraceae* rise to high values. *Poaceae* progressively increases to very high values, as does charcoal. *Polygonum* reaches high values.

Zone RK2–8, 0.5 m – 0.0 m, c.150 BP to present

Palmae, *Sophora*, and *Triumfetta* disappear completely, but *Urticaceae/Moraceae* survive. *Poaceae* and charcoal reach their highest values of all. Wetland taxa, including *Polygonum*, remain abundant, as do ferns.

Key to plant taxa

Palmae	palm trees
Poaceae	grasses
Asteraceae (tubuliflorae)	shrubs of the Dandelion family
Coprosma	evergreen shrub
Sophora (toromiro)	evergreen shrub
Triumfetta	herbs or shrubs
Polygonum	herbs, some aquatic
Urticaceae	herbs or shrubs
Moraceae	trees or shrubs
Scirpus	subaquatic herb

Interpretation

Zone RK2–1, 21 m – 20.3 m, c.10500 to 10000 BP

The vegetation appears to have been a dense palm forest, allowing almost no grasses. A sub-tropical rainforest is suggested. The background charcoal is probably carried a long distance from South America and/or Australia (Butler 2008). The climate was most likely warm and wet.

Zone RK2–2, 20.3 m – 19 m, c.10000 to 9600 BP

The palm forest declined and was partially replaced by shrubs such as *Asteraceae (Tubuliflorae)*, *Sophora* and *Triumfetta*. The vegetation was more open, allowing grasses and ferns to thrive. A peak of charcoal suggests a fire, most likely a natural fire on the island. This fire was probably volcanic in origin since volcanic ash was recorded in Rano Raraku slightly earlier than these dates (Flenley et al. 1991). This period was probably a natural climatic oscillation as occurred in many places around this time. A similar one a little earlier was recorded from Rano Raraku by Azizi and Flenley (2008). The climate probably became temporarily cooler and drier.

Zone RK2–3, 19 m – 14 m, c.9600 to 1900 BP

This period represents the post-glacial forest, dominated by palms, but with an understorey which included *Sophora* and *Triumfetta*. This was a moist, dense forest allowing only a minor presence of grasses. It almost certainly contained other species listed by Orliac and Orliac (2005) and was a sub-tropical rain forest, not the "woodland" described by Mieth and Bork (2010). The term woodland implies an open canopy, as defined by Costin (1954). Sub-tropical rainforest had a dense canopy of trees, with a sub-canopy of small trees and shrubs. It was generally too densely shading to allow much growth of grasses.

The climate was sufficiently moist for this forest to thrive, but the sedimentation rate in the swamp was rather low. This could have been the result of absorption of nutrients by the dense forest, allowing few to leach into the swamp and even fewer into the more central parts of the caldera's swamp. Alternatively, it could be that the climate was drier but this seems unlikely given the dominance of the forest.

Zone RK2–4, 14 m – 13 m, c.1900 to 1850 BP

This is the first good evidence of disturbance of the forest. Palm pollen decreased and charcoal increased. There appears to have been fire, and the palm forest was drastically reduced. Regrowth of *Sophora* occurred. Grasses flourished, as did the ferns. Whether this disturbance was caused by climate, volcanicity or people is uncertain, and will be discussed below.

Zone RK2–5, 13 m – 11 m, c.1850 to 1000 BP

The forest partially recovered during this phase, at least within the crater. The walls of the crater were perhaps partly used for cultivation of paper mulberry (pollen of *Urticaceae/Moraceae*) for making tapa-cloth.

At the end of this zone, there appears to have been a dramatic increase in precipitation. This not only led to a rise of the water, but probably flooded the marginal gardens around the edge of the swamp as the water level progressively rose by several meters. The extra precipitation probably also led to land-slipping, that destroyed terraced gardens on the caldera slopes. The extra precipitation doubtless made other, drier parts of the island more suitable for agriculture, and probably led to migration of people out of the crater to other, now more favorable, parts of the island.

Water Gap, 11 m – 3 m, c.1000 BP or later

The interpretation of the water gap is unclear. It could be the result of a climatic change at some time in the last millennium, which might correlate with the ending of the hiatus in deposition at Rano Raraku

(Mann et al. 2008; Saez et al. 2009). Alternatively, it could be a more local phenomenon.

Zone RK2–6, 3 m – 2 m, c.1000 to 600 BP

The forest within the crater partially recovered during this phase, possibly because of migration of people out of the crater. Agriculture continued outside the crater, as shown by the charcoal values indicating burning. It is also possible that human populations varied during this period as people migrated to and away from the area around Rano Kau.

Zone RK2–7, 2 m – 0.5 m, c.600 to 150 BP

Age determinations in years BP are measured from AD 1950, so this phase runs from c. AD 1350 to c. AD 1800. This is the major phase of final deforestation of the island. The palm forest disappears, along with the *Sophora* and the *Triumfetta*. *Brousonettia* (paper mulberry) continues to thrive in the crater, where it survives to this day. High levels of burning led to grassland prevailing over the lower parts of the island where they were not in cultivation.

Zone RK2–8, 0.5 m, c.150 BP to present

The final extinction of the *Paschalococos* palm and the *Sophora* has occurred, and *Triumfetta* is reduced to the few shrubs remaining in the crater today. Burning continues, with grasses totally dominating the vegetation especially since the introduction of sheep, horses, goats and cattle. In the marginal swamp, the medicinal *Polygonum* thrives.

Discussion

At this point we must first discuss whether the presence of charcoal in the core with a date of c. AD 100 (Zone RK2–4) could possibly represent the time of first arrival of people to the island. Alternative possibilities such as natural fires resulting from lightning or volcanism could explain the decline of forest and rise of charcoal at this time. It must be noted that the decline of palm pollen, and the rise of charcoal, affected numerous samples, not just one. Thus the decline of trees lasted for some time, and in fact charcoal values remain elevated fairly continuously after that time. So it was probable that a repeated burning caused this environmental signature.

Perhaps climate change leading to longer droughts and lightning fires could have been responsible. But it is worth noting that lightning is actually rather rare in the Pacific islands, as shown on the world lightning map of Doswell (2002). In fact, I understand that some island languages do not even have a word for lightning. Also, when lightning occurs, it is commonly accompanied by heavy rain, so it rarely lights fires, and when these occur in a rainforest environment they rarely spread. This is certainly so in New Zealand (Flenley 2004). Also, there is no clear evidence of climatic change at this time.

The volcanic hypothesis for the origins of charcoal in the core deserves serious consideration on a totally volcanic island. Most of the island is well over 100,000 years old (Bahn and Flenley 2011) but a more recently active area appears to have been Hiva-hiva, c.10 km north of Rano Kau. The formation date of this location was reported as <2000 BP (González-Ferrán et al. 2004). It now appears very questionable as to whether there was still any volcanic activity on the island in AD 100 when the forest began to decline. The main activity at Hiva-hiva has been dated at 130,000 to 110,000 years BP (Vezzoli and Acocella 2009).

Having discounted the above hypotheses, another possibility is the start of a human presence on the island that must now be considered. We have noted that in the pollen diagram, the palm pollen does not just decline in a steady manner (see Figure 5.2): it declines and then recovers. In fact it does this repeatedly. There are at least four phases of forest decline and three of forest recovery. There are also five peaks of charcoal, which roughly, but not exactly, coincide with forest decline. The forest recovery phases include Zone RK2-6 (roughly 1000 to 600 BP) (i.e., AD 950 to AD 1350) when forest showed almost 100% recovery compared to levels earlier in the record. Possible explanations for this could include migration out from the crater by people who had previously lived within it. Although the pollen diagram shows a regional record, it might be less regional than it seems at first sight.

There is, however, an alternative explanation. Some years ago, before we had the new dates, Anthony Cole and John Flenley (Cole and Flenley 2005) considered the possibility that there was a relationship between the forest decline phases and human population growth. It seems reasonable to state that more people would lead to more forest clearance for agriculture, firewood, canoe building and possibly statue moving. At the time we considered the possibility that the floating mat and the uppermost lake mud were in fact duplicating the sedimentary record and giving a false impression of numerous declines and recovery episodes giving the false impression of repeated decline and recovery events? We now know, from the new dates, that this is unlikely in Rano Kau. But the idea of forest decline indicating human population increase, and forest recovery indicating human population decline is still a possibility.

Most writers discussing the population growth of Rapa Nui have assumed a fairly steady growth rather than a process of population growth and decline, alternating. But other possibilities must also be considered. A major one is internal warfare. It is generally accepted that the island had various tribes, but Hunt and Lipo (2011) suggest the island was peaceable. Bahn and Flenley (2011) quote Owsley (2003) as stating that examination of skeletons suggests general warfare. But this was only in the 17th and 18th centuries. A better suggestion is that intermittent fish poisoning occurred, as is recorded in the Marquesas (Rongo et al. 2009). Fish poisoning can be very serious when it happens because many people can be affected before the cause is understood.

If one were to accept the concept of colonization about AD 100, one would have to reject the late arrival hypothesis (Wilmshurst et al. 2011). That hypothesis is claimed to apply to New Zealand and to Polynesia. It has however been strongly challenged in relation to New Zealand (Elliott et al. 1995), Central Polynesia (unpublished) and Easter Island (Bahn and Flenley 2011).

One other possibility must be considered. Could the demise of the Easter Island palm tree (*Paschalococos disperta*) be the result of attack by rats, as suggested by Hunt and Lipo (2011) (see also Bahn and Flenley 2010). The palm tree appears to be closely related to the Chilean Wine Palm (*Jubaea chilensis*), and they may well be the same species, as proposed by Grau (1996). When the island was fully forested there may have been 16 million palm trees (Bork and Mieth 2003).

Each tree deposited its nuts (fruits) on the ground. Most of those found later show evidence of gnawing by rats. In about AD 1200, the rat *Rattus exulans* was introduced to the island. It propagated rapidly. Is it possible that rats caused extinction of the palm? It must be remembered that the Chilean palm tree lives for approximately 2000 years (Grau 1996). So it seems unlikely that extinction could have occurred by AD 1800. Rats do not seem to have caused extinction of other species on other islands. But they may well have been a contributing factor.

Conclusion

We are not suggesting that the evidence presented here is conclusive. The arrival of people in Rapa Nui could have been as early as AD 100, or as late as AD 1200. Most writers seem to prefer an intermediate date, perhaps around AD 700.

It is relevant to consider the Rapa Nui language. It appears to have been isolated from other Pacific languages in the first few hundred years AD (Bahn and Flenley 2011; Barthel 1978).

Apart from the language, there are few indications of early arrival of people. The decline of forest as early as AD 100 (see above) is not very convincing, because it must be understood that the first arrivals were coming to an island which was probably the world's greatest sea bird colony. The birds probably nested all over the island, not just on the cliffs. So the availability of young birds as food would have been most attractive. The people would have brought tropical crops with them and these would have to be planted and nurtured. So a few trees would have to be removed to create space, but why spend great effort on cultivation when there are sea-birds available for eating in quantity.

The same argument applies to large offshore marine food – fish such as sharks and abundant tuna. We know from the excavation near the shore of Anakena that these items were important in early times (Hunt and Lipo 2011). To do this fishing would have required canoes, so some trees had to be felled. But this would have needed less effort than the large-scale felling for agriculture, which occurred later. So in general the forest clearance for agriculture is not an indication of first arrival of people (Bahn and Flenley in press).

Most writers discussing the population growth of Rapa Nui have envisaged a fairly steady growth rather than an alteration of growth and decline. Internal warfare could have caused such an alternation, but there is no evidence for this until the 17th and 18th centuries, as discussed by Hunt and Lipo (2011) and Bahn and Flenley (in press). Possibly some people could have left the island in canoes, and visited South America. The arrival of *kumara* on Rapa Nui supports this idea (Bahn and Flenley 2011).

The possibility of illness on the island, caused by fish poisoning, has been proposed. It appears to have happened on the Marquesas (Rongo et al. 2009). It appears to affect fish on coral reefs. On Rapa Nui there are some offshore corals, but no reefs, so this illness is rather unlikely.

References

Azizi, G. and J. R. Flenley. 2008. "The Last Glacial Maximum Climatic Conditions on Easter Island." *Quaternary International* 184: 166–176.

Bahn, P. G. and J. R. Flenley. 2010. "Of Rats and Men." Book Review. *Rapa Nui Journal* 24(6): 68–70.

Bahn, P. G. and J. R. Flenley. 2011. *Easter Island, Earth Island*. Third Edition. Santiago: Rapa Nui Press.

Bahn, P. G. and J. R. Flenley. in press. *Easter Island, Earth Island*. Fourth Edition. Lanham, MD: Santiago Press and Rowman and Littlefield.

Barthel, T. 1978. *The Eighth Land*. Honolulu: University Press of Hawaii.

Bork, H.-R. and A. Mieth. 2003. "The Key Role of *Jubaea* Palm Trees in the History of Rapa Nui: A Provocative Interpretation." *Rapa Nui Journal* 117(2): 119–122.

Butler, K. 2008. "Interpreting Charcoal in New Zealand's Palaeoenvironment – What Do Those Charcoal Fragments Really Tell Us?" *Quaternary International* 184: 122–128.

Butler, K. and J. R. Flenley. 2001. "Further Pollen Evidence from Easter Island." In *Proceedings of the Fifth International Conference on Easter Island and the Pacific*, edited by C. M. Stevenson, G. Lee, and F. J. Morin, 78–86. Los Osos, CA: Easter Island Foundation.

Butler, K. and J. R. Flenley. 2010. "The Rano Kau 2 Pollen Diagram: Paleoecology Revealed." *Rapa Nui Journal* 24(1): 5–10.

Cole, A. and J. R. Flenley. 2005. "Human Settlement of Easter Island, A Far-from-Equilibrium Model." In *The Renaca Papers: VI International Conference on Easter Island and the Pacific*, edited by C. M. Stevenson, J. M. Ramirez A., F. J. Morin, and N. Barbacci, 35–54. Los Osos, CA: Easter Island Foundation.

Costin, A. B. 1954. *A Study of the Ecosystems of the Monaro Region of New South Wales*. Sydney: Government Printer.

Doswell, C. A. 2002. "In the Line of Fire: First Global Lightning Map Reveals High-Strike Zones." *National Geographic Magazine* 202(2): vii.

Elliott, M. B., B. Striewski, J. R. Flenley, and D. G. Sutton. 1995. "Palynological and Sedimentological Evidence for a Radiocarbon Chronology of Environmental Change and Polynesian Deforestation from Lake Taumatawhana, Northland, New Zealand." *Radiocarbon* 37(3): 899–916.

Ferdon, E. N. Jr. 1961. Report 11. "Stone Houses in the Terraces of Site E-21." In *Archaeology of Easter Island*, edited by T. Heyerdahl and E. N. Ferdon, Jr., 313–321. London: Allen and Unwin.

Flenley, J. R. 2004. "Aspects of the Late Quaternary Environment in Aotearoa-New Zealand." In *Glimpses of a Gaian World: Essay in Honour of Peter Holland*, edited by G. Kearsley and B. Fitzharris, 171–191. Dunedin: University of Otago.

Flenley, J. R., A. S. M. King, J. Jackson, C. Chew, J. T. Teller, and M. E. Prentice. 1991. "The Late Quaternary Vegetational and Climatic History of Easter Island." *Journal of Quaternary Science* 6: 85–115.

González-Ferrán, O., R. Mazzuoli, and A. Lahsen. 2004. *Geologia del Complejo Volcanic Isla de Pascua, Rapa Nui*. Santiago, Chile: Centro De Estudios Volcanologicos.

Gossen, C. 2007. "The Mystery Lies in the Scirpus." *Rapa Nui Journal* 21(2): 105–110.

Grau, J. 1996. "*Jubaea*, the Palm of Chile and Easter Island." *Rapa Nui Journal* 10(2): 37–40.

Hunt, T. and C. Lipo. 2011. *The Statues That Walked: Unraveling the Mystery of Easter Island*. New York: Free Press.

Jacobson, G. L. and R. H. W. Bradshaw. 1981. "The Selection of Sites for Palaeovegetational Studies." *Quaternary Research* 16: 80–96.

Mann, D., J. Edwards, J. Chase, W. Beck, R. Reanier, R. Mass, B. Finney, and J. Loret. 2008. "Drought, Vegetation Change, and Human History on Rapa Nui (Isla de Pascua, Easter Island)." *Quaternary Research* 69: 16–28.

Mieth, A. and H.-R. Bork. 2010. "Humans, Climate or Introduced Rats – Which Is to Blame for the Woodland Destruction on Prehistoric Rapa Nui (Easter Island)?" *Journal of Archaeological Science* 37(2): 417–426.

Orliac, C. and M. Orliac. 2005. "R. La Flore Disparue de I'Ile de Pasques." *Les Nouvelles de l'Archeologie* 102(4): 29–33.

Rongo, T., M. Bush, and R. van Woesik. 2009. "Did Ciguatera Prompt the Late Holocene Polynesian Voyages of Discovery?" *Journal of Biogeography* 36: 1423–1432.

Saez, A., B. L. Valero-Garces, S. Giralt, A. Moreno, R. Bao, J. J. Pueyo, A. Hernandez, and D. Casas. 2009. "Glacial to Holocene Climate Changes in the SE Pacific: The Raraku Lake Sedimentary Record (Easter Island, 27°S)." *Quaternary Science Reviews* 28(25–26): 2743–2759.

van Steenis, C. G. G. J. 1935. "Open Air Hothouses in the Tropics at 3100 Metres Altitude." *Gardens Bulletin Straits Settlements* 9: 64–69.

Vezzoli, I. and C. Acocella. 2009. "Easter Island, SE Pacific: An End-Member Type of Hotspot Volcanism." *GSA Bulletin* 126: 869–886.

Wilmshurst, J. M., T. L. Hunt, C. P. Lipo, and A. J. Anderson. 2011. "High-Precision Radiocarbon Dating Shows Recent and Rapid Human Colonization of East Polynesia." *Proceedings of the National Academy of Sciences* 108(5): 1815–1820.

5 Subsistence strategies on Rapa Nui (Easter Island)
Prehistoric gardening practices on Rapa Nui and how they relate to current farming practices

Joan A. Wozniak

Introduction

Archaeological, archaeobotanical, zooarchaeological, geoarchaeological, and ethnographic studies conducted on Rapa Nui (Easter Island) over the past century have helped establish the island's prehistoric subsistence patterns and especially the nature of various gardening strategies used over the past millennium – the focus of this review. The Rapanui people subsisted on native marine and land resources and on food production – crops and domesticated animals introduced by the original Polynesian settlers. Archaeological studies suggest early cultivation began with plantings in the midst of the native palm forest. As the forest canopy was diminished, other cultivation techniques were developed. These include the use of small surface rocks that provided a "lithic mulch" (or "stone mulch"). Other noteworthy prehistoric gardening techniques on Easter Island include the use of concave geomorphic landforms into which runoff would collect after rainfall, rock alignments or furrows which directed rainwater to plant roots, and construction of walled structures (*manavai*) which served both as garden walls and as containment structures for plantings. Analyses of microfossils (pollen, phytoliths, starch grains) and macrofossils (e.g. seeds) and charcoal have provided evidence that Polynesian and prehistorically introduced American cultigens were cultivated in these contexts. Ethnographic studies indicate that some of these same cultivation techniques have been continued historically to grow both traditional plants and those cultigens introduced in the 19th and 20th centuries.

Environment and culture

Past weather patterns on Rapa Nui have shown that the island is subject to periods of droughts or high precipitation, often in rapid succession. There are no permanent fresh water sources other than three caldera marshes and fresh water pools and lava tubes that empty into the sea at sea level (Englert 1977: 219). Rapa Nui at one time was home to a palm savanna biome with few endemic plants, and about three dozen pan-Pacific species (Skottsberg 1920; Flenley 1991; Orliac 2000). Endemic land birds and pan-Pacific marine birds lived or nested on the land along with at least one skink species. The only other vertebrates that had made their way to the island were those of migrating sea mammals, turtles, and pelagic fishes (Hucke-Gaete et al. 2014). Most of the fish around the island were and are near shore species; invertebrates, such as lobsters, snails, and chitins, living in the waters around the island (Randall 1976). When the Polynesians colonized the island, they brought with them a host of edible Southeast Asian plants and animals. These settlers placed their homes near the fresh water sources close to the coast and cleared land around their settlements to cultivate these crops.

Routledge (1919: 277–278) recorded an origin legend of Rapa Nui from local informants regarding the colonization of the island by Polynesians. The legend related that the *ariki mau*, named Hotu Matu'a, sent men from his homeland (neighboring islands called Marae Renga and Marae Tohio) to examine a new island in the east (Rapa Nui) and initiate food production. Later Hotu Matu'a and his subjects sailed to Rapa Nui in two large canoes, along with more plants and animals. Plants, such as yams, bananas, gourds, and fowl, i.e., traditional island foods, which were necessary for life on a new island, are specifically named in the legend.

As the oral tradition conveys, food production (cropping of cultigens and animal husbandry of chickens and possibly rats) was extremely important to people colonizing islands like Rapa Nui in the Eastern Pacific. Native terrestrial and marine faunal resources of Rapa Nui were limited in kinds and numbers by the island's size and isolated geographic position. Nonetheless, marine resources were an important part of the Polynesian economy (Reinman 1967). Limited native resources became reduced through exploitation by a growing population (Ayres 1986; Steadman 1995) as occurred elsewhere in Polynesia (Allen 2002).

Ayres (1986) proposed that chiefly control of resources and the lack of suitable canoe material resulted in limited fishing or hunting offshore during later prehistory, while near-shore marine exploitation increased. For this reason, Yen (1988) also suggested that cultivation and animal husbandry of chickens had become a more important part of the larger subsistence system on the island during late prehistory. Not only was the population density potentially higher, but more wealth was needed to support an increased ranking of chiefs and their demands for carved images (*moai*) to be erected on platforms (*ahu*) in each settlement. Yen believed that there were subsistence changes with time, specifically the increased use of domesticated plants and animals, and that there was a decreased use of foraged animals, such as marine mammals and birds, pelagic fish, and turtles, because remains of these animals retrieved from the later archaeological contexts are rare.

By the end of the 17th century the environment and the natural ecosystem on Rapa Nui had been greatly altered. This understanding – oral history not withstanding – is based, not only on ethnohistoric texts, but also on the identification of charcoal found in prehistoric ovens on Rapanui (Orliac 2000) and by pollen studies (Flenley and King 1984; Peteet et al. 2003). Orliac found that many hardwood species became extinct on the island, charcoal pieces became smaller, and that more herbaceous plants than hardwoods were burned after the 17th century. These archaeobotanical studies and ethnohistoric texts (e.g., Lapérouse 1968 [1799]) showed that most of the former palm forest had disappeared by AD 1700.

Deforestation initiated by the Rapanui and possibly exacerbated by natural climatic changes between the 16th and 19th centuries (McCall 1993, 1994) would have encouraged innovation of the various gardening techniques in the ensuing environmental changes that occurred. Many of these have recently been identified in the archaeological record (e.g. McCoy 1976; Bork et al. 2004; Mieth and Bork 2003; Stevenson et al. 1999; Wozniak 2003).

Cultivation of Polynesian crop plants likely provided the major portion of the general Rapanui subsistence as population grew. These crops supplemented the fishing and gathering of near-shore sea life and native birds. The population of Rapa Nui has been estimated at between 3000 and 6000 by early explorers (Boersema 2015 and see Chapter 8 this volume; Roggeveen 1908; Forster 1778) and some ethnographers (Englert 1977: 123; Métraux 1940: 22). Some anthropologists and geographers, however, believe that as many as 10,000 people to 35,000 people may have lived on the island at its peak population (Diamond 2005). Whatever the average or peak size of the population on Rapa Nui, it can be assumed that a great deal of land and many people within this island society participated in production of food staples to feed themselves, their chiefs, their craftspeople (e.g., those who constructed *ahu* and carved and erected *moai*), their fisher people, and their inter-clan competitors (e.g. the Birdman competition), and warriors.

Early Rapanui gardeners raised cultigens that had originated in the Island Southeast Asia and Papua New Guinea area (see e.g., Denham et al. 2003, 2004). These cultigens were domesticated by, or were adopted by, the early Austronesian language speaking settlers in the Pacific, who then transported them throughout the Pacific islands (Zizka 1990). The transported plants cultivated on Rapa Nui include *Dioscorea alata* yams, *Colocasia esculenta* and *Alocasia* taros, *Musa* bananas, *Saccharum officinarum*, *Cordyline*, *Curcuma longa* – turmeric, and *Broussonetia papyrifera* – paper bark mulberry, used to make *mahute* – the local name of Polynesian tapa cloth on Rapa Nui, which was used to clothe the people. Other tropical cultigens, such as breadfruit and coconuts, were brought to and grown in many parts of tropical Polynesia including the likely immediate homeland of the Rapanui and Mangarevan peoples – the Marquesas. There is no evidence that breadfruit and coconuts and several other tropical trees widely used within Polynesia were grown on Rapa Nui prehistorically. Either these trees were not conveyed to Rapa Nui at the time of Polynesian colonization or temperature and/or moisture conditions were not conducive to their successful cultivation upon arrival. However, in addition to the Island Southeast Asian cultivars, the Rapanui people (and other East Polynesians) also ate young gourds and sweet potatoes, *Ipomaea batatas*, which have their origins in the Americas. *Lagenaria siceraria* gourds were used when mature to hold water. Both of these plants were introduced from South America prehistorically, likely by Polynesian navigators themselves (Yen 1974; Green 1998, 2000; Montenegro et al. 2008).

On Rapa Nui, most if not all ancient gardens received moisture from rainfall rather than from some form of irrigation or water diversion as on other Polynesian islands. Annual precipitation fluctuates, varying between 50 and 200 cm (Wright and Diaz 1962). The average precipitation on Easter Island approximates 120 cm. According to www.easter-island.climatemps.com/, total annual precipitation averages 1224 mm (48.2 inches). Although at higher elevations rainfall can average 200 cm (78.7 inches), much of the cultivation was carried out along the coastal region where people had their house gardens (Vargas 1998; Wozniak 1998a). The rains on Rapa Nui often are heavy inundations even during the warmer, dryer summer months (January to March). Rapa Nui experiences seasonal temperatures (10° C differences between summer and winter). During the warmer growing season, evaporation rates are elevated owing to high insolation and constant winds that tend to desiccate the soil

According to European visitors to Rapa Nui during the 18th century, large areas of Rapa Nui had rectangular field systems, earth mounds several meters in diameter, or depressions and furrows in which banana plants grew aligned in rows within rectangular field systems that covered an estimated 10% of the total land surface (Cuming 1827–28; Lapérouse 1968 [1799]). Lapérouse also mentioned use of a field system on the West Coast where:

> this space abounds with a kind of herbage...[covering] large stones lying on the surface. These stones, which were found very troublesome in walking, are a real benefit to the soil, because they preserve the coolness and humidity of the earth, and in part supply the salutary shade of the trees, which the inhabitants have had the imprudence to cut down, no doubt at some very distant period. This has exposed their soil to the burning ardor of the sun, and has deprived them of ravines, brooks, and springs.
>
> (Lapérouse 1968 [1799]: 312)

European voyagers of the 18th and 19th centuries who visited the island (such as Lapérouse 1968 [1799]; Cuming 1827–28) described (though often superficially) various foods and horticultural techniques used by the Rapanui farmers. In the early 20th century, ethnographic studies provided more in-depth knowledge of subsistence strategies that had been passed on from, or adapted from, the Polynesian ancestors (Routledge 1919;

Métraux 1940). Still many of the techniques used in cultivation were not described fully.

Archaeological research carried out since the 1960s (McCoy 1976; Cristino et al. 1981; Stevenson 1999; Wozniak 2003; Stevenson et al. 2015), environmental studies (Mieth and Bork 2003; Ladefoged et al. 2010) and botanical research, such as microfossil analyses – pollen, phytoliths, starches – (Horrocks and Wozniak 2008; Wozniak et al. 2010; Commendador et al. 2013; Horrocks et al. 2015), macrofossil remains identification – seeds – (Pearthree 2003) and wood charcoal identification (Orliac 2000) have expanded both our knowledge of the nature and extinction rates of natural resources and our understanding of prehistoric gardening practices. The results from the various research studies and surveys and the early Westerner eyewitness reports have contributed to the following view of prehistoric and early historic (protohistoric) Easter Island horticulture. Although rock covered and non-rock covered field systems were noted by Lapérouse and other Western sailors, more obvious garden structures such as the *manavai*, planting circles (circular rock alignments), small terraces, meter deep rock accumulations encompassing planting wells holding individual plants (*pu*), and water diversion features were not discussed in ethnohistoric texts. This has led to some conjecture that such obvious structures as *manavai* may have been more recent structures possibly built to keep European introduced animals away from the plants. If these structures had existed in the 18th century would they not have been mentioned along with the "well divided fields" (Behrens 1722) of bananas and other cultigens.

Below I will discuss recent archaeological, environmental, and botanical work related to understanding prehistoric agriculture on Rapa Nui. Then I will discuss how these ancient gardening techniques are currently being used as farming practices on the island.

Recent archaeological studies of ancient Rapanui gardening

Surveys by McCoy (1976), the Universidad de Chile (during the period 1970s to 1990s), Stevenson (1997), Stevenson et al. (1998, 1999, 2002), and Stevenson et al. (2006) have exposed small gardens, open fields and intensively cultivated plantations both on the coastal and on the elevated regions of Rapa Nui. Mieth and Bork (2003), Hunt and Lipo with the University of Hawaii field schools (from 2003 to 2009) and more recently with the University of Oregon field school, and Wozniak's dissertation research (conducted in 1996 and 1999), and the recent island-wide survey by Haoa and her team have continued to find additional gardening locations and structures not previously recognized as such. Some of the field systems do have a surface layer of rocks (i.e., lithic mulch), as described by Lapérouse, and these have only recently been identified archaeologically as prehistoric gardening features during archaeological surveys (Bork and Mieth 2004;

Ladefoged et al. 2013, Stevenson and Haoa 1998; Stevenson et al. 1999; Wozniak 1998a, 1998b, 2003).

Stevenson (1997) in his survey of the settlement on Maunga Tari near Vaitea, identified several alignments of rocks in garden areas he interpreted as water diversion or water conservation structures. He believes that Maunga Tari, with its house sites, *ahu*, and agricultural features, was evidence for seasonal intensive agricultural production between AD 1200 and 1600.

A geoarchaeological survey was done at Te Niu in 1996 and 1999 by Wozniak (1998b, 2003). One aspect of the research design was to discover the "cultivated fields" on Rapa Nui described in ethnohistoric texts, and to describe and define the makeup of Rapanui agricultural soils. It was here that Ap soil layers (*plaggen* soil – i.e., agricultural sediments), or "Ag soils" as defined by Stevenson et al. (2006) containing morphological evidence of planting pits (pits filled with darker, looser sediments than the matrix of the Ap agricultural layer) were found under surface layers of small rocks. This rock layer was identified as a "lithic mulch" as defined by Lightfoot (1994, 1996). Interviews with local Rapanui during the past two decades have also brought to light several other rock structures used for specialized gardening. These topics are discussed below.

Research of lithic mulch gardens and fields

"Lithic mulch" is the term used by Lightfoot (1994, 1996) to describe a layer of gravel or rocks covering agricultural soil in prehistoric mountain gardens of the American Southwest. Lightfoot's (1996) survey of the literature uncovered that using rocks or gravel as mulch was a strategy used in many locations around the world. The utilization of gravel or rocks to mulch food crops has been identified in many different climatic environments (usually in areas subject to extremes – cold or hot and dry areas) and wherever gravel or rocks are abundant. Rock mulch is used where the cultivated crops are in need of protection – often where there is a need to extend the length of the growing season. Earlier, McFadgen (1980) had used the term Maori *plaggen* soils to describe gravel-rich surface sediments in New Zealand gardens, where *kumara* – sweet potatoes – were grown prehistorically.

The use of lithic mulch in places such as Rapa Nui may have been implemented because there was a ubiquitous supply of vesicular (porous) lava rocks, and because the hot summer climate resulted in low crop production after shade producing trees had been removed from garden areas. A thick surface layer of small rocks has a mulching property because it protects the soil from desiccation by reducing the soil's evaporative surface. The rocks also facilitate water permeability and provide minerals to the soil as they weather. The surface rocks help prevent water and aeolian erosion, and also rapid fluctuations in soil temperature (Fairbourne 1973; Edwards et al. 1984).

During the 1996 survey (Wozniak 1998a, 1998b, 2003) excavation units were placed at 50 m intervals along several axes within one kilometer of *Ahu Te Niu*. Additional units were placed in suspected garden areas (under surface layers of lithic mulch, such as that shown in Figure 5.1). Soil samples, charcoal for radiocarbon dating, and obsidian for hydration dating were collected from these units. The charcoal and the volcanic glass tools from garden pits were dated to determine when these gardens had been used. Soil samples collected during these excavations were examined for microfossils (Cummings 1998; Wozniak et al. 2010) such as pollen, starch, and phytoliths. Microfossils of both native plants and cultigens were abundant in these samples.

Stevenson et al. (1999) compared and contrasted lithic mulch gardens found in several parts of the island starting during the late 1990s. As the topography, geology, and microclimate of garden areas differed, so did their composition of the rocks used as mulch. Lithic mulch typical of the Northwest coast of Rapa Nui consisted of 20–30 cm deep layers of small, usually round to subrounded rocks with occasional larger boulders scattered on top of the small rocks. The mulch on the hill tops of Lapérouse was less thick, more like a "veneer". Some hillsides with thick accumulations of rocks in which single plants grew in depressions within the rock layer were called "*pu* gardens" (*pu* means 'hole' or depression in Rapanui).

Figure 5.1 Lithic mulched garden at Te Niu
(Photograph by Wozniak taken in 1996)

Stevenson et al. (2002) revised the definitions of garden types, doing away with the term "lithic mulch" or "rock mulch". He defined garden soils as "mulched soils" (i.e. "mulched soils are similar to the original "lithic mulch" but include the Ap soils in which some or most of the surface mulch may have become incorporated into the agricultural soil layer), veneer surfaces (where the rocks were still wholly on the surface), stacked boulder concentrations (where larger rocks were stacked on the surface layer of rocks, presumably to provide shade or wind protection), *pu* (thick accumulations of rocks with depressions excavated in the rocks to plant one or more plants – historic use is for planting taro).

Bork et al. (2004) questioned whether the source of the stones used in lithic mulch was man-made or the consequence of natural processes. They also asked if there was a tendency to have lithic mulched gardens in some parts of the island more than in others. Because their studies of 500 sites showed that the rocks in suspected lithic mulched gardens were evenly spread and the diameters and volumes of rocks in various lithic mulched gardens were similar, and that garden sediments were present under the rock layer, they concluded that surface rock accumulations over cultivated soil were "man made", i.e. rocks were collected and placed on the garden surface by humans. The authors also note that mulching stones covered 76 km^2 of the total 166 km^2 of the island.

Bork and Mieth (2004) found lithic mulching was not carried out on Poike. This may be because Poike has few surface rocks or outcrops (because the original rocks had been weathered into fine soil particles over time). Bork and Mieth (2004) also noticed a lack of lithic mulching on the steep slopes of the extinct volcanoes, on the cliffs, and on the upper slopes of Terevaka (Terevaka is often in cloud cover but is also subject to high winds). Their study made at Orito (discussed below) and published as Stevenson et al. (2006) went on to support a late introduction of lithic mulching to cultivation practices on Rapa Nui, after the extensive loss of the palm dominated forest.

Baer et al. (2008) has further defined garden types allowing "for statistical analyses and empirically-based conclusions" and for its level of labor investment per unit of land. Baer et al. (2008) define the rock mulched garden as types depending on the distribution of rock by size and surface coverage on top of the garden soils. These are Type 1 (generally smaller stones but with percentages of rock sizes quantified; also percentage of land coverage by rocks is quantified), Type 2 (predominately boulders but with calculated percentage of smaller rocks; land coverage quantified), Type 3 (mostly medium stones – often with multiple layers – with a low level of small pebbles but surface coverage higher than Types 1 and 2). Type 4 gardens are put into subsets of 4.1, 4.2, and 4.3 (all generally have equal amounts of small and medium rocks but surface coverage varies from low to high with increasing number). In addition, Baer et al. (2008) define four zones of elevation (0–100, 100–200, 200–300, and 300–400 meters above sea level), with everything above 200 meters asl (above sea level) generally corresponding to the "upland area".

Now that the general category of lithic mulch gardens have been better defined and differentiated in the literature, details about the mulched soils within these garden types are being examined. Between 2005 and 2009 Ladefoged et al. (2010) also conducted a survey and excavation project at Te Niu in 19 potential garden areas (i.e., land covered with small rocks), in five areas they believed were not used previously for gardening purposes, and at Hanga Ho'onu on the northeast side of the island at La Pérouse, where they intensively sampled three separate gardens and three areas just outside of each garden. Their "integrated soil samples" from both garden and non-garden areas immediately surrounding the sampled gardens were analyzed for their nutrient value. Their aim in both cases was to identify the fertility of agricultural and uncultivated sediments. They also conducted excavations along a transect from the Northwest coast to the South coast of Rapa Nui (shown in Figure 5.1 of their paper). In this Ladefoged et al. survey, sediments were collected every 250 meters along the trans-island transect "to investigate the relationships between soil nutrient levels, rainfall, and the age of geologic substrates". Ladefoged et al. (2010: 83) also recorded temperature fluctuations in lithic mulch garden structures over long periods of time to see how much a layer of rock mulch would ameliorate the temperature of the agricultural sediments.

Ladefoged et al. (2010: 83) found that the soil under the rock mulch was several degrees cooler than the average ambient temperatures and therefore moisture content of the soil was presumably increased. They concluded, from their admittedly "limited temperature data of subsurface sediments in a rock mulch garden, that considerable climatic benefits could have been gained from such features" (i.e., lithic mulches) because the rocks would have lowered excessive temperatures and raised the moisture content of the growing medium.

In addition, Ladefoged et al. (2010) proposed that rock gardens could have also functioned as "physical foci for increased mulching" (composting) of organic wastes deposited by the human inhabitants, thereby raising soil nutrients needed for crop growth. Their alternative hypothesis was that the segments of land on which gardens were placed may have been "sweet spots", i.e., soils with naturally high levels of nutrients. The presence of lithic mulch over these "sweet spots" would have presumably been added after several growing seasons during which the cultigens in these areas grew better than in other areas. It may also be that the gardeners enhanced the nutrient area near their home site by continual deposition of food wastes and humic material, possibly including algae as do Polynesians on other islands (Abbott 1991).

The results of the Wozniak and the long term Stevenson-Haoa-Ladefoged surveys and the work of Bork and Mieth (2004) demonstrates that many coastal areas of Rapa Nui had been transformed into a mixed-crop, dryland production system. Indeed, almost half the total land mass of Rapa Nui was used at one time or another for lithic mulched gardening according to Bork and Mieth's calculations. The microfossil analyses (e.g. pollen, phytoliths, and starch grains) of soils collected during the Wozniak study at Te Niu further supported the findings that the Ap soil layer (see Wozniak 2003, Chapter 7) found under lithic mulch layer was used to grow such crops as sweet potato, yams, and taro (Horrocks and Wozniak 2008; Wozniak et al. 2010). Cummings (1998) reported similar results plus noticed the presence of banana phytoliths in soils collected at La Pérouse. Specifics of this botanical study are discussed below.

Gardens lacking lithic mulch and other surface features associated with food production

As noted above, almost half of the island appears to have been mulched with small rocks (76 km^2 according to Bork et al. 2004). However, some portions of Rapa Nui were not mulched with rocks because either the land was too steep, or the soil not conducive to productive harvests, or the gardens were at high elevations on Terevaka where rainfall is higher than along the coast, or some locales were considered *tapu* (i.e., the *ahu* and plazas). Likely cultivation took place in various locations on favorable landforms on Rapa Nui without the use of rock mulch or other rock structures because mulch was not needed (e.g. soils were naturally thick and moist). In addition, cultivation at a specific location may not have been continuous but intermittent. Agricultural soils (the Ap layer) have been found in contexts suggesting direct planting in the surface soil took place at La Pérouse (Wozniak and Stevenson 2008), on Poike (Mieth and Bork 2003; Bork et al. 2004) and at the western base of the obsidian quarry at Orito (Stevenson et al. 2006) among others.

Meters long profiles of the stratigraphy at both the Orito and the Poike locations beautifully illustrate evidence that gardens or fields were used without the benefits of surface rocks. In both Poike and Orito, it appears that land was first cleared of low vegetation among the palm forest in the twelfth or 13th centuries AD.

At Orito, Stevenson et al. (2006) found evidence – a deep Ap soil layer – of extensive gardening following forest clearance. The garden later suffered erosion and subsequent sedimentation, possibly during periods of extreme weather, e.g., a period of drought followed by heavy rainfall. The authors date these environmental change events to the 17th century at both locations. After the 17th century, portions of the garden area were mulched with surface rocks and boulders on Orito.

Although land amid the trees of the original palm forest on Poike was cultivated beginning in the 13th century, these gardens were never covered with lithic mulch. According to Mieth and Bork, gardening on the segment of Poike they studied appears to have ceased completely in the 17th century.

Colluvial sediments cover the cultivation (Ap) layer. Why did the gardeners desist from cultivation on Poike at this time rather than follow the example of other gardeners on the island, we might ask? Possibly, the land did need mulch, but as rocks were not as readily available on Poike, the gardeners either moved to other districts on Poike or on the island to cultivate their crops, rather than move rocks to their gardens.

In the La Pérouse area, Wozniak and Stevenson (2008) found an Ap layer in swale landforms where soils were naturally deeper (>1.5 meters). The Ap layer was covered with colluvial sediments but there was no evidence of application of rocks to form a mulch. Radiocarbon dating showed these soils were cultivated between the 13th and the 19th centuries. Lithic mulched gardens, with Ap sediments dated to as early as the 11th century, were found nearby but in landforms with thin soils.

In addition to prehistoric garden plots cultivated with, and without, the aid of mulch, other gardening constructions have been identified. For example, Stevenson (1997) found linear rock alignments and planting circles (circular alignments made of rocks) at the productive area around Mauga Tari near the center of the island at the base of Terevaka. Here, intermittent streams form after rain storms. Planting circles made of single tiers of rocks do not seem as common as *manavai* or lithic mulched gardens in the archaeological record of Rapa Nui. However, these circular alignments would help retain water around the roots of whatever plant was planted within the circle. Variations of these structures are still in use on the island.

Manavai – rock wall enclosures that protect against wind – have been located around the island, but as with all other garden types and structures, the *manavai* are more common along the coast (Stevenson et al. 2002: 19). The construction age of these structures has not been determined and the use of walled gardens was not mentioned in the 18th-century texts written by Western visitors. *Manavai* have been associated with gardening in ethnohistoric references (Barthel 1974; Métraux 1940) however.

The free-standing *manavai* structures provide benefits similar to lithic mulching. The walls create a wind break for plants and the wall of stones retains moisture while shading the roots from the sun. *Manavai* may represent family cultivation areas according to Stevenson et al. (2002), as they were constructed in areas with high residential densities and for this reason the majority of the *manavai* are mainly found within 100 m of the coastline.

Bradford (2009), using 3 sets of recent satellite imagery, has identified at least 2553 circular to oval walled structures on Rapa Nui (most within 2 kilometers of the coast) she interprets as intact or partially intact *manavai* structures. She indicates such structures enclose almost 10% of the island surface. The 10% figure for *manavai* land coverage seems very high. Not all circular features were or are *manavai*. For example, at Te Niu on the northwest coast, the total surveyed area, from coast to 1500 meters inland, was 750,000 square meters. I found 13 *manavai* enclosing 4535 square meters (0.6% of total surveyed area at Te Niu), while other circular edifices were single tier rock outlines of various types of *hare*. All garden areas, *manavai* and lithic mulched gardens at Te Niu do cover approximately 9% of the total land mass surveyed (Wozniak 2003: 337). Some of circular structures Bradford included in her calculations may be features not intended for gardening, such as *hare umu* (cooking house) or *hare oka* (traditional house feature) foundations, or they may be *manavai* historically constructed on private *parcelas* over the past century as this garden protection technique has been readily used after the introduction of free roaming herbivorous animals, such as sheep, cows, and horses.

In addition to *manavai*, another possibly late prehistoric or protohistoric feature associated with food production is the *hare moa* or chicken house. Chickens were an important protein source (although the Polynesian rats were also eaten) and were often used as an offering at feasts and celebrations. *Hare moa* are often associated with *manavai* but may be free standing in the middle of a house site. The construction of the *hare moa* suggests it is a place to put the family's chickens at night, rather than have them vulnerable to predators (human or otherwise).

Botanical evidence of cultivation

Microfossil analyses of soils from suspected gardens have supported the findings of the archaeological work. For example, most of the nineteen soil samples collected at Te Niu in 1996 (as described above) contained microfossils. Cummings examined seven samples for pollen, phytoliths, and spores and Horrocks examined 12 for pollen, phytoliths, spores, and starches (see Wozniak et al. 2010 for details). The presence of fern spores in dated soil samples demonstrates that land clearing commenced circa AD 1300 along the coastal region inland of Ahu Te Niu. The vegetation proceeded to become dominated by grasses, ferns, and herbaceous weeds. However, evidence of many of the traditional Polynesian cultigens is also seen at this time and evidence of taro, yams, and sweet potatoes were identified in samples date from the 14th century to the mid 1800s.

Dating the charcoal and volcanic glass found in soil layers, especially in the sediments of garden pits, were used to estimate the age of the microfossil deposition in those same samples to the prehistoric period. In the microfossil analyses at Te Niu, starch of sweet potatoes and yams was found not only in the garden sediments, but also at the *ahu*, indicating that these tubers or root crops may have been used during feasts or left as offerings on or near the *ahu*.

Starch grains of *Dioscorea alata* and of *Ipomoea batatas* were identified in all cultural sediments from Te Niu examined by Mark Horrocks, while starch of *Colocasia esculenta* was identified in fewer of the samples. Putative (because of poor pollen preservation) bottle gourd (*Lagenaria siceraria*) pollen suggests that gourds were grown at Te Niu (and likely elsewhere on the island in the past). The high percentages of yam and sweet potato starch in all cultural levels at Te Niu suggest these were extensively cultivated. Pollen of *Curcuma longa* and *Broussonetia papyrifera* were also present, although these were considered a tentative identification because pollen of these species is difficult to differentiate from other species in their respective families. Although evidence of bananas was not found at Te Niu, Cummings (1998) did find *Musa* banana phytoliths in sediments from the La Pérouse area on the north coast of Rapa Nui.

Pearthree (2003) found macrofossils of sugarcane in *umu* ovens from several locations on Rapa Nui, along with several cultivated plants, such as sweet potatoes, *Cordyline,* and putative taro and yam remains.

These botanical studies verify the ethnohistoric references as to which plants were grown in ancient Rapa Nui. However, the techniques, tools, and cultivation procedures used to prepare the garden for planting and harvest each of these crops were not recorded. Ethnographic studies inform as to how the plants were likely cultivated.

Ethnohistoric and ethnographic evidence of gardening techniques

Foods presented to the earliest Western visitors consisted of several tuber crops, bananas, and chickens according to historic texts. In AD 1722, Bouman (1994: 99), who accompanied Roggeveen, recorded that at least 10 % of the land of Rapa Nui was cultivated. Bouman noted that "the inhabitants have their fields square and well divided by dry ditches, which they have planted with yams and other tubers . . . as well as sugar cane".

Cook (1821) described "fields laid out with a cord" with "rows of banana plants that extended half a league". Forster (1996: 321), one of Cook's two naturalists on this trip, "saw but few plantations towards the north end, the land being much more bluff or steep there . . . (but saw) more plantations on the east coast". He described the cultivation of bananas, sugar cane, sweet potatoes, yams, eddoes (taro), and nightshade (*Solanum*), and the use of grass as a manure or mulch. Forster and his father (Forster 1996: 110–111) remarked on the scarcity of wood, noting that there were "few plants but cultivated ones, despite the fine climate". Beechey (1831) noted in the early 19th century that taro was grown on the banks of natural gullies made by intermittent streams although this phenomenon has not been reported in the archaeological sense.

Lapérouse (1968 [1799]) also described the use of *Solanum forsteri (poporo)*, grasses, and ferns that were either turned in as green matter, or were burned and applied to the soil to supply nutrients. Lapérouse described plantations of bananas planted in quincunx (parallel rows of features, offset every other row) patterns within rectangular plots. As noted above, he also described how the Rapanui used rocks as mulch on the northwest coast.

Ethnographic work on Rapa Nui did not begin until the late 19th and early 20th centuries (Geiseler 1995; Handy 1923; Linton 1926). Traditionally,

Pacific islanders who live in the tropics use traditional horticultural swidden practices (slash-and-burn). Swiddening normally is used on Pacific islands, not only to clear land to make room for crop plants, but also to regenerate nutrients in soil. In swidden agriculture, one or several seasons of cultivation are followed by several years of fallow (no cultivation). In much of the Pacific, gardeners used 7 to 20 year fallows or "rest intervals" between plantings. There is no archaeological or ethnohistoric evidence that suggests long term fallows were practiced on Rapanui. Because Rapa Nui is not within the tropics and had few of the fast growing native plants which define the tropics as a lush forest or jungle, one can imagine that once the forest was cleared it did not grow back to its original density during fallow periods of several years. On Rapa Nui, evidence that short-fallow swiddening took place was described by Lapérouse (1968 [1799]) in the late 18th century, which was later verified by Métraux (1940).

The ethnohistoric texts lack descriptions of the fine points of gardening and general food production. For example, were cultigen starts placed into level soil or were they planted in shallow mounds or in ditches or troughs (to collect rain water around the roots)? How did the Rapanui gardeners plant yams, sweet potatoes, taro, and bananas – their major starch crops? Recent ethnographic work on gardening informs on the likely details of traditional gardening practices on Rapa Nui (Wozniak 2005), some of which I will relate here. These practices leave no trace in the archaeological record. One reason for this was the constant re-use of garden soils. The planting pits observed in the agricultural soils indicate where the roots and tubers grew but do not inform as to where the original start was placed.

Garden soil was prepared for cultivation using a variety of wooden or stone tools or one's hands traditionally. In areas where lithic mulch was used, the gardener removed enough rocks to expose the ground surface or the plant being harvested; the edible part (usually a tuber or corm) was removed and the top part of the plant that would sprout roots was replanted. The weeds or previous crop remains are mixed into the soil (as a green manure). Although there is no chemical evidence that algae was used as fertilizer, in the past algae may have been added to gardens relatively close to the coast. As the gardens were close to the living area of the gardeners, their families, and their animals (chickens and rats) meal wastes and charcoal from the *umu* ovens were added to garden soil. There is archaeological evidence for this (Wozniak 1998b) – organic debris in the agricultural soil. After preparation of the soil gardeners made hills (for sweet potatoes or yams) or troughs (for bananas) and placed the starts into these.

Historically horses with metal plows or metal hand tools have been used to loosen the soil and today tractors are used to disc the fields. Animal manure from horses and cattle is often used to provide nutrients for the plantings. In these cases rocks are apparently not used as mulch.

Rapanui farmers (e.g. NH and JH) who lived during the 20th century were aware of lithic mulching and other cultivation methods and discussed the techniques with this author (see Wozniak 2005). Currently some Rapanui gardeners have continued to use these traditional constructions when farming on their parcelas, and especially when gardening in remote places they visit during forays to fish along the northern and western cliffs. Figure 5.1 shows a lithic mulched garden known to JH. *Xanthosoma* taro (American introduction) can be seen growing within the garden about 100 meters from the edge of the cliff at Te Niu. The taro is harvested and replanted during fishing trips. Even so, this elder of Rapa Nui was not convinced at the extent of rock mulched gardens in the Te Niu area, although he knew and used this particular garden.

Figures 5.2a and 5.2b illustrate the "nursery" of taro varieties on a parcela along the south coast. The owner of this *parcela* grows extensive fields of

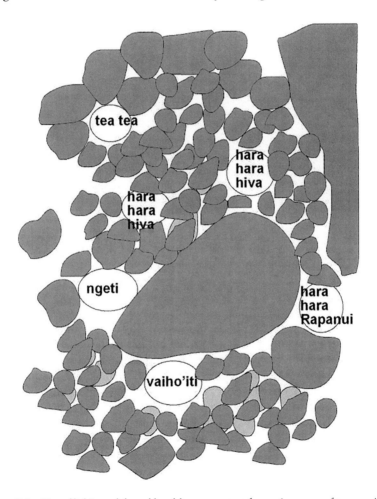

Figure 5.2a Use of lithic mulch and boulders to protect farmer's source of taro varieties on his *parcela*. Here five taro varieties grown on this *parcela* are shown
(Diagram by Wozniak.)

Figure 5.2b Taro cultivars grown on Rapa Nui and shown mapped in the sketch in *Figure 5.2a*: Taro *tea tea*, taro *hara hara hiva*, taro *ngeti*, taro *vaiho'iti*, and taro *hara hara* Rapanui

(Photograph by Wozniak.)

various *Colocasia* taros and other traditional Rapanui crops (some, such as manioc, which was introduced historically but has been on the island for well over 100 years). He maintains a nursery of cultigens in a lithic mulched garden consisting of small rocks and larger boulders, as well as in several *manavai*. Both rock constructions, he feels, protect his cultigens from fire and animals. He uses no rocks in the cultivation of plants he grows for the market.

In the early 20th century there were dozens of varieties of yams grown on Rapa Nui (Englert 1977). Gardeners on Rapa Nui in the 21st century know of 3 or 4 varieties still present on the island. Many of the yam varieties grown in the past generally developed tubers that were one meter or more in length. There are (or, were) a few Rapanui varieties that formed tubers less than 30 cm long also. Modern Rapanui farmers who still grow yams make sure the soil is thick enough to accommodate the yam tuber if they plant the larger varieties, or they place the yam starts in mounds of soil (Figure 5.3).

Figure 5.3 Yam plant growing in hill mound on Rapa Nui
(Photograph by Wozniak taken in 2006)

According to several elder Rapanui farmers, oral tradition indicates that there are areas of the island traditionally associated with yam production. Thicker soils may have been selected for yam production or mounds built in some of these districts. However, within one district on Terevaka the traditional way to grow yams involves constructing *manavai* approximately one meter in diameter. A local Rapanui farmer has identified the location of such structures along the south coast (Figure 5.4a). The technique used involved placing a flat stone at the base of the *manavai* and then filling the structure with soil. The yam start, which takes at least one year to grow a harvestable tuber, is then placed at the top of this soil during spring rains. As the tuber grows down to the base of the structure its rootlets touch the flat rock and downward growth is arrested. Then lateral growth continues, producing a thick diameter tuber as long as the *manavai* is tall. A sketch of how this walled structure would function is shown in Figure 5.4b.

Fields of banana "trees" were described as grown in large fields of quincunx rows by the 18th century visitors (Lapérouse 1968 [1799]). This is still the technique used on Rapa Nui (Wozniak 2005). The finer details of cultivating the banana plant can be seen in Figure 5.5. This photo demonstrates that the young *"poki"* or banana start had been placed in a small mound surrounded by a circular trough. The banana plant produces a bunch of

Figure 5.4a Set of *manavai* structures along the South Coast of Rapa Nui having 1 meter inner diameters. These *manavai* are filled with soil. These represent possible yam growing structures, likely used prehistorically or protohistorically

(Photograph by Wozniak taken in 2006)

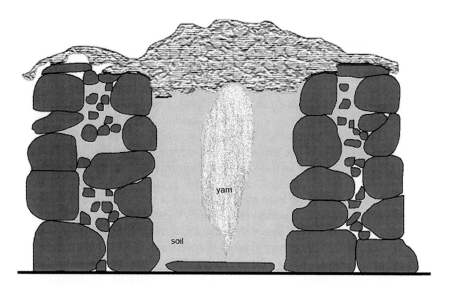

Figure 5.4b Sketch of yam growing *manavai* structure – soil-filled rock wall approximately 1 meter high, with flat rock at base of soil

Subsistence strategies on Rapa Nui 105

Figure 5.5 Banana on Rapa Nui planted in small mound surrounded by a shallow circular trough which collects rain water around the plant's roots

(Photograph by Wozniak taken in 2006)

bananas about a year after it is planted. The main stem dies after producing a bunch of bananas, however, by harvest time new shoots have emerged around the main stem of the banana. These are dug up for replanting in early spring (during the rainy season).

Discussion: ancient subsistence on Rapa Nui – gardening strategies

The subsistence strategy on prehistoric Rapa Nui consisted of harvesting marine life and growing traditional Polynesian cultigens and animals in whatever method was most favorable to produce food for the general population and to create an economic surplus, which supported an increasingly ranked society. This subsistence strategy can be applied to Polynesia in general. Polynesians moved from island to island to take advantage of marine resources and grow their crops.

Above I have summarized the archaeological and environmental evidence for gardening methods used for food production on Rapa Nui during the prehistoric and protohistoric periods, i.e., over much of the past thousand years. I have included the ethnohistoric and ethnographic observations describing traditional cultivation techniques on this particular island. What this overview demonstrates is that gardening techniques were adapted to both the physical (environmental) landscape and to the climate. As these attributes varied, so did the techniques used to sustain food production.

Gardening techniques used by ancient Rapanui gardeners seem to vary with local differences in the island environment. For example, swales (concave landforms) at Te Niu constitute many of the gardens found situated on this rather steep hillside on the western side of Terevaka (see Wozniak 2003). Gardens positioned between 100m (the lowest elevation at Te Niu given its position at the top of a cliff) and 250m elevation have garden soils, whether thick and thin, that are covered with lithic mulch. However, at higher elevations (above 250 meters) rocks were not used to mulch the soil. This is likely the case because the pattern of orographic rainfall is such that on the upper elevations of Terevaka rainfall is greater and the peak at this elevation is often surrounded by clouds providing a humid environment. There may be another explanation for the lack of rocks at higher elevations. This explanation is related to the apparent source of rocks used for lithic mulch.

Because it appears that almost half the island surface supports lithic mulch gardens, this must have been a most important strategy for food production. Diamond (2005: 92) assesses these gardens to be a "huge effort to construct, because they required moving millions or even billions of rocks". This may be so, but in all likelihood the rocks could have been collected for another purpose and then re-used.

Although there continues to be controversy regarding the techniques used to move the *moai* to *ahu* around the island, we do know hundreds of *moai* were moved to *ahu* around the island. Dozens more lay along the Moai Roads that circle the island. RR, an informant in my ethnographic study on gardening (Wozniak 2005), has suggested that small rocks were used, not only to raise the *moai* onto the *ahu*, but to move the *moai* over land. The smaller rounded or subrounded rocks, he says, worked as ball bearings to help move the *moai* up or down gentle slopes. The Rapanui people also used rocks to raise the *moai* onto the *ahu* – namely by enlarging the pile of rocks under a prone *moai* until the image stood upright. One may observe the pile of rocks used in a failed attempt to right a *moai* near Ahu Akahanga on the south coast. The fallen *moai* is located head down next to a small *ahu* south of the main *ahu*. Rocks were piled under the *moai* and as levers slowly righted the *moai* to an upright position on the *ahu*, more rocks were added. In the case of Ahu Akahanga we see the righting procedure did not go as planned. Apparently, the end of the 17th century marks the period during which *moai* production and transport apparently ceased. What happened to all the rocks used to move and raise the *moai*? The rocks collected for *ahu* construction and *moai* placement were present within the community and proximal to their gardens. At Te Niu, for example, there is a rocky tongue of lava leading from the Road of the Moai down 100 m to Ahu Te Niu (where several large and small *moai* reside). Lithic mulched gardens with Ap soils now cover much of the swale inland of the *ahu*.

Some rocks may have been used in the re-construction of image *ahu* into semipyramidal *ahu* in the 18th and 19th centuries. Piles of rocks cover the bones of Rapanui people who died in great numbers by the introduction of disease by Western visitors at the *ahu*. But could not a major source of the rocks used as lithic mulch also be the rocks littering the land after *moai* transport? If indeed moving *moai* onto the coastal *ahu* in each settlement was carried out using small rocks, then rocks used during this process – likely collected from outcrops – were available nearby for other uses. At the end of the *moai* phase rocks were scattered in every settlement to varying degrees. The amount of energy needed to scavenge rocks for lithic mulch gardens was less than the effort required to obtain rocks to move the *moai*. Similarly, rocks were scavenged repeatedly to construct other structures used for food production. Water-worn cobbles and carved *paenga* from house foundations were used in *manavai* and in *hare moa*.

Because re-use of land and resources was necessary on Rapa Nui, what we observe in our archaeological surveys is what came after what was before. We have not been able to fully assess the early agricultural pursuits and strategies of the first centuries of Polynesian occupation on Rapa Nui. Likely some of the techniques used for animal husbandry and cultivation have been obliterated by the more recent constructions evident on the landscape.

For example, traditional Polynesian methods of swidden agriculture involved long fallow periods alternating with a few years of cultivation in one piece of land (Barrau 1965; Yen 1973). This gave rise on Rapa Nui to constant reuse of garden plots as the population grew and expanded to settle the entire island. Without the benefits of tree cover for shade after turning their forest land into agricultural land, or of irrigation to provide water to their plants, the Rapanui gardeners developed methods of conserving their soil and the moisture necessary to grow their crops. Apparently they found it beneficial to cover their gardens with small rocks or to grow their crops plants in walled gardens – *manavai*. They varied these techniques according to a given environmental situation or to a specific geomorphic setting. The clans on Rapa Nui cultivated land held by their clan and thus they needed to improvise their techniques to maximize their production output on that land. For this reason we would expect to find variations of a theme as to what methods produced the best or most food for a given period of time in a given location on the island.

With time, we may uncover additional evidence of early food production on Rapa Nui, and may better understand why certain methods were chosen for one location and not another. The Rapanui people were inventive in procuring local foods and growing those Southeast Asian and American crops that they introduced the isolated island in the Southeast Pacific one thousand years ago. Now faced with a century of increasing climatic perturbations, many of the techniques used by their ancestors could aid the 21st century Rapanui people in maximizing locally produced foods.

References

Abbott, I. 1991. "Polynesian Use of Seaweed." In *Islands, Plants, and Polynesians*, edited by P. A. Cox and S. A. Banack, 135–145. Portland, OR: Dioscorides Press.

Allen, M. S. 2002. "Resolving Long-Term Change in Polynesian Marine Fisheries." *Asian Perspectives* 41(2): 195–212.

Ayres, W. S. 1986. "Easter Island Subsistence." *Journal de la Société desOcéanistes* 80 (Tome XLI): 103–124.

Baer, A., T. N. Ladefoged, C. Stevenson, and S. Haoa. 2008. "Surface Rock Gardens of Prehistoric Rapa Nui." *Rapa Nui Journal* 22(2): 102–109.

Barrau, J. 1965. "L'Humide et le Sec: An Essay on Ethnobiological Adaptation to Contrastive Environments in the Indo-Pacific Area." *Journal of the Polynesian Society* 74(3): 329–346.

Barthel, T. S. 1974. *The Eighth Land: The Polynesian Discovery and Settlementof Easter Island*. Translated by A. Martin. Honolulu, HI: University Press of Hawaii.

Beechey, F. W. 1831. *Narrative of a Voyage to the Pacific and Beerings Strait*. 2 vols. London, England: H. Colburn and R. Bentley.

Behrens, C. F. 1722 (1908): *The Voyage of Captain Don Felipe Gonzalez to Easter Island, 1770–1: Preceded by An Extract from the Official Log of Mynheer Jacob Roggeveen in 1722*. Trans. and edited by B.G. Corney, Ser. II, Vol. 13: 131–137. Cambridge: Hakluyt Society.

Boersema, J. J. 2015. *The Survival of Easter Island: Dwindling Resources and Cultural Resilience*. Translated by Diane Webb. Cambridge: Cambridge University Press.

Bork, H.-R., A. Mieth, and B. Tschochner. 2004. "Nothing but Stones? A Review of the Extent and Technical Efforts of Prehistoric Stone Mulching on Rapa Nui." *RapaNui Journal* 18(1): 10–14.

Bouman, C. 1994. "The Complete Journal of Captain Cornelis Bouman, Master of the Ship Theinhoven, Forming Part of the Fleet of Jacob Roggeveen, from 31 March to 13 April 1722 During Their Stay Around Easter Island." *Rapa Nui Journal* 8(4): 95–100.

Bradford, I. 2009. *Archaeological Surveying with Satellite Imagery: Mapping Subsistence Features on Rapa Nui Using Remote Sensing Techniques.* Unpublished Thesis Presented to the Department of Anthropology. Long Beach, CA: California State University.

Commendador, A. S., J. V. Dudgeon, B. P. Finney, B. T. Fuller, and K. S. Esh. 2013. "A Stable Isotope (d13C and d15N) Perspective on Human Diet on Rapa Nui (Easter Island) ca. AD 1400–1900." *American Journal of Physical Anthropology* 152(2): 1–13.

Cook, J. 1821. *The Three Voyages of Captain James Cook Round the World III.* 6 vols. London, England: Longman, Hurst, Rees, Orme, and Brown.

Cristino, C., P. Vargas, and R. Izaurieta. 1981. *Atlas Arqueologica de Isla de Pascua.* Santiago, Chile: Universidad de Chile.

Cuming, H., MS. 1827–28. *Journal of a Voyage from Valparaiso to the Society and the Adjacent Islands Performed in the Schooner Discoverer, Samuel Grimwood Master, in the Years 1827 and 1828, by Hugh Cuming.* MS 1336 (CY Reel 194). Sydney, Australia: Mitchell Library.

Cummings, L. S. 1998. A Review of Recent Pollen and Phytolith Studies from Various Contexts on Easter Island. In *Easter Island in Pacific Context*, edited by C. M. Stevenson, G. Lee, and F. J. Morin, 100–106. Los Osos, CA: Easter Island Foundation.

Denham, T. P. 2004. "The Roots of Agriculture and Arboriculture in New Guinea: Looking Beyond Austronesian Expansion, Neolithic Packages and Indigenous Origins." *World Archaeology* 36(4): 610–620.

Denham, T. P., S. G. Haberle, C. Lentfer, R. Fullagar, J. Field, M. Therin, N. Porch, and B. Winsborough. 2003. "Origins of Agriculture at Kuk Swamp in the Highlands of New Guinea." *Science* 301: 189–193.

Diamond, J. 2005. *Collapse: How Societies Choose to Fail or Succeed.* New York: Penguin Books.

Edwards, W. M., P. F. Germann, L. B. Owens, and C. R. Amerman. 1984. "Watershed Studies of Factors Influencing Infiltration, Runoff, and Erosion on Stony and Non-Stony Soils." In *Erosion and Productivity of Soils Containing Rock Fragments.* SSSA Special Publ. No. 13, edited by J. D. Nichols, L. Brown, and W. J. Grant. Madison, WI: Soil Science Society of America.

Englert, S. 1977. *La Tierra de Hotu Matu'a.* Santiago, Chile: Editorial Universitaria.

Fairbourne, M. L. 1973. "Effect of Gravel Mulch on Crop Yields." *Agronomy Journal* 65: 925–928.

Flenley, J. R. 1991. "The Late Quaternary Vegetational and Climatic History of Easter Island." *Journal of Quaternary Science* 6: 85–115.

Flenley, J. R. and S. M. King. 1984. "Late Quaternary Pollen Records from Easter Island." *Nature* 307(5): 47–50.

Forster, J.R. 1996 (1778). Observations Made during a Voyage Round the World. N. Thomas, H. Guest, and M. Dettelback, eds. Honolulu: University of Hawaii Press.

Geiseler, W. 1995. *Geiseler's Easter Island Report: An 1880's Anthropological Account.* Translated by W. S. Ayres and G. S. Ayres. Asian and Pacific Archaeology Series 12. Honolulu: University of Hawaii at Manoa.

Green, R. C. 1998. "Rapanui Origins Prior to European Contact – The View from Eastern Polynesia." In *Segundo Congreso Internacional de Arqueologia de Isla de*

Pascua y Polinesia Oriental, edited by Patty Vargas Casanova, 87–110. Santiago, Chile: Anales de la University de Chile.

Green, R. C. 2000. "Origins for the Rapanui of Easter Island before European Contact: Solutions from Holistic Anthropology to an Issue No Longer Much of a Mystery." *Rapa Nui Journal* 14: 71–76.

Handy, E. S. C. 1923. "The Native Culture in the Marquesas." *Bulletin of the Bernice P. Bishop Museum* 9: 3–358. Honolulu: Bishop Museum Press.

Horrocks, M. and J. A. Wozniak. 2008. "Plant Microfossil Analysis Reveals Disturbed Forest and a Mixed-Crop, Dryland Production System at Te Niu, Easter Island." *Journal of Archaeological Science* 35: 126–142.

Horrocks, M., W. T. Baisden, M. A. Harper, M. Marra, J. Flenley, D. Feek, S. Haoa-Cardinali, E. D. Keller, L. Gonza'lez Nualart, and T. E. Gorman. 2015. "A Plant Microfossil Record of Late Quaternary Environments and Human Activity from Rano Aroi and Surroundings, Easter Island." *Journal of Paleolimnology* 54: 279–303.

Hucke-Gaete, R., A. Aguayo-Lobo, S. Yancovic-Pakarati, and M. Flores. 2014. "Marine Mammals of Easter Island (Rapa Nui) and Salas y Gómez Island (Motu Motiro Hiva), Chile: A Review and New Records." *Latin American Journal of Aquatic Research* 42(4): 743–751.

Ladefoged, T. N., C. M. Stevenson, S. Haoa, M. Mulrooney, C. Puleston, P. M. Vitousek, and O. A. Chadwick. 2010. "Soil Nutrient Analysis of Rapa Nui Gardening." *Archaeology of Oceania* 45: 80–85.

Ladefoged, T. N., A. Flaws, and C. M. Stevenson. 2013. "The Distribution of Rock Gardens on Rapa Nui (Easter Island) as Determined from Satellite Imagery." *Journal of Archaeological Science* 40: 1203–1212.

Lapérouse, J. F. G. 1968 [1799]. *A Voyage Round the World, Performed in the Years 1785, 1786, 1787, and 1788 by the Boussole and Astrolabe Under the Command of J.F.G. de la Perouse*. Vol. 1. (translated from the French). New York, NY: Plenum Publishing.

Lightfoot, D. R. 1994. "Morphology and Ecology of Lithic-Mulch Agriculture." *Geographical Review* 84(2): 172–185.

Lightfoot, D. R. 1996. "The Nature, History, and Distribution of Lithic Mulch Agriculture: An Ancient Technique of Dryland Agriculture." *The Agricultural History Review* 44(2): 206–222.

Linton, R. 1926. *Ethnology of Polynesia and Micronesia Guide Part 6*. Chicago, IL: Field Museum of Natural History.

McCall, G. 1993. "Little Ice Age: Some Speculations for Rapanui." *Rapa Nui Journal* 7(4): 65–70.

McCall, G. 1994. *Rapanui: Tradition and Survival on Easter Island*. Honolulu, HI: University of Hawaii Press.

McCoy, P. C. 1976. *Easter Island Settlement Patterns in the Late Prehistoric and Protohistoric Periods* (Bulletin No. 5). International Fund for Monuments, Inc.

McFadgen, B. G. 1980. "Maori Plaggen Soil in New Zealand, Their Origin and Properties." *Journal of the Royal Society of New Zealand* 10(1): 3–19.

Métraux, A. 1940. *Ethnology of Easter Island*. Bernice P. Bishop Museum Bulletin 160. Honolu: Bishop Museum Press.

Mieth, A. and H.-R. Bork. 2003. "Diminution and Degradation of Environmental Resources by Prehistoric Land Use on Poike Peninsula, Easter Island." *Rapa Nui Journal* 17(1): 34–41.

Montenegro, A., C. Avis, and A. Weaver. 2008. "Modeling the Prehistoric Arrival of the Sweet Potato in Polynesia." *Journal of Archaeological Science* 35(2): 355–367.

Orliac, C. 2000. "The Woody Vegetation of Easter Island between the Early 14th and the Mid-17th Centuries AD." In *Easter Island Archaeology: Research on Early Rapa Nui Culture*, edited by C. M. Stevenson and W. S. Ayres, 211–220. Los Osos, CA: Easter Island Foundation.

Pearthree, E. 2003. "Identification des Restes Carbonizés de Plantes Non-ligneuses Découverts sur Trios Sites d'habitat à L'île de Pâques." In *Archéologie en Océanie Insulaire: Peuplement, Societes et Paysages*, edited by C. Orliac, 172–183. Paris, France: Editions Artcom.

Peteet, D., W. E. Beck, J. Ortiz, S. O'Connell, D. Kurdyla, and D. Mann. 2003. "Rapid Vegetational and Sediment Change from Rano Aroi Crater, Easter Island." In *Easter Island Scientific Exploration into the World's Environmental Problems in Microcosm*, edited by J. Loret and J. T. Tanacredi, 81–92. New York, NY: KluwerAcademic /Plenum Publishers.

Randall, J. E. 1976. "The Endemic Shore Fishes of the Hawaiian Islands, Lord Howe Island and Easter Island." *Travaux et documents O.R.S.T.O.M.* 47: 49–73.

Reinman, F. M. 1967. "Fishing: An Aspect of Oceanic Economy." *Fieldiana: Anthropology* 56(2): 95–208.

Roggeveen, J. 1908. *An Extract from Mihnheer Jacob Roggeveen's Official Log of His Discovery of and Visit to Easter Island in 1722.* Cambridge: Hakluyt Society 2nd series, No. 13 (xv–xxvii).

Routledge, C. S. 1919. *The Mystery of Easter Island.* London: Sifton, Praed and Co. Ltd.

Skottsberg, C. 1920. "Notes on a Visit on Easter Island." In *The Natural History of Juan Fernandez and Easter Island*, Vol. 1. Uppsala, Sweden : Almqvist & Wiksells Boktryckeri.

Steadman, D. W. 1995. "Prehistoric Extinctions of Pacific Island Birds: Biodiversity Meets Zooarchaeology." *Science* 267: 1123–1131.

Stevenson, C. M. 1997. *Maunga Tari: An Upland Agricultural Complex.* Los Osos, CA: Bearsville Press & Cloud Mountain Press.

Stevenson, C. M. and S. Haoa. 1998. "Prehistoric Gardening Systems and Agricultural Intensification in the La Perouse Area of Easter Island." In *Easter Island in Pacific Context: South Seas Symposium*, edited by C. M. Stevenson, G. Lee, and F. J. Morin, 205–213. Los Osos, CA: Easter Island Foundation.

Stevenson, C. M., J. A. Wozniak, and S. Haoa. 1999. "Prehistoric Agricultural Production on Easter Island (Rapa Nui), Chile." *Antiquity* 73: 801–812.

Stevenson, C. M., T. Ladefoged, and S. Haoa. 2002. "Productive Strategies in an Uncertain Environment." *Rapa Nui Journal* 16(1): 17–22.

Stevenson, C. M., T. L. Jackson, A. Mieth, H.-R. Bork, and T. N. Ladefoged. 2006. "Prehistoric and Early Historic Agriculture at Maunga Orito, Easter Island (Rapa Nui), Chile." *Antiquity* 80(310): 919–936.

Stevenson, C. M., T. N. Ladefoged, and S. Haoa. 2006. "An Upland Agricultural Residence on Rapa Nui: Occupation of a *Hare oka* (18–473G) in the Vaitea Region." *Archaeology in Oceania* 42: 72–78.

Stevenson, C. M., C. O. Puleston, P. M. Vitousek, O. A. Chadwick, S. Haoa, and T. N. Ladefoged. 2015. "Variation in Rapa Nui (Easter Island) Land Use Indicates Production and Population Peaks Prior to European Contact." *PNAS* 112(4): 1025–1030.

Vargas Casanova, P. 1998. "Rapa Nui Settlement Patterns: Types, Function and Spatial Distribution of Households Structural Components." In *Easter Island and East Polynesian Prehistory*, edited by P. V. Casanova, 111–130. Santiago, Chile: Instituto de Estudios Isla de Pascua.

Wozniak, J. A. 1998a. "Settlement Patterns and Subsistence on the Northwest Coast of Easter Island." In *Easter Island and East Polynesian Prehistory*, edited by P. V. Casanova, 171–178. Santiago, Chile: Instituto de Estudios Isla de Pascua/Universidad de Chile.

Wozniak, J. A. 1998b. "Settlement Patterns and Subsistence on the Northwest Coast of Rapa Nui." In *Easter Island in Pacific Context*, edited by C. Stevenson, G. Lee, and F. J. Morin, 161–175. Los Osos, CA: Easter Island Foundation.

Wozniak, J. A. 1999. "Prehistoric Horticultural Practices on Easter Island-Lithic Mulched Gardens and Field Systems." *Rapa Nui Journal* 13: 95–99.

Wozniak, J. A. 2003. *Exploring Landscapes on Easter Island (Rapanui) with Geoarchaeological Studies: Settlement, Subsistence, and Environmental Changes*. Dissertation, Department of Anthropology. Eugene, OR: University of Oregon.

Wozniak, J. A. 2005. "An Ethnoarchaeological Study of Horticulture on Rapa Nui." In *The Reñaca Papers, Sixth International Conference on Rapa Nui and the Pacific*, edited by C. M. Stevenson, J. M. Ramírez, F. J. Morin, and N. Barbacci, 137–147. Los Osos, CA: Easter Island Foundation, and Valparaíso, Chile: University of Valparaíso.

Wozniak, J. A. and C. M. Stevenson. 2008. "Archaeological and Geomorphological Investigations of Rapa Nui Gardens and Agricultural Field Systems." In *Prehistoric Rapa Nui*, edited by C. M. Stevenson and S. C. Haoa, 41–78. Los Osos, CA: Easter Island Foundation.

Wozniak, J. A., M. Horrocks, and L. Cummings. 2010. "Plant Microfossil Analysis of Deposits from Te Niu, Rapa Nui, Demonstrates Forest Disruption c. AD 1300 and Subsequent Dryland Multi-Cropping." In *The Gotland Papers: Selected Papers from the VII International Conference on Easter Island and the Pacific: Migration, Identity, and Cultural Heritage*, edited by H. Martinsson-Wallin and P. Wallin, 111–124. Visby, Sweden: Gotland University Press 11.

Wright, C. S. and V. C. Diaz. 1962. *Soils and Agricultural Development of Easter Island (Hotu-Matua)*. Quarterly Report Supplement No. 1. Santiago, Chile: Ministry of Agriculture.

Yen, D. E. 1973. "The Origins of Oceanic Agriculture." *Archaeology and Physical Anthropology in Oceania* 8: 68–85.

Yen, D. E. 1974 *The Sweet Potato and Oceania*. Honolulu: Bishop Museum Press.

Yen, D. E. 1988. "Easter Island Agriculture in Prehistory: The Possibilities of Reconstruction." In *First International Congress: Easter Island and East Polynesia*, edited by C. Cristino, P. Vargas, R. Izaurieta, and R. Budd, Vol. 1, 59–80. Santiago, Chile: Universidad de Chile, Instituto de Estudios Isla de Pascua.

Zizka, G. 1990. "Easter Island Flora." In *State and Perspective of Scientific Research in Easter Island Culture*, edited by H. M. Esen-Baur, 189–207. Frankfurt, Germany: Courier Forschunginstitut Senckenberg.

6 By the Quebrada of Ava Ranga Uka A Toroke Hau – about landscape transformation and the significance of water and trees

Burkhard Vogt and Annette Kühlem

Introduction

When Easter Island was settled by the end of the 1st millennium AD the Rapanui started to transform their island to a large extent by introducing new plant and animal species, building settlements and ceremonial centers, exploiting quarries and installing vast rock gardens. One of the most noticeable interventions was the cutting down of the palm tree vegetation that covered the island by the time settlers arrived. This resulted in a dramatic degradation of the soils and consequent erosion. Even though the idea of an ecological collapse in pre-contact times (Diamond 2005) is now rejected by the majority of scholars, it remains unclear why the Rapanui applied protective measures in some cases (see below) but failed to do so in others. Landscape transformation was markedly affected by water and the management strategies adopted by the Rapanui, but the role that water played in this general process has only recently been a subject of research.

The role of water in Polynesian culture

Traces of ancient hydraulic architecture and water management are omnipresent on many of the Pacific islands. However, it was only in the 1950s that ethnographers began to systematically classify the variability of irrigation and drainage systems (Damm 1951; Barrau 1965), that included wells and cisterns, fish ponds and intertidal fish traps. Polynesian triangle anthropological studies mostly by Anglo-American scholars, were dedicated especially to irrigation systems such as on the Marquesas (Addison 2001), Hawaii, Wallis and Futuna, the Cook Islands (Kirch 1994) and in New Zealand (Barber 2001). By studying the visible surface remains of abandoned field systems, or the traditional active wet farming, investigations primarily focused on the different types of management and agricultural intensification, the choice of crops (Spriggs 1990), the discussion of Wittfogel's theories on hydraulic societies and oriental despotism (Wittfogel 1957), as well as the social prerequisites and effects of irrigation agriculture. To our knowledge, however, the role of water in the context of ritually transformed landscapes has never been investigated by larger-scale archaeological excavations in the Pacific.

The state of knowledge about the use of water on Easter Island was, until recently, rather limited and based on ethnographic data. Subtropical Easter

Island has an annual mean precipitation of up to 2000mm but the unpredictability of the rainfall and the long drought periods increased the risk of rainfall agriculture (Mann et. al. 2008, Ladefoged et. al. 2005). Early visitors like Cook and La Pérouse complained about the poor and brackish quality of the fresh water on the island and hinted at the complete lack of rivers and creeks as they were otherwise reported in large numbers from most of the inhabited Pacific islands. Authors of the 19th and 20th centuries referred to the crater lakes of Rano Kau, Rano Aroi, and Rano Raraku as the main sources for fresh water. Only Father Sebastian Englert (1948) provided a comprehensive list of wells and cisterns. He also emphasized the fact that the Rapanui considered months of little or no rainfall as periods of drought, which they tried to counter with technical measures and even with rituals (see below).

The site of Ava Ranga Uka A Toroke Hau

Since 2008 excavations have been conducted at the site of Ava Ranga Uka A Toroke Hau under the direction of the German Archaeological Institute – a project which demonstrates for the first time that hydraulic engineering and intensive anthropogenic landscaping were an integral part of ritual practices on Easter Island (Vogt 2009, 2013; Vogt and Moser 2010a, 2010b; Kersten et al. 2009; Fassbinder et al. 2009). The site is located almost exactly at the center of the island (Figure 6.1) at a place where the ancient tribal areas may have intersected (cf. Routledge 1919). Within these territories the various resources – such as obsidian and basalt for lithic products, soils, tuff, but also fresh water – were very unequally distributed.

Ava Ranga Uka A Toroke Hau is found at an elevation of 270 meters above sea level on the Quebrada Vaipú, a small creek that today bears water only after heavy downpours. Its catchment is very small (estimated less than 10 square kilometers) and so is its run-off. It extends from Rano Aroi, the crater lake of the volcano Terevaka, to the shore at Akahanga on the island's south coast. Judging by a couple of cement-plastered hydraulic installations erected by Williamson & Balfour between 1903 and 1953, the *quebrada* must have carried water until recent times, although to such a small extent that the creek was never explicitly mentioned as such. Systematic survey in the *quebrada* has not yet been undertaken but it was established that settlement structures along the *quebrada* were not more frequent than the general site distribution in the interior of the island (e.g., Cristino et al. 1981). The existence of fresh water thus did not result in a preference for settlement activities in its vicinity. Could the access to the water in the Quebrada Vaipú have been socially sanctioned and thus restricted?

The site of Ava Ranga Uka A Toroke Hau can be divided into three complexes (Figure 6.2; Figure 6.3):

1. the Ahu Hanua Nua Mea (= rainbow ahu) with a single moai on the eastern bank as one of the few image ahu in the interior;
2. a small settlement in the west;

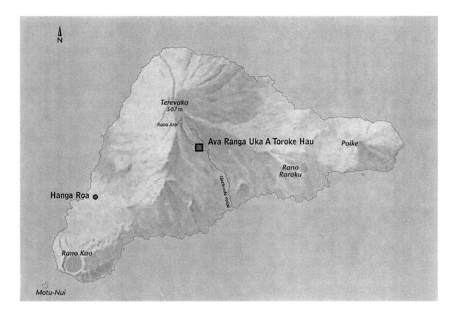

Figure 6.1 Easter Island with the location of Ava Ranga Uka A Toroke Hau (H.P. Wittersheim)

Figure 6.2 Ava Ranga Uka A Toroke Hau, general view at the beginning of excavation
(Photograph by B. Vogt.)

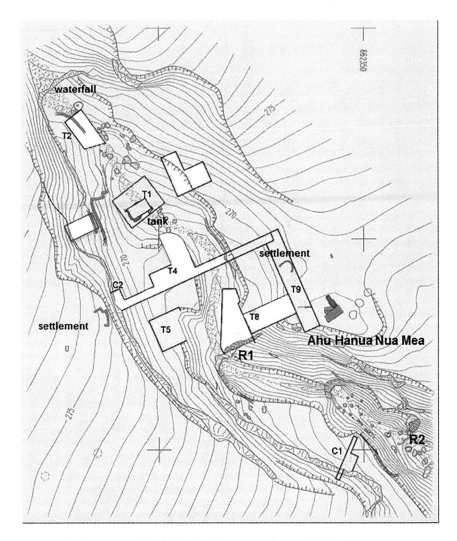

Figure 6.3 Ava Ranga Uka A Toroke Hau, general map (C. Hartl-Reiter)

3. and an assemblage of monumental structures in a small widening of the streambed, which at times must have been hydraulically active.

Such a combination of different kinds of architecture had never been reported from Easter Island before. The central sector of the site measures 80 by 50 meters and was strongly altered by an erosional gully that destroyed part of the installations but at the same time created optimal stratigraphic profiles by cutting through a maximum of six meters of deposits. The installations that survived destruction are two successive dam-like structures, a megalithic stone basin, canals, bank enforcements, terraces, extensive pavements and anthropogenic use-surfaces on different stratigraphic levels.

The dam-like earthworks R1 and R2

The most prominent hydraulic installations are the two dam-like constructions R1 and R2 which at an interval of 45 meters blocked the valley completely. They functioned as a system. According to radiocarbon dates the assemblage was probably set up in the late 13th/early 14th century (see Table 6.1), and perhaps simultaneously destroyed by an extraordinary flood event several decades before the arrival of the first Europeans in 1722. An undated oral tradition concerning the toponym of the site supports the assumption that flash floods were a real and sometimes fatal threat during the time of the occupation of Ava Ranga Uka A Toroke Hau: the name of the site can be translated as "where the body of Uka, daughter of Toroke Hau, was floating in the streambed" (Englert 1948). The occurrence of such heavy floods must be seen in the context of the preceding dramatic erosion that could be reconstructed for other parts of the island during later pre-contact times (Mieth and Bork 2012).

Originally, the two dam-like constructions were just 15 meters long. Structure R1 eventually reached a height of ca. 3 meters while R2 was about 5 meters high. Excavation (R1) and surface cleaning (R2) showed a similar construction: a structure made mainly from coarse gravel and

Figure 6.4 Ava Ranga Uka A Toroke Hau, dam-like earthwork R1 with three-phased supporting wall

(Photograph by B. Vogt.)

earth supported by a thin quarry stone and boulder wall on the valley-side (Figure 6.4). It is this kind of "facing" that gives them an appearance so markedly different from the "un-faced" dams as they are still used today in traditional Polynesian agriculture.

At Ava Ranga Uka A Toroke Hau the supporting wall of R1 and also the stratification of its earthwork provide evidence for three construction phases, which may reflect repairs and heightening after destructions and damages caused by flash floods. Neither outlet nor spillway could be detected; in fact, they may never have existed. The most striking discovery in the area immediately upstream of structure R1, upon which excavation and also the geomorphological studies of Hans-Rudolf Bork and Andreas Mieth (University of Kiel) have focused, was the scarceness of alluvial sediments which were to be expected in the riverbed that could have functioned as a reservoir (see below). Consequently a larger body of water was not retained here, although upstream of structure R2 fine-layered sediments could be recorded in a protected niche which may support its interpretation as a very small reservoir or retaining basin.

It definitely did not escape the builders' attention that the rare and unexpected floods could carry with them a substantial freight of gravel, boulders, and mud. For that reason the Rapanui regulated the flow of the Quebrada Vaipú along its entire course: to decelerate its force they built low cascades in the riverbed or constructed enforcements (Heyerdahl and Ferdon 1961) and terraces along its banks. The widely practiced lithic mulching is another indication for the Rapanui's ability to cope with erosion (Stevenson et al. 1999). The observations hitherto made on the two earthworks make it very plausible, however, that at least R1 was not a dam or weir in the sense of classical hydraulic engineering. We rather assume that the two earthworks were used as measures of "aquatic" landscape architecture manifesting itself in monumentality and representative appearance. The assumption of a non-utilitarian use of the installations in the streambed is supported by the stratigraphic and geomorphological analysis.

The stratigraphy of the site

The cultural deposits with their temporal depth and stratigraphic detail are one of the features that make Ava Ranga Uka A Toroke Hau a unique site on Easter Island. The geomorphological analysis of the profiles demonstrates that most strata owe their formation not to alluvial transport but to anthropogenic intervention creating even use-surfaces (Figure 6.5). Some layers were formed by deliberately transporting sediment to the site, leveling and compacting it, while for other layers the material was carried down the *quebrada* by water and then spread out horizontally by hand. In many cases the material was selected due to certain characteristics such as grain-size or even color. What could have been the motives for such selective behavior and energy expenditure? The intensions for burying labor-intensively

Figure 6.5 Ava Ranga Uka A Toroke Hau, T4 N section (photogrammetric image C. Hartl-Reiter)

Figure 6.6 Ava Ranga Uka A Toroke Hau, trench T4, pavement after the end of 2012 field season

(Photograph by B. Vogt.)

constructed features such as the pavements remain unclear. Functional or operational reasons cannot be concluded yet, but could the purpose of this overlaying have been a ritual sealing?

Fire places, planting pits, pits for the production of pigment, coral fragments, gaming pieces and basalt and obsidian artifacts were found on different levels in the aforementioned contexts. Under these layers an extensive, elaborate stone pavement – only the uppermost of four – seems to have covered the entire valley from its bottom up to the slopes (Figure 6.6). The anthropogenic use-surfaces and the pavements can be considered the most extensive architectural and landscape transformations so far known on Easter Island. The pavements in Ava Ranga Uka A Toroke Hau are especially unique not only because of their spatial extent and their labor-intensive execution, but also due to the fact that comparable pavements generally occur only in front of *ahu* or the boat-shaped elite houses.

Pavements, planting pits, and canals

Outstanding features amid the upper pavement were circular stone-rimmed planting pits that showed the typical traces of palm root channels (Figure 6.7), as they are exclusively known on Easter Island for the now-extinct endemic *Jubea sp.* (Mieth and Bork 2004). During a later flood event the palm trees were destroyed by the force of sediment freight washed down the *quebrada* or they were felled by hand. In the younger strata above, garden soil was brought in and a second type of planting pits was dug; there is no evidence of palm root holes but root casts for different, yet unidentified plants. Therefore, we conclude that the function of the site had changed markedly during its final occupation.

In the context of the uppermost pavement and the palm tree planting pits, three parallel canals were discovered (Figure 6.8). Both the respective starting points and ends have not yet been located. The canals provide evidence for at least two phases and types of construction; that of relatively wide ditches and stone-lined conduits. Much effort was invested into their execution. A couple of *in situ* capstones indicate that one canal was a temporarily

Figure 6.7 Ava Ranga Uka A Toroke Hau, T4, detail of palm tree planting pit
(Photograph by B. Vogt.)

Figure 6.8 Ava Ranga Uka A Toroke Hau, T4, top pavement with canal 2
(Photograph by B. Vogt.)

subterranean construction and, at later times, still accessible by a sort of manhole to allow cleaning the canal-bed. The alluvial sediment fill suggests that the canals were used to conduct the flow of water along the *quebrada*. Whether they stood in a functional relationship to the palm tree plantation remains unclear.

The megalithic basin T1

The two earthworks R1 and R2 and the canals at Ava Ranga Uka A Toroke Hau are not the only installations in the streambed that were hydraulically active, although their precise interaction is not known. Just a few meters upstream of R1 are the remains of the megalithic basin T1 (Figures 6.9; Figure 6.10), perhaps the latest hydraulic installation on the site. The elaborately built water basin (interior dimensions 5 by 2.75 meters; depth 1.5 meters) was made from large, neatly dressed and pecked basalt *paenga*, of which one was clearly re-used from a boat-shaped house foundation. At its southeast corner is a small box-shaped annex through which water from the *quebrada* was diverted into the basin. The basin is founded on bedrock which shows the faint traces of three petroglyphs: a human footprint, a fish or dolphin and an abstracted double canoe. Along the south wall, the floor was levelled by an undisturbed stone pavement which covered an oblong pit of 50 centimeters depth.

The fill of the pit was composed of dark grey mud alternating with thin bands of fine white volcanic ash. It contained a unique collection of archaeological artifacts and botanical macro-remains, the preservation of which was owed to the permanent moist milieu of the fill and its covering. A first preliminary study recorded branches, leaves, root fibers, gourd seeds and some 220 nutshell fragments of the local palm tree (*Jubea sp.*) identified by Catherine Orliac (pers. comm). Associated with these remains were

Figure 6.9 Ava Ranga Uka A Toroke Hau, T1, megalithic basin with pavement (Photograph by B. Vogt.)

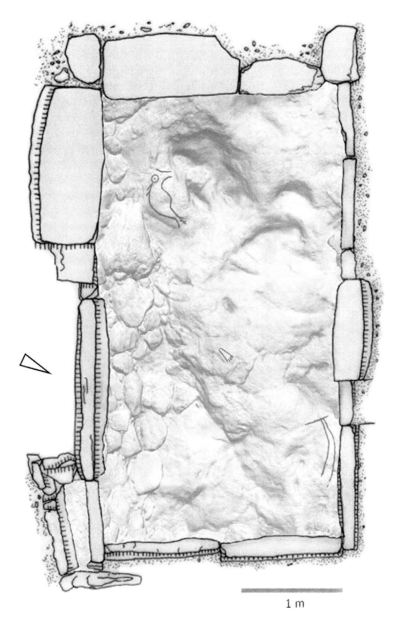

Figure 6.10 Ava Ranga Uka A Toroke Hau, T1, megalithic basin with three petroglyphs
(Drawing W. Herberg and M. Vogt.)

three wooden tools (awls) and some 250 modified obsidian and basalt pieces – several of these miniaturized, others partly polished – as well as innumerable bluish-gray beach pebbles (*poro*) which had been brought up from the coast. These small manuports are commonly encountered as ritual offerings primarily from the vicinity of *ahu* (cf. Martinsson-Wallin 1994). The association of the basin's stone pavement with the petroglyphs and the varied composition of the inventory of the pit suggest an offering deposit or *cache*, which is yet without parallel on Easter Island.

On the basis of four radiocarbon samples (from uncharred nutshells) the basin and the offering pit could be dated to the 16th/early 17th century (calibrated; see Table 6.1). While most of the island had already been deforested at that time (Mieth and Bork 2004), a palm tree plantation was still present at Ava Ranga Uka A Toroke Hau itself as proven by the archaeological evidence. The ultimate disappearance of the *Jubea sp.* palm can certainly not be associated with the interference of the Polynesian rat (*contra* Hunt 2006), since only two out of 220 nutshell fragments show traces of rat gnawing.

Table 6.1 AMS datings from stone basin T1.

lab. #	years BP	δC13	corrected cal. 1σ	corrected cal. 2σ	remarks
Erl-13247	384 ± 40	–27.4	AD 1479–1512 20.2% AD 1544–1623 48.1%	AD 1458–1631 95.4%	soil with organic remains; directly above pavement; E: 662294.16 N: 7000406.53 H: 266.78 – 266.96 Sample # 1, profile
Erl-13248	360 ± 39	–23.4	AD 1502–1592 58.2% AD 1613–1629 10.1%	AD 1463–1469 1.5% AD 1476–1642 93.9%	nutshell; under pavement E: 662296.56 N: 7000407.20 H: 266.79
Erl-13249	307 ± 39	–22.8	AD 1509–1575 38.7% AD 1620–1657 29.6%	AD 1497–1601 50.5% AD 1607–1672 38.6% AD 1743–1756 1.7% AD 1761–1770 1.1% AD 1779–1796 3.5%	nutshell; under pavement E: 662296.84 N: 7000407.03 H: 266.73
Erl-13250	349 ± 40	–24.9	AD 1504–1588 56.1% AD 1616–1635 12.1%	AD 1464–1468 0.7% AD 1477–1647 94.7%	charcoal; from SW corner; directly above pavement E: 662292.60 N: 7000406.79 H: 267.06; southwestern corner

Figure 6.11 Ava Ranga Uka A Toroke Hau, Ahu Hanua Nua Mea during excavation (Photograph by B. Vogt.)

The Ahu Hanua Nua Mea

In 2012, the team laid a first test trench across the small Ahu Hanua Nua Mea and its plaza in order to investigate its chrono-stratigraphic relation towards the nearby installations at the valley bottom. Set on the slightly elevated east bank of the *quebrada* the *ahu* is – not unlike the above mentioned dam-like structures – built basically as an earthwork (Figure 6.11). The builders had used only a very few random and undressed stones for the construction of the low front wall of the platform's west wing and for the small central pedestal of its single *moai*. The rest of the platform has been made from gravel and earth, while hundreds of bluish-gray beach pebbles (*poro*) dominated the fill close to its surface. The sounding made inside the fill revealed a temporary abandonment of the monument, when garden soil was spread over the low platform – only to be later superimposed by a second phase of the platform fill.

Within the limits of the test trench no disturbance was visible on the surface. In the lower and earlier phase of platform construction the contours of a rectangular stone cist (140 by 50 centimeters) came to light, an enclosure just big enough for an extended articulate burial. Capstones were not found. Several molar fragments at the southern end of the cist indicate the approximate position of the skull. Immediately outside at its northern end was a group of four small stones piled upon the remains of a cremation (Figure 6.12). Only later anthropological and stratigraphic study will clarify whether both modes of burial were indeed contemporaneous.

Figure 6.12 Ava Ranga Uka A Toroke Hau, T9, sounding inside Ahu Hanua Nua Mea with cist burial
(Photograph by B. Vogt.)

Excavation in the plaza produced further unexpected results. Its extensive stone pavement shows later interventions and disturbances in places reaching down to bedrock. In front of the platform a small circular pit contained an irregularly shaped slab bearing *toki* marks which was inserted in an upright position (Figure 6.13). This configuration strongly recalls similar installations for example in front of the *marae* on the Society Islands where such slabs have been interpreted as seats of chiefs or as back-rests.

Further north the pavement of the plaza is disturbed by a circular stone house foundation (*hare oka*). Its ring-shaped foundation is made from re-used pavement stones and its interior is filled with a packing of small stones. Into the underlying soft and strongly weathered bedrock, an artificial planting pit had been carved out and filled with garden soil. It reveals the same typical root-holes as previously documented in the pavement of the streambed. This is evidence that *Jubea sp.* palm trees were also planted on the plaza of the *ahu*. Mieth and Bork found evidence for palm tree planting pits at Rano Raraku (Mieth and Bork 2004: 58–59). There, the palm trees can also be interpreted as part of a ritual context (for the ritual character of Rano Raraku see Van Tilburg 1994; Cauwe 2011). The same applies for Ava Ranga Uka A Toroke Hau, where the plantations are an integral component

Figure 6.13 Ava Ranga Uka A Toroke Hau, T9, stone seat or back-rest
(Photograph by B. Vogt.)

not only of the transformed landscape but also of a ritual architecture. The new findings from the plaza of the *ahu* and the pavement in the central area give evidence that the palm trees on Easter Island were not only cut down but in some rare cases also deliberately planted. Their stone-rimmed planting pits, as integral parts of the elaborately finished pavement, are so far unparalleled on the island.

Figure 6.14 Ava Ranga Uka A Toroke Hau, T8, crematorium on top of dam-like earthwork R1

(Photograph by B. Vogt.)

Figure 6.15a and 6.15b Ava Ranga Uka A Toroke Hau, stone phallus (?), height 14 cm (T8); and stone komari (?), height 55cm (T3)
(Photographs by B. Vogt)

The eastern slope and the crematorium

Another focus of excavation was the slope between the *ahu* and the hydraulic installations in the streambed. The stratigraphic sequence showed that when the construction site of the *ahu* and its plaza was prepared, the heavily weathered bedrock was partly cut off and the spoil was dumped elsewhere in order to level the terrain. Directly on top of R1 a small stone platform had been erected (Figure 6.14). Many scorched stones and tiny bone fragments lead us to hypothesize that this structure once served as the crematorium, as these features are frequently found close to *ahu*. The stratigraphic interfacing of the crematorium with the dam-like earthwork R1 makes it highly probable that *ahu* and hydraulic installations were not only contemporaneous but there might also have been a connection between burial practices and the ritual use of water. A further indicator for a water-related fertility cult, a *komari*-shaped stone idol, has been discovered on the slope, while a small stone phallus (?) was found on the terrace on the opposite bank of the *quebrada* (Figure 6.15a and b).

Conclusion

Ava Ranga Uka A Toroke Hau with its transformation of nature and landscape, monumental architecture, hydraulic installations, substantial cultural deposits, *ahu* and funerary constructions formed a complex multi-facetted ensemble which is without parallel among ritual sites on Easter Island. While this combination is unique, beach pebbles, corals, petroglyphs, extensive pavements and monumental architecture as individual parameters have already been reported from ritual contexts of the Rapanui elite.

The Rapanui were well acquainted with the basic techniques and functional principles of hydraulic engineering, although on the site they did not apply them to the storage of water or large-scale irrigation. Instead, a special form of water management was practiced at Ava Ranga Uka A Toroke Hau – one which included a strong ritual component that determined the special characteristics of the site that make it significant.

The occupation of Ava Ranga Uka A Toroke Hau shows repeated changes in the use of the site as can be seen by the burying of pavements. Cauwe (2011) postulates that taboos motivated the intentional sealing of the *moai* quarries at Rano Raraku, the attached road system and of several *ahu*. This might also be a possible explanation for similar observations concerning the deliberate covering of features in the central part of Ava Ranga Uka A Toroke Hau. Especially in the light of limited resources, taboos might have confined the availability of the water of the Quebrada Vaipú making it a valuable commodity. Thus its restricted access and use can be best explained with Ava Ranga Uka A Toroke Hau as the central site of a water cult under the control of a Rapanui elite – perhaps for Hiro, the Polynesian god of rain and fertility. The installations and the plantation of palm trees in the streambed within the wider spatial context of the site can be seen as the intricately constructed architectonical framework for these cult practices.

Métraux (1940: 330) reports how in times of drought when the crops were threatened the Rapanui asked the king for help who then called on his priest (*ariki paka*) to address prayers to the god Hiro. The king took the role as an intermediary between the people and the priest. The priest was painted with red and black pigment and presided over the ceremony. He collected corals and fresh seaweed soaked with seawater, to take them to the top of a hill (possibly Terevaka) and there prayed to the god for rain, which was called "the long tears of Hiro" by the Rapanui. He stayed on the hill at the place of prayer until the rainfall started and then ran downhill so that the clouds might follow him to the fields. Could this be a possible scenario that took place on the *quebrada* of Ava Ranga Uka A Toroke Hau during periods of drought as part of a presumed fertility cult?

Acknowledgments

The field work at Ava Ranga Uka A Toroke Hau is a joint project under the direction of the German Archaeological Institute cooperating with the Consejo de Monumentos Nacionales de Chile and Hanga Roa, and Comisión

Aserora del Consejo de Monumentos Nacionales, Hanga Roa, the Museo Antropológico Padre Sebastian Englert, Hanga Roa, and its director Francisco Torres Hochstetter, the Consejo National Forestal, Hanga Roa, the Mata Ki Te Rangi Foundation, Hanga Roa, and from Germany, the HafenCity Universität Hamburg, the Christian- Albrecht- Universität Kiel, the Bayrisches Landesamt für Denkmalpflege Munich, and the Fachhochschule Potsdam (all Germany). From the very beginning many colleagues and students from Rapa Nui, Chile and different European countries joined the fieldwork, many of them for more than one season: Merahi Atam Lopez, Hans-Rudolf Bork, Roland Botsch, Claudia Bührig, Vittoria Buffa, Melinka Cuadros Hucke, Jörg Faßbinder, Sorobabel Fati Teao, Camila Guerra, Christian Hartl-Reiter, Werner Herberg, Itaya Hey Chavez, Anja Igelmann, Peter Im-Obersteg, Catalina Kemp, Thomas Kersten, Peter Kozub, Maren Linstaedt, Friedrich Lüth, Klaus Mechelke, Andreas Mieth, Johannes Moser, Mahina Pakarati Trengóve, Oswaldo Pakarati Arévalo, Francisca Pakomio Villanueva, Sheba-Celina Schilk, Nikolaus Schlüter, Werner Schön, Kristin Schreyer, Alexander Sedov, Joaquín Soler Hotu, Alan Tepano, Miriam Vogt, and Kai Zabel. We are very grateful to all our collaborating partners, colleagues and the many students that helped us to make the project a big success. Special thanks go to Cathérine Orliac for studying our paleobotanic collection from the megalithic basin T1, but especially we are very much indebted to our colleague Sonia Haoa Cardinali from Hanga Roa, who introduced us to the site, shared her unlimited knowledge on Easter Island archaeology and who was always extremely helpful with her advice when minor and major problems needed to be solved.

References

Addison, D. J. 2001. "Irrigation in Traditional Marquesan Agriculture: Surface Survey Evidence from Hatihe'u Valley, Nuku Hiva." In *Pacific 2000: Proceedings of the Fifth International Conference on Easter Island and the Pacific*, edited by C. M. Stevenson, G. Lee, and F. J. Morin, 267–272. Los Osos, CA: Easter Island Foundation.

Barber, I. G. 2001. "Wet or Dry? An Evaluation of Extensive Archaeological Ditch Systems from Far Northern New Zealand." In *Pacific 2000: Proceedings of the Fifth International Conference on Easter Island and the Pacific*, edited by C. M. Stevenson, G. Lee, and F. J. Morin, 41–50. Los Osos, CA: Easter Island Foundation.

Barrau, J. 1965. "L'humide et Sec: An Essay on Ethnobiological Adaptation to Contrastive Environments in the Indo-Pacific Area." *Journal of the Polynesian Society* 74: 329–346.

Beck, R. Reanier, M. Mass, J. Loret. 2008. "Drought, vegetation change, and human history on Rapa Nui (Isla de Pascua, Easter Island)." *Quaternary Research*, 69 (1), 16–28.

Cauwe, N. 2011. *Easter Island: The Great Taboo: Rebuilding its History after Ten Years of Excavation*. Vdersant Sud: Louvain-la-Neuve.

Cristino, C., P. Vargas, and R. Izaurieta. 1981. *Atlas Arqueológico de Isla de Pascua*. Santiago, Chile: Universidad de Chile.

Damm, H. 1951. "Methoden der Feldbewässerung in Ozeanien." In *South Sea Studies in Memory of Felix Speiser*, 204–234. Basel.

Diamond, J. 2005. *Collapse: How Societies Choose to Fail or Succeed*. New York: Penguin Books.

Englert, S. 1948. *La Tierra de Hotu Matu'a. Historia, Etnología y Lengua de la Isla de Pascua*. San Francisco: Padre Las Casas [1948] (reprint Editorial Universitaria, Santiago de Chile, 2006; also Rapanui Press).

Fassbinder, J. W. E., K. Bondar, B. Vogt, and J. Moser. 2009. "Magnetometerprospektion und magnetische Eigenschaften von Basalt-Böden am Beispiel der Osterinsel (Isla de Pasqua) Chile." *Metalla* 2: 41–44.

Heyerdahl, T. and N. Ferdon, eds. 1961. *Archaeology of Easter Island: Reports of the Norwegian Archaeological Expedition to Easter Island and the East Pacific*. Santa Fe, New Mexico: Monographs of the School of American Research and the Museum of New Mexico, Vol. 1, 24 Part 1.

Hunt, T. 2006. "Rethinking the Fall of Easter Island: New Evidence Points to an Alternative Explanation for a Civilization's Collapse." *American Scientist* 94(5): 412–419.

Kersten, T., M. Lindstaedt, and B. Vogt. 2009. "Preserve the Past for the Future – Terrestrial Laser Scanning for the Documentation and Deformation Analysis of Easter Island's Moai." *Photogrammetrie Fernerkundung Geoinformation* 1: 79–90.

Kirch, P. A. 1994. *The Wet and the Dry: Irrigation and Agricultural Intensification in Polynesia*. Chicago: The University of Chicago Press.

Ladefoged, T. N., C.M. Stevenson, P.M. Vitousek, O.A. Chadwick. 2005. "Soil nutrient depletion and the collapse of Rapa Nui society." *Rapa Nui Journal* 19 (2): 100–150.

Martinsson-Wallin, H. 1994. *Ahu – The Ceremonial Stone Structures of Easter Island*. Uppsala: Aun 19.

Métraux, A. 1940. *Ethnology of Easter Island*. Bernice P. Bishop Museum Bulletin 160. Honolulu: Bishop Museum Press.

Mieth, A. and H.-R. Bork. 2004. *Easter Island – Rapa Nui: Scientific Pathways to Secrets of the Past*. Kiel: Man and Environment 1.

Routledge, C. S. 1919. *The Mystery of Easter Island*. London: Sifton, Praed and Co. Ltd.

Spriggs, M. 1990. "Why Irrigation Matters in Pacific Prehistory." In *Pacific Production Systems/Approaches to Economic Prehistory*, edited by D. Yen, 174–189. Dunedin, New Zealand: XV Pacific Science Congress, 1983.

Stevenson, C. M., J. Wozniak, and S. Haoa. 1999. "Prehistoric Agricultural Production on Rapa Nui." *Antiquity* 73: 801–812.

Van Tilburg, J. 1994. *Easter Island: Archaeology, Ecology, and Culture*. Washington, DC: Smithsonian Institution Press.

Vogt, B. 2009. "Osterinsel – Wasserbau unterm Regenbogen." *Archäologie in Deutschland* 4: 12–16.

Vogt, B. 2013. "Archäologische Forschungen zur voreuropäischen Wassernutzung in Ava Ranga Uka A Toroke Hau, Osterinsel (Rapa Nui/Isla de Pascua, Chile) 2007-2009." *Zeitschrift für Archäologie Außereuropäischer Kulturen* 5: 7–45.

Vogt, B. and J. Moser. 2010a. "Ancient Rapanui Water Management: German Archaeological Investigations in Ava Ranga Uka A Toroke Hau." *Rapa Nui Journal* 24(2): 18–26.

Vogt, B. and J. Moser. 2010b. "Feldforschungen 2007 und 2008 auf der Insel Rapa Nui (Osterinsel/Isla des Pascua), Chile." *Zeitschrift für Archäologie Außereuropäischer Kulturen* 3: 244–252.

Wittfogel, K. 1957. *Oriental Despotism: A Comparative Study of Total Power*. New Haven: Yale University Press.

7 Re-use of the sacred

Late period petroglyphs applied to red scoria topknots from Easter Island (Rapa Nui)

Georgia Lee, Paul Bahn, Paul Horley, Sonia Haoa Cardinali, Lilian González Nualart, and Ninoska Cuadros Hucke

Introduction

The corpus of Easter Island rock art, comprising several thousand designs (Lee 1992: 4), is one of the most impressive in Oceania. A wide array of motifs were executed on a large variety of carving surfaces – cave entrances and ceilings, house entrances, the inner side of *paenga* slabs delimiting houses, stones in the vicinity of water sources, *moai* quarries at Rano Raraku, *pukao* quarries at Puna Pau, basalt boulders at the ceremonial center of 'Orongo, as well as countless carved flat lava panels (*papa*) scattered over the island. Such abundance and diversity, beyond any doubt, emphasize the high importance of rock art in the ceremonial and everyday life of the ancient Rapanui society. The petroglyphs might have served as signs of power, shrines, illustrations of folklore, delimiters of clan territory, or *tapu* markers.

Being such a versatile vessel for artistic, cultural, and political expression, rock art was also used to reflect the changes in the society, including weakening of hereditary monarchy, development of the birdman cult, and contact with European civilization (Love 2012; Boersema 2017; Richards 2017). Such strong cultural changes manifested themselves in a variety of ways, most notably in the development of new petroglyph types for depiction of the sacred birdman (Lee 1992: 20–22, 65–70) or European ships and vessels (Barthel 1962: 112–120; Lee 1992: 112–113; Pollard et al. 2010: 570–571; Shepardson et al. 2013: 70; Kühlem and Hartl-Reiter 2015). Another manifestation of a new ideology was focused on erasure, correction, and replacement of the monuments characteristic of the previous ideology. Thus, during the shift of emphasis from the ancestor cult to the new birdman order, the monolithic *moai* (mostly toppled by then) were carved with the "signs of the victor": Makemake face masks (see, e.g. Mulloy and Figueroa 1978: 163, Figure 7.5) and birdman designs.

Essentially, the same cultural pattern governed the re-use of *pukao* that once crowned the statues standing on the ceremonial platforms. The scoria used for the topknots is of low density and porous, which undoubtedly simplified the placement of the topknot on the head of the *moai* (Bahn and Flenley 2011: 233). On the other hand, porosity also facilitated the secondary carvings: "it is significant that red scoria was one of the primary targets of these added carvings; the color red had strong ritual connotations and was associated with kingship and sacrifice" (Lee 1992: 126). Considerable scientific attention has been paid to the secondary petroglyphs adorning *pukao* (Lavachery 1939: 60–63; Van Tilburg and Lee 1987: 142–147; Lee 1992: 122–126) and facia of the *ahu* (Lee et al. 2015–16: 157–209).

These secondary petroglyphs are of essential importance for understanding of cultural changes that took place in the society during the transition from the classical *ahu moai* phase to the *huri moai* phase. The carving of the monolithic statues and construction of the ceremonial platforms were most likely established, financed, and supervised by the ruling elite – either the chiefs of individual tribes or a hereditary king *'ariki mau*. These monuments were considered to contain the *mana* of venerated ancestors and thus were *tapu*. The mere act of destroying once-sacred ceremonial structures marks a profound change in the social order, when the traditional elites were seemingly unable to exert the authority required to protect the normal functioning of the ceremonial site. The application of secondary petroglyphs on statues and topknots can be considered as further sacrilege. On the other hand, they might have deeper meaning. This paper presents detailed analysis of the motifs used for secondary carvings with the hope of improving our understanding of underlying social change.

Background to the petroglyph study

The early European visitors marveled greatly at the Easter Island statues, as well as the red "baskets" balanced on top of them. Subsequent expeditions clarified that these adornments were made of red stone and possibly represented a headgear. The archaeological data suggest that the addition of the topknots was a late development in the ceremonial architecture of Easter Island (Stevenson 1984: 174). The number of *pukao* associated with ceremonial platforms – 58 (Englert 1948: 111) – is less than the number of statues that once stood on the *ahu* – 269 (Van Tilburg 1994: 28). In total, about a hundred *pukao* were produced, including 31 specimens located in the quarry of Puna Pau (Englert 1948: 111). To simplify further discussion, we will use the numbering scheme proposed by Lipo and Hunt (2009) for addressing individual *pukao*, with a minor numbering correction for *pukao* blanks located at Puna Pau quarry.

The topknots, so highly prized for their red color, were added only to selected ceremonial sites, many of which already manifested their special status through elaborate architecture and superb masonry techniques: Ahu Nau Nau at the royal residence of 'Anakena, two *ahu* at Vinapu, Ahu Hanga Poukura, Ahu Hanga Te'e (Vaihu), Ahu Akahanga and nearby Ahu Ura

Uranga te Mahina, Ahu One Makihi, Ahu Tongariki, Ahu Te Pito Kura, Ahu Heki'i, and Ahu Tepeu. After the statues were overthrown in the late period of island history, the topknots ended up on the ground, where they could be measured and studied:

> Their dimensions range from 1.2 meters to 2 meters in height and from 1.6 to 2.7 meters in diameter. The top of some cylinders has a knob or boss the length of which ranges from 15 to 60 cm. The lower surface has a slight depression which fitted over the top of the image's head. The concavity is not in the center, but near one side so that the cylinder projected over the eyes.
>
> (Métraux 1940: 300)

Such asymmetry, according to Métraux, complicated their interpretation:

> The theory that these crowns were merely a crude attempt to ornament the statues with a structure similar to a topknot (*pukao*) is the most logical assumption. The only problem is the projection which overhangs the eyes.
>
> (Métraux 1940: 301)

Today, we have at least two answers to this "controversy". The asymmetry of *pukao* in the first place follows from engineering issues. If one needs to raise a multi-ton topknot (Bahn and Flenley 2011: 232) almost 10 meters to crown the *moai* Paro, how could it be done? It was far more efficient to raise the topknot from the front side of the *moai*, because the rear wall of the *ahu* started almost immediately at its back. In the case of Ahu Te Pito Kura, on which the *moai* Paro once stood, it may not be an issue, as its rear wall is quite low. Yet at Vinapu or Heki'i, where the statues also had *pukao*, the rear wall is several meters tall. Working from the front, independently of the approach used (raising the *pukao* along a kind of inclined plane or raising it vertically with a tower of rocks piled beneath), it was necessary to ensure the stability of the system at the very conclusion of the process, when the topknot was pushed over the top of the statue. If the concavity for the image's head were to be located at the center of the *pukao*, it would require a larger displacement of the topknot from a supporting structure, which automatically increased the risk of toppling the statue backwards. In contrast, with the concavity made closer to the back side of the *pukao*, the required displacement was considerably reduced. As long as the concavity includes the center of the cylinder's base – which would correspond to a projection of the topknot's center of mass – the *moai-pukao* system will be stable. Thus the asymmetric design of the topknot represents an ingenious optimization of the considerable engineering task of crowning an already-standing statue with a topknot. The other benefit of the asymmetric placement of the *pukao* became evident after the discovery of the coral eye inlay at Ahu Nau Nau in

136 *Georgia Lee et al.*

1978 – the projecting topknot (Figure 7.1a) would partially protect the eye sockets and coral sclera of the inlay from the elements.

The most common shape of the *pukao* is cylindrical (Figure 7.1), which may be further stylized to a form resembling a truncated cone (Figure 7.1a,

Figure 7.1 Original shapes and adornments of the topknots: a) *pukao* #65–68 at Ahu Nau Nau; rectangular tenons on b) *pukao* #14, Ahu Hanga Poukura, c) *pukao* #34 and d) *pukao* #38, Ahu Akahanga; e) *pukao* #49, Ahu Tongariki. Parallel lines carved on f) *pukao* #10, Ahu Hanga Poukura and g) *pukao* #73, Ahu Te Pito Kura. Photographs b)–d) were taken in 2002, a) and e)–g) in 2013

pukao #65 crowning the foreground *moai*). The top of the *pukao* may have a knob of varying length (Figure 7.1a, c–f). It is unclear if the shape of the knobs conveyed some meaning, yet at certain sites they are pronouncedly high and cylindrical (Ahu Nau Nau, Figure 7.1a) while on others the knobs are low (Ahu Akahanga, Figure 7.1c, d). The knobs may be accompanied by rectangular tenons of different geometry (Figure 7.1b–e) or by longitudinal grooves (Figure 7.1f–g). Bearing in mind that the *pukao* were most possibly a stylized representation of a hairdo with a topknot, it is tempting to suggest that the different *pukao* designs reflect a certain aesthetic canon, which determined how the chiefs of the lineages wore their hair. In real life, braids or cords may have been used to achieve the desired form. Adding these characteristic features to the topknots may have served to identify the clan to which the statue belonged. It is worth mentioning that, contrary to popular belief, every *moai ma'ea* has individual fully-recognizable facial features, which nevertheless remain within the general artistic canon of Easter Island statuary. Thus the *moai* wearing a topknot with distinctive marks may have achieved a far greater degree of personalization, perhaps up to the level of exact identification with a certain revered ancestor.

At present, many topknots feature cup-shape depressions or cupules (Figure 7.1b, f and g), usually about 10cm in diameter, which "may be a case of trying to extract the *mana* from them, or to release, and thus destroy, the *mana* inherent in them" (Lee 1992: 124). The idea that *mana* contained inside an object can be accessed/tapped into by proper manipulation is known from other Polynesian societies:

> The impact of Cook's arrival [to Hawai'i] by ship with sails reminiscent of the *tapa* hung from a wooden cross, symbol of the god Lono . . . would be consistent with the veneration Hawaiians held for the *ali'i* [hereditary king]. Recalling the many women who directed their men folk to place *piko* stumps [umbilical cord of newborns] into cracks and crevices of Cook's ships, it is clear that Hawaiians believed the *mana* of a man-god could be extended to his possessions.
> (Lee and Stasack 1999: 66)

If the cupules were made for "*mana*-harvesting" purposes, it is natural to expect that their placement would be random, which is clearly the case in the topknot of the largest image, Paro (Figure 7.1g).

For other *pukao*, such as topknot #10 from Hanga Poukura, the situation is radically different. It features cupules located at the ends of a band marked with longitudinal grooves (Figure 7.1f). On the other side (not pictured), the same *pukao* has three cupules placed symmetrically inside a similar band. These signs of deliberate placement may be the vestiges of advanced *pukao* decoration, possibly serving as sockets for the insertion of *poro* beach cobbles or disks made of other materials (obsidian, coral), with colors contrasting with the red scoria of the topknot.

Indeed, some early explorers of the 18th century noted that the statue topknots had white objects (possibly bones or *poro*) piled on their tops (Bahn and Flenley 2011: 233). Even more remarkably, the illustrations of *moai* crowned with *pukao* in the maps produced by the Spaniards in 1770 feature a row of small circles around the upper rim of the topknot (Mellén Blanco 1990: 131), suggesting that at least some topknots might have been adorned with inlays made of different materials.

The earliest record of petroglyphs adorning the *pukao*, to the best of our knowledge, dates back to the 1868 expedition of HMS *Topaze* (Van Tilburg 2006: 30, Fig. 44). The documented artifact was a topknot blank in Puna Pau quarry. The reported abundance of these carvings brought a lingering hope of finding groups of signs resembling an inscription: "Palmer (1875: 286) likens topknot signs more to the '1770 signatures' [of the islanders on the Spanish proclamation by Felipe González y Haedo] than to RR[*rongorongo*]; it is uncertain what he means here, especially as *pukao* 'inscriptions' have yet to be published" (Fischer 1993: 180). In the 1930s, about forty of these carvings were documented by the Franco-Belgian Expedition to Easter Island (Lavachery 1939: Figs. 246–283). Although Lavachery's drawings of Rapanui rock art were rough and sketchy, he tried to make some sense out of these designs:

> One is struck by the similarity that the petroglyphs of Punapau present with those that one discovers on scoria slabs of the *ahu* of the South coast. They appear, like them and at first sight, completely meaningless. However, one distinguishes among these arabesques the semblance of the known designs, such as heads of sea-birds . . . additionally one can dare to recognize shapeless sketches of boats . . . But be that as it may, the petroglyphs of PunaPau and in general all those carved on red tuff do not have anything in common with the images so clearly traced on lava panels.
> (Lavachery 1939: 63, translated from the French by the authors)

Petroglyph documentation methods

In the 1980s, the Easter Island Petroglyph Documentation Project directed by Georgia Lee established a new standard in documentation of Rapa Nui rock art using a grid of strings, producing accurate drawings of several *pukao* petroglyphs (Lee 1992: 21, 105, 106, 124 and 125). More tracings were published following the analysis of symbolic stratigraphy (Van Tilburg and Lee 1987: 142, 144, and 145), mostly identified as stylized images of boats.

The main difficulties associated with the recording of topknot carvings are illustrated in Figure 7.2. First of all, the cylindrical shape of the *pukao* precludes photographic documentation with a single picture. Even when numerous images of the same objects are taken (Figure 7.2a, b), it is difficult

Figure 7.2 Petroglyphs made on *pukao* #18 from Ahu Hanga Te'e (Vaihu), pictures taken in a) 2002 and b) 2013; c) two topknots at Ahu Akahanga featuring a small *manutara* carving (*pukao* #35) as well as a two-headed bird, a large *manutara*, and a sitting anthropomorph (*pukao* #36), photo 2013. Note that the shape of the *pukao* may significantly complicate the search for optimal lighting conditions to reveal the entire design, as is the case with the *manutara* adorning a curved surface of *pukao* #35 (Figure 7.2c, left side). Its wings are clearly seen in slanting light, yet its tail is hidden in shadow. The head of the *manutara*, despite being carved with a contour of the same depth as the wings, is almost invisible due to a different angle of the image surface

to make a continuous tracing of a carving "flowing" around the object because of unavoidable image distortion. The designs were easily chiseled into the friable scoria, which is prone to erosion. With the passing of time the contours became blurred through the action of the elements. The ancient artists "amended" degradation of the carvings by deepening the existing contours and adding new ones, so that the final composition may be difficult to interpret (Figure 7.2a, b). The interplay of light and shadow over a cylindrical object is another issue (Figure 7.2c), making it necessary to take pictures at different times of day to catch the best lighting for a particular design carved on a *pukao*.

On top of this, several topknots are overgrown with lichens (Figure 7.1c, g) that may partially conceal the carvings. Therefore, it will be important to develop accurate and non-intrusive documentation methods that can overcome all the aforementioned difficulties – light-and-shadow patterns, lichen growth, and perspective distortion of the images. All these benefits can be achieved with modern 3D modeling techniques, which have been successfully used in Polynesian archaeology (Mulrooney et al. 2005; Van Tilburg 2007; Kersten et al. 2010), but due to the considerable cost of laser scanning equipment, it was decided to test cheaper solutions based exclusively on digital photography with further 3D photogrammetric reconstruction (Kersten and Lindstaedt 2012; Pitts et al. 2013). For 3D modeling and 3D visualization we used Agisoft PhotoScan Standard Edition from Agisoft LLC, Blender from Blender Foundation, and MeshLab from Visual Computing Lab – ISTI – CNR. Each 3D model contained from 2 to 3 million faces. The dimensions of the modeled *pukao* were reconstructed from published drawings and maps (Mulloy 1961: Fig. 133; Smith 1961: 186, Fig. 50; Lee 1992: 125, Fig. 4.133) or obtained from comparison with measurements of the nearby *moai* (Shepardson 2009). To alleviate the issues of shadows, lichens, and perspective distortions (Figure 7.3a), the models were rendered in isometric projection without any texture (Figure 7.3b). This approach was useful for detecting surface formations hidden in shadows, such as an irregular curve connecting the shallow cupules carved on the knob of topknot #15, Ahu Hanga Poukura (Figure 7.3b).

It is worth noting that the Phong shading technique commonly used in 3D visualization represents only local illumination, without taking into account the general geometry of the object. We sought to improve the situation by using the method of ambient occlusion developed to obtain realistic images in motion pictures (Landis 2002); the impact of the ambient occlusion method was recognized by a Scientific and Technical Award of the Academy of Motion Picture Arts and Sciences (Robinson 2010). The method consists of the calculation of shadowing degree for every point of the object under diffuse lighting. The points exposed at the surface can collect light from a large number of directions, and thus will be mapped with a bright tone. The points located at the bottom of cavities can be reached by a limited

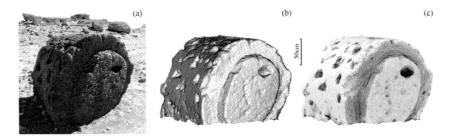

Figure 7.3 Illustration of the approach used: a) photograph of *pukao* #15, Ahu Hanga Poukura; b) 3D model of the same *pukao* rendered in isometric projection. To emphasize the volumetric details, the model was rendered as a reflective object devoid of texture; c) the same view of the *pukao* rendered with ambient occlusion, marking the cavities with a darker tone

number of light sources, and thus are mapped with a dark tone. As one can see from Figure 7.3c, this method produced good results for the 3D model of a *pukao*, clearly revealing cupules and surface defects with a darker tone. The intensity of the tone is roughly proportional to the depth of the cavity. However, it should be remembered that the ambient occlusion method will render wider cavities in a lighter tone than narrower ones.

Results of the petroglyph analysis

Ahu Hanga Te'e and Ahu Akahanga

Among the numerous topknots associated with ceremonial platforms, only a few are adorned with secondary petroglyphs. *Pukao* # 18 at Ahu Hanga Te'e (Vaihu) features a complex curvilinear composition (Figure 7.2a, b) that is difficult to interpret. It is worth noting that for proper identification of petroglyph orientation it is necessary to consider that the topknots of Hanga Te'e spent a considerable time lying on their side in the shallow bay, from which they were recovered in 1986. Two topknots from Ahu Akahanga (Figure 7.2c) feature carvings of birds, the most elaborate of all the secondary petroglyphs applied to red scoria topknots and facia of the *ahu*. Perhaps these designs were mentioned by Englert (1948: 111): "some of the crowns were marked with figures, made in low relief, the so-called '*rona*', with preference for the figures of a 'bird-man'" (translation from Spanish by the authors). It should be noted that the only motif resembling a bird-man (or, rather a figure similar to the "sitting-man" sign in the *rongorongo* script) appears on top of *pukao* #36 (Figure 7.2c). The two-headed bird from the same topknot also appears in the *rongorongo* script, as well as in the petroglyphs of Mata Ngarahu, 'Orongo (Lee 1992: 71, 73). As one of the heads of the two-headed bird is carved on a horizontal surface beside the knob, which would be invisible to a ground-based beholder when the *pukao* was still on its statue, it is completely safe to conclude that this carving together with that of a sitting man (carved on the knob itself) were made only after the topknot was toppled. The orientation of the *manutara* design on the nearby topknot #35 (Figure 7.2c) also suggests that it was carved on a toppled *pukao*.

Ahu Heki'i

Another prominent site, Ahu Heki'i, is located on the North shore at Hanga Ho'onu, displaying every feature of an important ceremonial center – high and robust rear wall, wide plaza in front of the *ahu*, multiple statues once crowned with *pukao*, and red scoria facia adorning the platform. The recent studies of Hanga Ho'onu (La Pérouse) and Ahu Heki'i produced much interesting and thought-provoking data on the settlement pattern for this region (see Stevenson and Haoa 1998, 2008; Martinsson-Wallin and Wallin 2000; Mulrooney et al. 2009). Two topknots associated with the *ahu* feature secondary carvings. *Pukao* #61 has at least six boats carved on its side (Figure 7.4a), oriented according to the present position of the topknot. All the petroglyphs are on the side that faces the ceremonial platform. *Pukao* #57 is located on the stone-covered ramp of the platform. It has secondary carving on its base, also facing the *ahu* (Figure 7.4b). Two crescent-shaped lines, possibly depicting stylized boats, are carved inside the cavity that once accommodated the head of the statue. Another boat, comprising a curved hull and relatively straight gunwale, is carved on the part of the *pukao* that projected over the *moai*'s forehead. All the designs are upside-down, suggesting that this topknot was rolled to its present position after the carvings were made.

Vinapu

Other topknots with secondary adornments can be found at the Vinapu complex on the South coast. One large topknot #4 was turned into a kind of ceremonial basin after significant deepening of the concavity originally designed to fit the statue's head. It is located in front of Ahu Vinapu 2 within a paved area surrounded by stones (Figure 7.4c, also Mulloy 1961: Fig. 35). The entire side surface of this topknot is decorated with schematic depictions of the boats. The first attempt to document the entire composition was made during the Easter Island Petroglyph Documentation Project, producing a roll-out image (Van Tilburg and Lee 1987: 145, Figure 7.7). We are pleased to present the image here, obtained by unrolling the 3D computer model, shaded according to the ambient occlusion method to reveal all the cupules and more than a dozen boat carvings adorning this *pukao* (Figure 7.4e). It

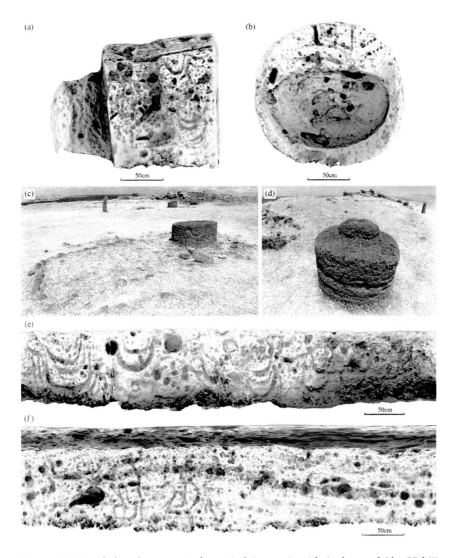

Figure 7.4 Toppled topknots: a) *pukao* #61 lying on its side in front of Ahu Heki'i with a series of boats carved on its lateral surface; b) *pukao* #57 lying on its side on the ramp of Ahu Heki'i with boats carved on its base. The upside-down carving orientation suggests that the *pukao* was rolled after the carvings were done; c) *pukao* #4 lying with its base up on a paved area in front of Ahu Vinapu 2. The boat carvings adorn the entire side surface of this topknot, so we illustrate it as a e) roll-out image; d) *pukao* #5 lying on its base at the corner of the ramp of Ahu Vinapu 2, also given in f) roll-out

is important to mention that the petroglyphs' orientation perfectly matches the current position of the *pukao*, indicating that they were applied after the topknot landed on the ground (upside-down) upon the toppling of its statue. We also produced a roll-out image for the nearby *pukao* #5 (Figure 7.4f), illustrating the carving of a boat, an outline that can be tentatively interpreted as a phallic symbol, and a complicated shape that was previously identified as a sitting anthropomorph (Van Tilburg and Lee 1987: 142, Table 2, the rightmost motif in the second line). The latter identification is not completely evident from the present roll-out image. However, the curve marking the spine of the would-be anthropomorph looks reasonably similar to a boat design carved at an angle. This petroglyph may suggest that *pukao* #5 did not land with its base flat to the ground, and spent some time lying on its side. During this period, the first boat image was added to it. Later, the topknot was moved to its present position (which is rather particular, marking the corner of the *ahu* ramp, Figure 7.4d), and new carvings were added to it. To counteract the tilted appearance of the first boat carving, the design was expanded with new curves.

Puna Pau quarry

The topknot blanks lying near the Puna Pau quarry (outside the crater) are profusely adorned with secondary petroglyphs (Figure 7.5a-f and Figure 7.6a-e). The flat base of the largest blank #77 was carved with more than a dozen boats (Figure 7.5a), marked with a single curved line, or double curved line (see, e.g., the design at upper right). The square with a vertical line running through it (Figure 7.5a, upper left) may represent the sail of a European ship. The hooked shape below it resembles the beak of a bird; the very shallow contour seen to its left seemingly depicts the head and the neck, yet we were unable to figure out the possible location of the body outline. It is important to mention that every boat carved on this topknot is properly oriented with a single exception – the boat appearing to the left of the rectangular object (Figure 7.5a, upper left). This observation suggests that, after the carving of the first boat at the bottom of the *pukao*, the topknot was rolled to its present position. A dark area in the center of the topknot marks a cavity made in the early 20th century to provide a shelter from rain. The other flat side of the same *pukao* blank (Figure 7.5b) bears the initials "J. C(H?)". Right below them, two boat carvings are discernible.

The nearby *pukao* #78 was considerably hollowed out and toppled to its side, making enough room for about six people (Lavachery 1939: 62). An elegant double outline of a boat is carved on the side of this topknot (Figure 7.5c); on its flat side, one can discern two stacked boat designs (the lower one is marred by cupules, Figure 7.5d). Above the boats, at least three inscriptions are seen: "?AMA", "MHMR(Y?)" and "G.I." *Pukao* #81 features an intriguing composition (Figure 7.5e) comprising an elegant deeply-carved boat on top of a circle; four wavy lines stand to the left of the boat.

Re-use of the sacred 145

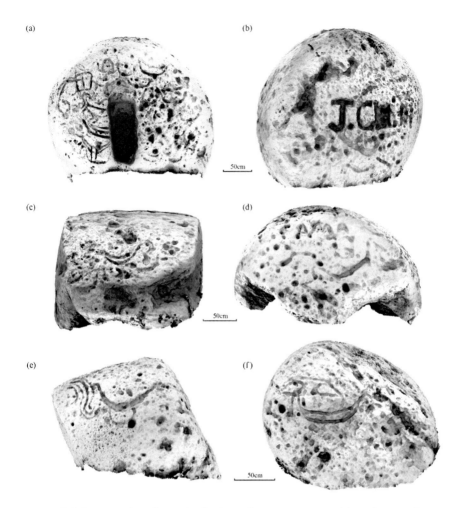

Figure 7.5 Decorated topknots in the Puna Pau quarry: a) and b) – front and rear views of *pukao* #77 showing multiple boat motifs and deeply carved initials; c) and d) side and rear views of *pukao* #78 showing boat shapes and initials; e) and f) side and front views of *pukao* #81 showing multiple boat forms and wavy lines

The front of the same *pukao* displays a boat marked with a double outline (Figure 7.5e) with a carving above it, possibly representing the teardrop-shaped "vigilant eyes" that frequently appear on the walls of the Rano Raraku and Puna Pau quarries (Lavachery 1939: Figs. 221, 221bis, 234, 235, 294; Hamilton 2015). A considerable displacement of the eye petroglyph relative to the boat design makes it difficult to determine whether both carvings belong to the same composition.

The remaining *pukao* at Puna Pau are less profusely decorated. Topknot #76 features two elegant boats marked with a double outline on its side (Figure 7.6a). It should be noted that this *pukao* has several sawing marks, seen as dark horizontal lines in the figure. *Pukao* #79 is adorned with several boats. The most recognizable is a deep carving in the center of its flat base (Figure 7.6b). There is at least one boat to the left of it, one boat right above it (embracing one of the cupules that seemingly were carved as an attempt to erase a graffiti inscription). There are at least three faint canoe designs at the bottom of this topknot (one is partially obscured by the dark vertical stripe on the right, which corresponds to a large-leaf plant

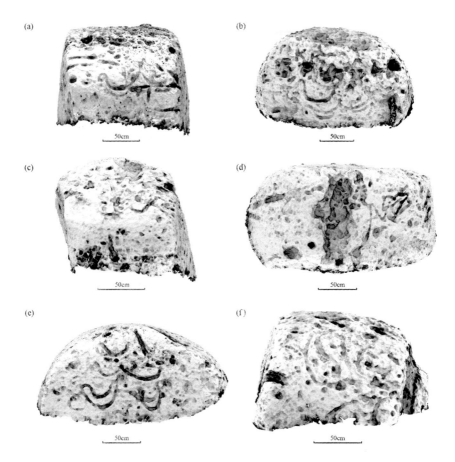

Figure 7.6 Decorated topknots at Puna Pau quarry (continued): a) *pukao* #76 with boat signs carved on its side; b) *pukao* #79 with multiple boat signs and initials carved on its front side; c) *pukao* #82; d) *pukao* #83 with a bird carving on its lateral side; e) *pukao* #84 with multiple boat carvings on its front side. Decorated topknot at Ahu Hanga Poukura: f) *pukao* #16 with curved lines carved on its lateral side

growing by the topknot). Topknot #79 also features some barely readable lettering, "K.R." (Figure 7.6b). *Pukao* #82 has two poorly-executed crescent shapes on its side (Figure 7.6c). Topknot #83 is special because it features a rough sketch of a bird (Figure 7.6d). The head with an eye and a pointed beak is carved with a deep contour; the sharp-angled outline of one of the wings is seen on the left. The design is unfinished. *Pukao* #84 bears a lovely composition of at least seven interlaced boats (Figure 7.6e). Now we can finally solve the "riddle" of the elliptic shape located at the bottom left. It looks very promising in photographs, because it bears a considerable resemblance to the "eyes" or "ears" of *rongorongo* glyphs. However, the 3D model clearly shows that the original shape is made up of two boats with gracefully curved ends.

Ahu Hanga Poukura

We would also like to illustrate here the topknot #16 from Ahu Hanga Poukura that features curved lines on its lateral surface (Figure 7.6f). They form a pattern that is difficult to interpret before one notices that two such lines disappear underground (Figure 7.6f, bottom right). This observation suggests that the carvings were done when the *pukao* was standing on its base. After rotating the image, it becomes obvious that we are dealing with the same crescent shapes that depict boats on other topknots. After the carvings were done, the *pukao* was half-buried to achieve its present position.

Iconographic analysis and possible ethnological implications

As we can conclude from the present research, the most characteristic design carved on the red scoria *pukao* is a stylized depiction of a boat. These motifs may overlap to form complex compositions. Judging from the orientation of the boat carvings (which frequently appear at an angle or even upside-down if one considers how the topknot was placed on the statue head), one becomes inclined to think that the secondary carvings were added to the topknots after *pukao* were toppled along with their *moai*. In some cases – such as topknot #16 from Ahu Hanga Poukura, *pukao* #57 from Ahu Heki'i and topknot blank #77 from Puna Pau – the tilted orientation of petroglyphs suggests that the topknot was rolled to its present position after the carving of the design.

The secondary application of boat carvings to the red scoria objects has extremely important cultural implications connected to the meaning of the *pukao* itself – the topknot of a revered ancestor, who becomes perpetuated a "living face" *aringa ora*, watching over his descendants. It is imperative to recall here one of many *tapu* connected with the paramount king, *ariki mau*:

> No one could touch any part of the king's body without running the risk of falling dead or of suffering severe pain. There is no doubt that

the head of the king was the most sacred part of his person – so sacred that he was obliged to let his hair grow without ever allowing the *mataa* (obsidian knife) to pass through it . . . The head of every man was more or less tapu . . . but probably only the king's head was so sacred that the hair on it could not be cut. When the missionaries wanted to cut the hair of the little Gregorio, the last king of the island, the child opposed it firmly and yielded only through force or fear. The anger was so general that the hairdresser was on the point of being stoned when he achieved his work.

(Métraux 1940: 131)

It is unclear if the *tapu* relating to the ancestors was as strong as that surrounding the living king, yet it seems safe to assume that the addition of the red *pukao* symbolizing a topknot overflowing with *mana* had considerably incremented the sacred powers of *moai ma'ea*.

With the statue toppled and its topknot rolled away, this *mana* was considerably weakened. Carving the motifs into the once-sacred topknots of the chiefs can be considered as further sacrilege. The other possible explanation concerns the re-use of the *mana* inherent to red *pukao* to add power to new designs. In both cases, the predominance of stylized boat motifs carved on toppled topknots is very thought-provoking. In line with the change of emphasis from ancestor worship to the cult of the bird-man, it would be far more understandable to find the images of a new cult – the eye masks of Makemake, profile views of *tangata manu* as well as images of *manutara* and *makohe* – to appear on the topknots. In a very few cases, bird images are indeed present, such as those on *pukao* #35 and #36 at Ahu Akahanga, as well as *pukao* blank #83 from Puna Pau. Yet the boat carvings on *pukao* dominate by sheer numbers, and were definitely the design of choice. Moreover, the very same boat designs appear in the red scoria facia of Ahu Akahanga and Ahu One Makihi, as well as on statues in the quarries of Rano Raraku, images left in transport, and even *moai* toppled from ceremonial platforms (Lee 1992: 107, Fig. 4.106), possibly suggesting that the "canoe symbol marked a victory or conquest over another section of the island" (Lee 1992: 126). It is worth noting that stylized face masks of Makemake were another frequent secondary carving applied to *moai* (Lee 1992: 124).

It goes without saying that sea-going vessels were of huge importance to Polynesian people, and the rock art of Easter Island certainly features dozens of canoes carved island-wide, with a particularly high concentration of these motifs in the vicinity of Ahu Ra'ai and Papa Vaka (see Lee 2000). These elegant canoe designs display a curved hull, frequently adorned with horseshoe-shaped extensions at their bow and stern (Figure 7.7a). These unusual formations were interpreted as frames for nets (Métraux 1940: 205), with at least one petroglyph from Ava o Kiri showing a fish on a line attached to such a frame (Lee 1992: 110). The canoes carved on the topknots are different; their stern and prow are gracefully curved; the body of

Re-use of the sacred 149

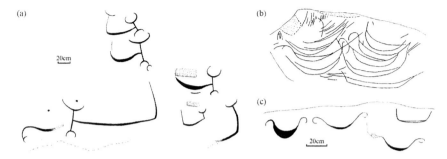

Figure 7.7 Iconography of boat designs: a) classical Polynesian canoes depicted at site 31–113 inland from Ahu Ra'ai; b) designs incised into a basalt boulder at Hanga Piko; c) boat petroglyphs added to *moai* 13-486-07 that fell in transport. The designs are carved on the right side of the statue just below its arm (all petroglyphs were traced by G. Lee in the framework of the Easter Island Petroglyph Documentation Project)

the canoe is depicted with two lines (Figure 7.7b) or a single shape carved in intaglio (Figure 7.7c). Such a shape is comparable with Rapa Nui canoes as depicted by Blondela from the La Pérouse expedition (Métraux 1940: 205, Figure 7.18a), yet the bow and stern in the drawing are not as curved as in the petroglyphs. A quite similar hull can also be found in double canoes from the Marquesas (Oliver 1989: Figure 7.10.7), but they do not match exactly the shape of the *pukao* boat motifs.

It is certain that secondary boat petroglyphs do not have a one-to-one correspondence to the stylized depictions of European ships known in Rapanui rock art (Barthel 1962: 112–120; Lee 1992: 112–113; Pollard et al. 2010: 571; Lee and Horley 2013: 28–31; Shepardson et al. 2013: 70). Nevertheless, the indirect evidence seemingly points towards historical vessels. The boats are carved into toppled topknots, which had probably crowned their *moai* in historic times. The González expedition of 1770 anchored at Hanga Ho'onu and charted the coast, showing the *moai* with *pukao* standing in locations that agree well with those of Ahu Heki'i and Ahu Te Pito Kura (Mellén Blanco 1990: 127, Figure 7.2), suggesting that the destruction of Ahu Heki'i (as well as the carving of the secondary boats on the *pukao*) postdated the European contact. The *moai* Paro from Ahu Te Pito Kura was the last statue to be overthrown (Routledge 1919: 197). The ceremonial center of Vinapu was still in fair shape when visited by Johann Reinhold Forster in 1774 (Captain Cook's expedition). His son Georg Forster wrote as follows:

> We reached the east side of the island, near a range of seven pillars or statues, of which only four remained standing, and one of them had lost its cap. They stood on a common pedestal, like those which we had seen on the other side, and its stones were square and fitted

exactly in the same manner. Though the stone of which the statue itself is formed seems to be soft enough, being nothing but the red tufa which covers the whole island, yet it was incomprehensible to me how such great masses could be formed by a set of people among whom we saw no tools; or raised and erected by them without machinery. The general appellation of this range was Hanga Tebòw; hanga being the word which they prefix to every range. The names of the statues were Ko-Tomoaï, Ko-Tomoèeree, Ko-Hòo-oo, Morahèena, Oomarèeva, Weenâboo, Weenapè.

(Forster 1968: 336)

The name of the Vinapu bay, Hanga Te Pau, was reported here for the first time. The suggested names of the statues, apart from the generic "*Ko te Moai*", also include allusions to the place name Vinapu. The text confirms that several statues were standing on the site, most possibly on Ahu Tahiri (Vinapu 1), some of them still wearing their *pukao*. Alas, we do not have enough data to prove that the decorated topknots lying beside Ahu Vinapu 2 (Figure 7.4c, d) were still on top of their images during Forster's visit.

By the second half of the 19th century all the statues had tumbled to the ground, and when John Linton Palmer visited the ceremonial center of Vinapu in 1868, he saw the site in ruins, with an improvised shelter constructed below the toppled *moai* of Ahu Tahiri. Importantly, the flank and the chest of the statues inside this shelter were adorned with paintings of boats (Van Tilburg 2006: 34, Images 54–55; Lee and Horley 2013: 26, Figure 7.16c).

Palmer described in detail the "Fifteen-image platform" (Palmer 1870: 175–176) that can be identified – at first glance – with Ahu Tongariki. Yet Palmer's map between pp. 167 and 168 marks this platform in the middle of the South shore, meaning that the only possible identification is that of Ahu Akahanga, which has three conjoined platforms with numerous broken *moai* (Van Tilburg 1994: 80). Palmer provides the following description:

At a little distance from this terrace, and about the centre point, was a short pillar or cylinder of red tuff (vesicular lava), standing in an area paved with large, smooth, sea-worn stones. It stood on a low slab, which was of the same material, and which served as a pedestal. It was about 6 feet high, and as much in diameter; the top was flat, and cut away on each side, so as to make a step or shelf. On it I found two skulls, very much perished, which, from the dentition, I judged to be those of youths of twelve to fourteen years old. The faces of the skulls were directed towards the platforms.

(Palmer 1870: 179)

The description and measurements enable us to make a positive identification of the cylinder as *pukao* #34 (Figure 7.1c). Palmer continues:

At Winipoo there is one similar. The upper part is paved with smooth sea stones of the size of a dinner plate. The measurement of the pillar, which is oval, is 7 feet by 5, and it was 4½ feet high. It stood also in a paved area.

(Palmer 1870: 179)

This description matches the *pukao* "basin" #4, Figure 7.4c. Palmer's mention of a "paved upper part" is perplexing; it may mean that the stones were deposited on top of the *pukao*. However, if that were the case one would rather expect him to use the corresponding wording. Looking carefully at the rolled-out image, one finds a possible explanation – there are two large holes carved in the upper part of the *pukao*, flanking two superimposed boat carvings. It may be that these holes were inlaid with *poro*, which would fit Palmer's description perfectly.

The existence of *pukao* petroglyphs was not mentioned in Palmer's early publications, which may suggest that the topknot #4 at Ahu Vinapu 2 was still in pristine condition without any boat carvings added. However, it is more likely that the boat petroglyphs were already there, but Palmer did not recognize them yet. Actually, he never mentioned any *pukao* carvings before becoming interested in Easter Island's *rongorongo* script (Fischer 1997: 64–69). Only then did he re-study his Rapa Nui watercolors, finally paying attention to a pattern of crescent motifs:

On the base of some of these crowns which were at the quarry [of Puna Pau], I found some scribbling, as I thought. I copied some, and found lately among them one or two figures identical with the so-called signatures of the chiefs mentioned by Gonzalez.

(Palmer 1875: 286).

Finally, the boats adorning the topknot blanks at the Puna Pau quarry were documented photographically in 1886 by William Safford, who came to the island on board the USS *Mohican* (Daisy Njoku 2013, personal communication). It is worth mentioning that Puna Pau offers a scenic view towards Hanga Roa bay where the ships of Cook and La Pérouse dropped their anchors.

Putting all the evidence together, an interesting picture emerges. The boat designs were carved on topknots that had toppled to the ground after the collapse of their statues, some of which were still seen standing in the time of early visitors. This suggests that at least some of the secondary boats were added to the topknots in the late 18th–early 19th centuries. It is quite reasonable to assume that the numerous boats of the very same style as those adorning the topknots at Vinapu and Heki'i might already have been carved into the topknot blanks of Puna Pau after the *pukao* production stalled during the *huri moai* phase. If one considers the worrying news about growing social unrest and toppling of the statues from early 19th century accounts

(Heyerdahl 1961: 65–67), it would suggest that *pukao* production ceased by approximately the end of the 18th century, providing plenty of time to produce all the secondary carvings recorded in Puna Pau. The quarry itself was not necessarily completely abandoned during this period, as it may have served as the birthplace of the cremation pillars seen by Palmer (1870: 144) at Akahanga and Vinapu.

This particular period in which the secondary petroglyphs were carved into the artifacts made of sacred red scoria makes one inclined to think that the boat motifs were connected more to the visiting ships and their lifeboats rather than being illustrations of Polynesian voyaging canoes. The double-contour motifs (Figure 7.4a, b, e, f; Figure 7.5a, c, f; Figure 7.6b, e; also Figure 7.7b, c) may have been intended to depict the multi-deck construction of a European ship. It is worth emphasizing that the major concentrations of boat petroglyphs carved into topknots occur in the places visited by the early expeditions (the ceremonial complex of Vinapu visited by the Cook and La Pérouse expeditions) or located in direct view of the anchored ships (the 1770 González expedition anchored in Hanga Ho'onu in view of Ahu Heki'i; the 1774 Cook and 1786 La Pérouse expeditions anchored at Hanga Roa, in view of Puna Pau).

Conclusions

We illustrate a promising technique that can be used for the detailed documentation of rock art adorning red scoria artifacts such as *pukao*, making a photogrammetric 3D model based on multiple photographs of the object. The resulting model, made up of millions of faces, makes possible an accurate study of fine carving details. In order to achieve a high-contrast visualization of petroglyphs, we have used the ambient occlusion method.

An analysis of petroglyphs decorating topknots from Ahu Tahiri (Vinapu 1), Ahu Vinapu (Vinapu 2), Ahu Hanga Poukura, Ahu Vaihu, Ahu Ura Uranga te Mahina, Ahu Akahanga, Ahu Te Pito Kura, Ahu Heki'i and Puna Pau has shown that the predominant secondary carving motif is a stylized boat with a curved stern and prow, carved either with a wide intaglio band or as an outline motif. In a few cases (Ahu Akahanga and Puna Pau), bird carvings were added to the topknots.

The prominence of the boat motif carved onto *pukao* toppled from the statues that were seen standing in historic times is very thought-provoking, emphasizing the need for further detailed study of the cultural impact of early European visitors (especially those of the 18th century) on Rapanui culture.

References

Bahn, P. and J. Flenley. 2011. *Easter Island, Earth Island*. Third Edition. Santiago: Rapa Nui Press.

Barthel, T. S. 1962. "Schiffsdarstellungen in der Osterinselkultur." *Tribus* 11: 111–137.
Boersema, J. J. 2017. "An Earthly Paradise? Easter Island (Rapa Nui) as Seen by the Eighteenth-Century European Explorers." In *Cultural and Environmental Change on Rapa Nui*, edited by S. H. Cardinali, K. B. Ingersoll, C. M. Stevenson, and D. W. Ingersoll, 156–178. London: Routledge.
Englert, S. 1948. *La Tierra de Hotu Matu'a*. Santiago: Padre Las Casas.
Fischer, S. R. 1993. "A Provisional Inventory of the Inscribed Artifacts in the Three Rapanui Scripts." In *Easter Island Studies: Contributions to the History of Rapanui in Memory of William T. Mulloy*, edited by S. R. Fischer, 177–181. Oxford: Oxbow Books.
Fischer, S. R. 1997. *Rongorongo, the Easter Island Script: History, Traditions, Texts*. Oxford: Clarendon Press.
Forster, G. 1968. *Werke: sämtliche Schriften, Tagebücher, Briefe*. Vol. 1. Berlin: Academie-Verlag.
Hamilton, S. 2015. "The 'Eye' Petroglyphs of Rano Raraku." In *Abstract Booklet of the 9th International Conference on Easter Island and the Pacific, Berlin, Germany, 21–26 June, 2015*, edited by B. Vogt, 26. Berlin: German Archaeological Institute, Christian-Albrechts-University Kiel and the HafenCity University Hamburg.
Heyerdahl, T. 1961. "An Introduction to Easter Island." In *Archaeology of Easter Island: Reports of the Norwegian Archaeological Expedition to Easter Island and East Pacific*, edited by T. Heyerdahl and E. Ferdon, Jr., 21–90. Santa Fe, New Mexico: Monograph of the School of American Research and the Museum of New Mexico, Vol. 1, Number 24.
Kersten, T., M. Lindstaedt, K. Mechelke, and B. Vogt. 2010. Terrestrial Laser Scanning for the Documentation of Archaeological Objects and Sites on Easter Island. *Computer Applications and Quantitative Methods in Archaeology 2010 – Fusion of Cultures*, Granada, Spain.
Kersten, T. and M. Lindstaedt. 2012. Generierung von 3D-Punkwolken durch Kamera-basierte Low-cost Systeme – Workflow und Praktische Beispiele. *Terrestrusches Laserscanning 2012 (TLS2012), Schriftenreihe des DVW, Band 69, Beiträge zum 121. DVW-Seminar am 13. und 14. Dezember 2012 in Fulda*, Wißner-Verlag, Augsburg, pp. 25–46.
Kühlem, A. and C. Hartl-Reiter. 2015. "'Looking Towards the Horizon' – a Ship Petroglyph on Rapa Nui and the Possibilities and Limits of 3D-Documentation." In *Abstract Booklet of the 9th International Conference on Easter Island and the Pacific, Berlin, Germany, 21–26 June, 2015*, edited by B. Vogt, 33. Berlin: German Archaeological Institute, Christian-Albrechts-University Kiel and the HafenCity University Hamburg.
Landis, H. 2002. Production-Ready Global Illumination. Course 16 notes, SIGGRAPH 2002. http://renderman.pixar.com/view/production-ready-global-illumination.
Lavachery, H. 1939. *Les Pétroglyphes de l'Ile de Pâques*. Antwerp: De Sikkel.
Lee, G. 1992. *The Rock Art of Easter Island: Symbols of Power, Prayers to the Gods*. Monumenta Archaeologica 17. Los Angeles: The Institute of Archaeology, University of California.
Lee, G. 2000. "Rock Art of the Ceremonial Complex at Ahu Ra'ai." In *Easter Island Archaeology: Research on Early Rapanui Culture*, edited by C. M. Stevenson and W. S. Ayres, 44–52. Los Osos, CA: Easter Island Foundation.

Lee, G. and E. Stasack. 1999. *Spirit of Place: Petroglyphs of Hawai'i*. Los Osos, CA: Bearsville and Cloud Mountain Press, Easter Island Foundation.

Lee, G. and P. Horley. 2013. "The Paintings of Ana Kai Tangata Cave, Easter Island (Rapa Nui)." *Rapa Nui Journal* 27(2): 11–32.

Lee, G., P. Bahn, P. Horley, S. Haoa Cardinali, L. González Nualart, and N. Cuadros Hucke. 2015-16. "Secondary Applications of Rock Art at Coastal Sites of Easter Island (Rapa Nui)." *Almogaren* 46–47: 157–209.

Lipo, C. P. and T. L. Hunt. 2009. Rapa Nui *pukao*. Geo-Referenced Image Database. www.terevaka.net/dc/databases/lipo_and_hunt_2009/Pukao.html.

Love, C. 2012. "Miro 'o'one (Wooden Boat made of Earth)." In *Abstract Booklet of the 8th International Conference on Easter Island and the Pacific, Santa Rosa, USA, 8–13 July, 2012*, edited by A. Padgett, 11. Los Osos, CA: Easter Island Foundation.

Martinsson-Wallin, H. and P. Wallin. 2000. "Ahu and Settlement: Archaeological Excavations at 'Anakena and La Pérouse'." In *Easter Island Archaeology: Research on Early Rapanui Culture*, edited by C. M. Stevenson and W. S. Ayres, 27–43. Los Osos, CA: Easter Island Foundation.

Mellén Blanco, F. 1990. "Cartografía Histórica de la Isla de Pascua en el Siglo XVIII, Acompañada de Algunos Datos Etnológicos y Arqueológicos." In *State and Perspectives of Scientific Research in Easter Island Culture*, edited by H.-M. Esen-Baur, Vol. 25, 123–137. Frankfurt am Main: Courier Forschungsinstitut Senckenberg.

Métraux, A. 1940. *Ethnology of Easter Island*. Bernice P. Bishop Museum Bulletin 160. Honolulu: Bishop Museum Press.

Mulloy, W. 1961. "The Ceremonial Center of Vinapu." In *Archaeology of Easter Island: Reports of the Norwegian Archaeological Expedition to Easter Island and East Pacific*, edited by T. Heyerdahl and E. Ferdon, Jr., 93–180. Santa Fe, New Mexico: Monograph of the School of American Research and the Museum of New Mexico, Number 24, Part 1.

Mulloy, W. and G. Figueroa. 1978. *The a Kivi – Vai Teka Complex and Its Relationship to Easter Island Architectural Prehistory*. Asian and Pacific Archaeology Series 8. Honolulu: University of Hawaii.

Mulrooney, M., T. Ladefoged, R. Gibb, and D. McCurdy. 2005. "Eight Million Points Per Day: Archaeological Implications of Laser Scanning and Three-Dimensional Modeling of Pu'ukoholā Heiau, Hawai'i Island." *Hawaiian Archaeology* 10: 18–28.

Mulrooney, M., T. Ladefoged, C. M. Stevenson, and S. Haoa. 2009. "The Myth of A.D. 1680: New Evidence from Hanga Ho'onu, Rapa Nui (Easter Island)." *Rapa Nui Journal* 23: 94–105.

Oliver, D. L. 1989. *Oceania: The Native Cultures of Australia and the Pacific Islands*. Vol. 1. Honolulu: University of Hawai'i Press.

Palmer, J. L. 1870. "Visit to Easter Island, or Rapa Nui, in 1868." *Journal of the Royal Geographical Society of London* 40: 167–181.

Palmer, J. L. 1875. "Davis or Easter Island." *Proceedings of the Literary and Philosophical Society of Liverpool* 29: 275–297.

Pitts, M., J. Miles, H. Pagi, and G. Earl. 2013. "The Story of Hoa Hakananai'a." *British Archaeology*, Issue 130, May/June: 24–31.

Pollard, J., A. Paterson, and K. Welham. 2010. "Te Miro O'one: The Archaeology of Contact on Rapa Nui (Easter Island)." *World Archaeology* 42: 562–580.

Richards, R. 2017. "The Impact of the Whalers and other Foreign Visitors before 1862." In *Cultural and Environmental Change on Rapa Nui*, edited by S. H. Cardinali, K. B. Ingersoll, C. M. Stevenson, and D. W. Ingersoll, 179–187. London: Routledge.

Robinson, A. 2010. Oscar 2010. Scientific and Technical Awards. www.altfg.com/blog/oscar-2010-scientific-and-technical-awards-489.

Routledge, K. 1919. *The Mystery of Easter Island*. London: Hazell, Watson and Viney.

Shepardson, B. 2009. Moai of Rapa Nui (Easter Island, Chile). Geo-Referenced Image Database. www.terevaka.net/dc/databases/shepardson_2009/Moai_pt1.html.

Shepardson, B., B. Atán, G. Droppelman, G. Pakarati, M. Wilkins, H. Falvey, B. Fornaiser, K. González, J. Hager, O. Haoa, H. Ika, M. Pakarati, V. Pakarati, E. Pakarati, F. Pérez, K. Redell, M. Tuki, and N. Tuki. 2013. "Terevaka.net Archaeological Outreach 2013 Field Report: Approaching Sustainability." *Rapa Nui Journal* 27(2): 66–70.

Smith, C. 1961. "A Temporal Sequence Derived from Certain Ahu." In *Archaeology of Easter Island: Reports of the Norwegian Archaeological Expedition to Easter Island and East Pacific*, edited by T. Heyerdahl and E. Ferdon, Jr., 181–219. Santa Fe, New Mexico: Monograph of the School of American Research and the Museum of New Mexico, Number 24, Part 1.

Stevenson, C. M. 1984. *Corporate Descent Group Structure in Easter Island Prehistory*. Ph.D. Dissertation, The Pennsylvania State University.

Stevenson, C. M. and S. Haoa. 1998. "Prehistoric Gardening Systems and Agricultural Intensification in the La Pérouse Area of Easter Island." In *Easter Island in Pacific Context: South Seas Symposium, Proceedings of the Fourth International Conference on Easter Island and East Polynesia*, edited by C. Stevenson, G. Lee and F. Morin, 205–213. Los Osos, CA: Easter Island Foundation.

Stevenson, C. M. and S. Haoa. 2008. *Prehistoric Rapa Nui*. Los Osos, CA: Easter Island Foundation.

Van Tilburg, J. A. 1994. *Easter Island: Archaeology, Ecology and Culture*. London: British Museum Press.

Van Tilburg, J. A. 2006. *Remote Possibilities: HMS Topaze on Easter Island*. Research Paper 158. London: British Museum Press.

Van Tilburg, J. A. 2007. Hoa Hakananai'a Laser Scan Project. www.eisp.org/10.

Van Tilburg, J. A. Lee, and G. Lee. 1987. "Symbolic Stratigraphy: Rock Art and the Monolithic Statues of Easter Island." *World Archaeology* 19(2): 133–149.

8 An earthly paradise? Easter Island (Rapa Nui) as seen by the eighteenth-century European explorers

Jan J. Boersema

Introduction

On 9th April, 1722, Dutch explorers, under the command of Jacob Roggeveen, were the first Europeans to set foot on Easter Island. They were later followed by explorers from Spain (1770), Great Britain (1774) and France (1786). Each of these expeditions produced accounts of their findings on this remote Polynesian isle: a variety of official logs, notes by crew members, reports by scientists and even 'second hand' writings. This chapter summarizes the main conclusions of the accounts. What do they tell us about the ecological and cultural situation at the time of these visits? Do they render reliable information on (over)population, weapons, food and/or (over)exploitation? How are the various reports to be interpreted in view of later scientific studies? The main conclusion is that the accounts do not confirm the reported collapse, suggested by Clive Ponting and Jared Diamond. Easter Island may not have been the 'paradise' that Jacob Roggeveen deemed possible, but it does appear to have been a sustainable society in the pre-European period, even after deforestation.

In recent decades, several different researchers have come to believe that on Easter Island in the pre-European period a collapse occurred as the result of over exploitation of the natural resources. This collapse is said to have commenced in the period prior to 1722, because in that year an expedition under the leadership of the Dutchman Jacob Roggeveen was the first European expedition to reach the island. In the same century, expeditions from Spain (1770), England (1774) and France (1786) also came to the island. The European visitors, with Roggeveen as their vanguard, are said to have witnessed a society in severe decline with hungry, belligerent people and wrote about this in their accounts of their expeditions. Later research confirmed these accounts and added additional detail.

The first to put forward the concept of a collapse was the American archaeologist William Mulloy. This he did in his article 'Contemplate the Navel of the World', which was published in 1974 in the little-known periodical *Américas*. In the years that followed, the theory appeared in all manner of formulations in literature relating to the environment, but none of these reached a broader audience. This did not happen until 1991, when the British historian Clive Ponting opened his bestseller *A Green History of the World* with a chapter in which he described the dramatic situation on Easter Island as Roggeveen would have found it. Shortly thereafter the collapse theory gained a certain scientific status through the work of the British archaeologist Paul Bahn and the New Zealand geographer and botanist John Flenley, two renowned Easter Island researchers. In their 1992 book *Easter Island, Earth Island,* they compare the computer models from the first report to the Club of Rome (Meadows et al. 1972) with their own reconstruction of the history of Easter Island. The analogy was striking: seriously declining natural resources, increasing pollution and, finally, a dramatic fall in population numbers. What the modelling scientists at MIT, reporting to the Club of Rome, a group of leading business people, foresaw for the world as a whole had apparently occurred already on Easter Island. In 1994, the film *Rapa Nui* was made, visualising the collapse story as told in Bahn and Flenley's book. Finally, it was the American geographer Jared Diamond who in 2005 with his book *Collapse: How Societies Choose to Fail or Survive* ensured that the story reached an audience of millions (see also Diamond 1995, 1997, 2000, 2004, 2007). To some extent as a result of this, the account of the collapse of the culture of Easter Island gained an iconic status in the environmental sciences. It became *the* lesson from ecological history, a grim warning to the world. If we are not more careful with our natural resources, the earth can also expect a similar collapse.

In this chapter, all the accounts of the four expeditions that visited Easter Island in the 18th century are discussed.[1] From it, what image emerges of the island and its inhabitants especially in regards to specific health and environmental conditions? How should these historical sources be weighed and interpreted? How do they relate to the research results of later periods? What conclusions do they allow to be drawn about the ecological history of Easter Island? First, we provide a brief discussion of the collapse theory and of the elements important to this theory.

The collapse theory

When does one speak of the collapse of a society or culture? What distinguishes a collapse from a 'fundamental change'? Some authors take a middle part in this, but from the descriptions that have been made there are two important points of distinction.[2] First, the period of time in which it occurs. A true collapse happens quickly; if such a process takes place over centuries it is a change rather than a collapse. It is particularly the tempo at which population numbers diminish that is high, and this rate of decrease is always very large, the population being decimated rather than being halved. With a collapse we tend to think of time spans such as decades or a maximum of a century, depending on the extent of complexity and the size of the society. A second characteristic is the scale of the phenomenon. This is not about a few elements of a society but includes a number of aspects. There must therefore be a certain complexity present in a society that is to a great extent wiped out by the collapse. In a collapse, the important social structures crumble, resulting in chaos, hunger, poverty and strife, together with rapidly reducing population numbers as the result of death or flight. In the light of the radical nature of the decline in numbers, there can be no question of recovery in a reasonably short space of time. It is for this reason that some authors speak of 'vanished civilizations'.[3]

The type of collapse that is said to have afflicted Easter Island distinguishes itself further by its cause: human (over-) exploitation of the natural environment. This is not about inescapable natural disasters, invading aggressors or unintentionally introduced diseases. It is about the consequences of our own depletion of the available resources. In the 1960s, concern about the consequences of exploitation by mankind increased greatly worldwide. In his article, Mulloy quoted Paul Ehrlich's 1968 book *The Population Bomb*, in which the latter foresaw hundreds of millions of deaths as the result of food shortages before the turn of the century. Bahn and Flenley referred to the first report to the Club of Rome. Clive Ponting – and after him Jared Diamond – suggest a general pattern in the green history of the world. If the cultures are unable to maintain some sort of a balance with the natural environment, not only will that environment be lost, they themselves will also perish. Easter Island was, in their eyes, no exception.

The theory posits a causal chain, in which there is a succession of cause and effect. At the foundation of the chain of occurrences on Easter Island was deforestation. Wood was the natural resource that gradually disappeared, from the time of the arrival of the Polynesian colonists and by their 'slash and burn' actions, so that in the 18th century the first European visitors encountered a bare, deforested island. Seaworthy canoes could no longer be built, and deep-sea fish disappeared from the menu. Transporting the statues by the use of rollers was no longer possible. As a result of the disappearance of the trees the soil became drier and crops that required water were more difficult to grow. The ground was susceptible to erosion and fertile soil was washed away. There was a decline in food production, followed by scarcity and after a while, hunger. The island's resources were insufficient for the size of its population. The hunger led to (food) wars. This not only had a high cost in human lives but also eroded the social structures. 'The society' according to Diamond 'spiralled down into chaos and cannibalism'. If we are to believe the reconstruction of Bahn and Flenley, this decline began well into the second half of the 17th century and continued until well into the 18th century.[4] Roggeveen arrived, as it were, in the middle of the collapse. This is also how Ponting described the situation (Ponting 1991, 2007). This was, for me, reason enough to study the written accounts of the experiences of the island's first visitors, in which I expected I would find descriptions that would support the collapse theory (Boersema 2002, 2011, 2015a, 2015b).

The accounts

For this article I draw in particular on the accounts of the visitors to Easter Island in the 18th century.[5] We can subdivide these into three categories.

First, there are the journals. A journal is an official logbook written by the leader of an expedition or by the captain of an individual ship, which has to include daily records of the weather conditions, the vicissitudes and the progress of the journey. On the basis of these data the owners of the ship or the directors could subsequently determine whether the expedition's leader or the captain had complied with his instructions and, if not, what the reason was for his non-compliance. All these matters were of importance when making the decision as to whether to pay the agreed salary. For example, Roggeveen had been instructed to look for the sandy Davis Island, which was said to lie off the coast of the unknown Southland (Terra Australis Incognita). When Easter Island did not match up to this description and thus could not be the island that he was instructed to look for, this was ascertained and in a well substantiated manner recorded in the journal at a special meeting of all three captains and their first pilots.

The second type relates to the reports of crew members, illustrators or scientists also taking part in the journey. These reports can follow specific themes, but can also give more general descriptions. Some of them are specifically written to correct other accounts like William Wales' 'remarks' on the account of Mr. Forster.[6]

Finally, there are 'second hand' accounts that have been written by people who themselves did not participate in the journey and who have therefore acquired their information indirectly. These could be publications relating to a special journey, written by writers of potboilers hoping to earn money from the story, but could also be reviews that relate to a number of journeys and that are intended as historical works. The latter are usually published many years after the journeys described in them. There are, however, exceptions. In the third volume of a collection of travel accounts by François Valentijn (1726), there is a short passage about Roggeveen's journey. This is the first published report but does not mention his visit to Easter Island.

It is clear that accounts of journeys can vary as to the extent of their reliability, some visitors are better observers than others, and this is certainly the case for Easter Island.[7] The journals are the most authoritative, but do not cover everything. The captains did not see everything on the island, and could make mistakes in matters of detail or interpretation. The scientists had more knowledge in certain fields, and they also wrote more systematically and generally more succinctly. The crew members, who wrote sometimes, felt free to record certain piquant or ostensibly unimportant facts. The accounts of journeys are sometimes one-sided or bear evidence of personal embroidery. This also applies to the prints and paintings that have been passed down from the 18th century expeditions. For example, in French accounts we read undisguised criticism relating to the accuracy of the work of the Englishman Hodges.[8] The sources can be complementary to one another, and apart from being assessed comparatively must also be judged on their own merits. In addition, the background of the writer must also be taken into account. Captain Cook, for example, who in his travels had acquired a large amount of knowledge about the Pacific, was quite ill when he anchored off the island. He and his crew had been roaming the seas for weeks and were in urgent need of fresh water and food. The expeditions that followed that of Roggeveen had some prior knowledge about the journey and the island from accounts that had been published previously and stories that had circulated.[9] These matters are also a factor in their descriptions and evaluation of the perceptions of Easter Island.

The second-hand stories about the Roggeveen expedition appear to have been the least reliable. The writer obtained his information from a returning crew member, and supplemented that insouciantly with his own speculations. We read of giants on Easter Island, beings that were some twelve feet tall, and under whose legs the Dutchmen could walk without having to stoop.[10] In order to make the publication more attractive, a local illustrator was asked to create a couple of pictures. In the *Tweejaarige Reyze* there are etchings by Matthijs Balen who, just as the printer Johannes van Braam, lived and worked in Dordrecht. The best known – 'Reyze naar het Zuydland' – portrays a large group of islanders armed with spears; they are being shot at by two sailors in a sloop, each with a gun. Offshore lie three European ships at anchor, and on the island we can see, in addition to a few trees, a block of stone with a head carved into it, apparently a *moai*, with islanders walking around it or kneeling before it. The print has been copied many times, often without the sloop, with, among other things, the caption 'the earliest known depiction of Easter Island'.[11] However, Roggeveen and Bouman write in their journals that they saw neither weapons nor trees. Shots were never fired from a sloop. Sadly, these journals did not turn up until many years later, so the conceptualisation of Easter Island in the decades that followed 1722 was mainly determined by less reliable sources.[12]

With these caveats in mind, the accounts of the four expeditions have been analysed on the observations and notes relevant to the collapse theory, and in particular with reference to the following subjects: (1) The presence of weapons, signs of warfare or strife, wounded people, the physical condition and the health of the inhabitants; (2) Data on population numbers; and (3) Water and food, the cultivation of food crops and the circumstances in which to cultivate them.

Signs of warfare or strife, injuries and physical condition

Polynesians are very keen to show their weapons to foreigners as a signal of 'being in power' in their territory, so the lack thereof on Easter Island is remarkable.[13] The absence of weapons is firmly attested in the first accounts of the 18th century, with that in the journal of Bouman being the clearest. The Dutch were apparently in fear of possible hostilities from the Easter Islanders, since both Roggeveen and Bouman reported that they should go exploring only if accompanied by a sufficient number of armed crew members. Their fear seems not to have been justified, as the Dutch saw nothing resembling weapons:

> 'they came on board unarmed, and the members of our crew that had been to the shore with the sloops also stated that they had seen not a single man with a weapon'.[14]

When after a couple of days the weather is favourable, they go ashore on Friday, April the 9th with '134 hands, and all of them armed with musket, cartridge bag and cutlass'.[15] As the whole group has come ashore and treks inland, in the rear-guard a tragic shooting incident takes place in which some 10 islanders are killed by some crew members who had panicked.[16] They claim later that the islanders had touched their flintlocks and clothing, and that a few had threatened to throw stones at them. Roggeveen and Bouman attach absolutely no value to their statement and heartily condemned their actions.

The German Carl Behrens has left us a testimony of two accounts of his travels, together with a report relating to Southland, drawn up for the Dutch East India Company (VOC), which contain several passages about Easter Island. The first account dates from 1728 and is written in verse. In this we read nothing relating to weapons. In the report for the VOC, Behrens does his best to make the existence of a Southland plausible. To that end he seeks the alliance of the claims that 'Capitein Ferdinandus Dequier' had published about this Southland. According to Dequier there live heathens who fight one another with spears and clubs. Behrens has also seen much heathenry and idolatry, *inter alia* on Easter Island, but mentions nothing of weapons there.[17] In his third report, which in a short space of time was published in French, German, and Dutch, and which in 1923 was once more rewritten and published, Behrens is clearer:

> 'It looks like the islanders possessed no weapons'.[18]

The Spanish expedition that reaches the island in 1770 also sees no weapons:

> 'They possess no arms'.[19]
> 'natives, all of them unarmed, and some nude, wearing plumes on their heads'.[20]

The Spanish also test the acquaintance of Easter Islanders with weapons by giving them a bow and arrows, but they showed absolutely no knowledge of what to do with them; in fact, they hung the bow around their necks like an ornament. Knives also appear to be unknown.[21] On some of the islanders the visitors do see 'wounds on the body, which we thought to have been inflicted by cutting instruments of iron or steel, we found that they proceeded from stones, which are their only defence and offence, and as most of these are sharp edged they produce the injury referred to'.[22]

Just as all the visitors, the English are received peacefully. Cook recounts:

> 'We landed at the sandy beach where about 100 of the Natives, who gave us no disturbance at landing, on the contrary hardly one had so much as a stick in their hands'.[23]

The accounts of the expedition in 1774 under the leadership of James Cook report explicitly for the first time the presence of weapons. Georg Forster described fairly precisely what he saw:

> 'We saw but few arms among them; some however had lances or spears, made of thin ill-shapen sticks, and pointed with a sharp triangular piece of a black glassy lava (*pumex vitreus* Linn.) commonly called Iceland agate. One of them had a fighting club, made of a thick piece of wood about three feet long, carved at one extremity; and a few others had short wooden clubs, exactly resembling some of the New Zeeland patoo-patoos, which are made of bone'.[24]

The 'fighting club' over which Forster here writes is later identified as an *ua*, a leader's staff with a worked head. A few examples of these have survived. Anders Sparrman mentions the following about the material:

> 'an island that hardly produces anything more than a few bushes of a mimosa-like appearance, and a *Hibiscus populneus*, from which switch-like spears and a few small clubs are made'.[25]

Father Johann Forster only provides a sort of summary:

> 'Their Arms are Lances with sharp black flints & clubs & *patta pattow*.'[26]

Cook's journal has a similar description, possibly wholly or partially extracted from Forster as Cook himself arrived ill, spending only a short period on land:

> 'As inoffensive and friendly as these people seem to be they are not without offensive weapons, such as short wooden clubs and Spears, the latter are crooked Sticks about six feet long arm'd at one end with pieces

of flint – they have also a weapon made of wood like the Patoo patoo of New Zealand'.[27]

The pieces of flint were almost certainly obsidian. Since this material is found spread all over the island, this is too easily taken to be evidence of the large-scale use of spears. In any case, in the 18th century there was no question of this, and recent research has revealed that most of these finds were identified incorrectly as arrowheads.[28] The use of the bow and arrow has never been documented for the pre-Western contact period on Rapa Nui.

Lieutenant Richard Pickersgill, who was sent by Cook to explore the island, reports the following:

> 'Not one of them had so much as a stick or a Weapon of any sort in their hands'.[29]

The other, often brief, accounts by Elliot, Clerke and Wales contain no information about weapons.

In 1786, the last major European expedition arrives. The expedition's leader is La Pérouse. A number of accounts of this visit have also survived. In his journal La Pérouse observes the following about weapons:

> 'These natives were unarmed; 3 or 4 at the most, in such a crowd, had a kind of club made of wood and hardly dangerous'.[30]

The French make the acquaintanceship of the islanders' practice of throwing stones. When a few inhabitants are successful in stealing an anchor, the pursuing soldiers are pelted with stones. It is only after the French have fired a few shots that the anchor is brought back. Nevertheless, in most accounts the Easter Islanders are described as friendly and peaceful. Georg Forster believes that he knows the reason for this:

> 'The disposition of these people is far from warlike; their numbers are too inconsiderable, and their poverty too general, to create civil disturbances amongst them'.[31]

The visitors are unanimously positive to very positive about the appearance and health of the Easter Islanders. They describe the inhabitants as being of attractive build, quite tall, powerful persons with sufficient flesh on their bones and excellent swimmers. Even Cook, who – as the result of his roaming the area – had a great deal of material for comparison and observed that the Easter Islanders are smaller than the inhabitants on some other islands, comes to a favourable general judgment:

> 'in general they are a very Slender race but very Nimble and Active, well featured with agreeable countenances'.[32]

The population, or at least the hundreds that were observed by the visitors, give the impression of being healthy. What is at least as remarkable for the visitors is absence of all manner of food or nutrient deficiency-related diseases. On the point the Spanish are the most outspoken. They see:

> 'No halt, maimed, bent, crooked, luxated, deformed, or bow-legged among them, their appearance being thoroughly pleasing'.[33]

All in all, this information from the 18th century accounts offers no support for the descriptions from the collapse literature. There is no question of warfare and strife, or of a starving and desperate population, let alone of cannibalism because of a lack of food. Some lived in caves, but not because it was unsafe above the ground. On the contrary, Roggeveen sees during his visit that a new house is being built.[34]

It goes without saying that the deforestation of the island has caused a shortage of wood, making it difficult to build large numbers of houses or to make good spears or hefty clubs. So if there were a question of bellicosity or tribal warfare then they must have had to 'manage' to accomplish this without the use of stone. From the accounts there appears little of this bellicosity which could have contributed to a declining population and certainly not with such a large number of victims that as a result population numbers declined.

It cannot be ruled out that in the pre-European period armed combat had occurred on the island. If significant loss of life had occurred in the past, the island had recovered from the fighting and had achieved a situation. Theoretically, people could have died through lack of food prior to the arrival of the European visitors because the island could not feed the greatly increased population. However, there is as yet no archaeological evidence of such a scenario.[35]

Population growth and size

If resources are reduced and population numbers continue to increase, there comes a time when the capacity of the whole is exceeded and the population enters a swift downward spiral. That is the essence of the collapse theory. What can be said about the rate of population growth and size of Easter Island? Unfortunately, there are no hard figures. We must work with estimation procedures. We have evidence that the size of the groups of Polynesian colonists varied between fifty and one hundred. We also know that on average the growth figures of pre-modern societies were low; never greater than 0.5% over a longer period, and mostly lower. These are then average figures in which all irregularities have been included. We do not know exactly when they had reached Easter Island. We have hard evidence of habitation from ca. 1100 AD (Lipo and Hunt 2016). If we calculate the population numbers using these data, the following picture emerges.[36]

An earthly paradise? 165

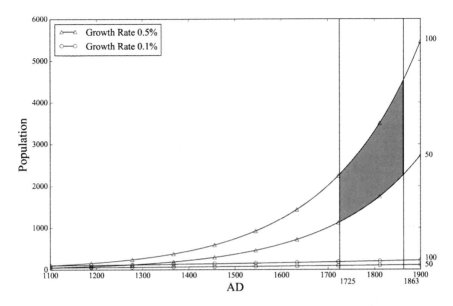

Figure 8.1 Population numbers (Y-axis); year (X-axis). Upper and lower boundaries assuming different number of settlers (50 minimum and 100 maximum) and different growth rates (0.1% and 0.5%). Grey area between vertical lines indicates the period of published estimates for eyewitnesses

How do these population growth curves relate to the estimates that we have from the earliest historical sources? In Table 8.1 below, all the numbers from the accounts have been put together. It appears that all numbers fall within the grey bounds of the calculations (Figure 8.1) rendering a sense of reliability to these historical estimates. A group of one hundred colonists and an average growth of 0.5% leads to approximately three thousand inhabitants at the end of the 18th century, a group of fifty leads to approximately one thousand five hundred. Even if one assumes a much earlier colonisation as Bahn and Flenley (2011) and Mieth and Bork (2015) appear to do, one can still arrive at the figures from the accounts if the growth-rate is on average considerably lower than 0.5%. This is not an unrealistic figure over such a long period.

In general, sex ratios in population should be equal, but on Easter Island there might have been a sex ratio disparity. All 18th century accounts point to a disparity; the European visitors saw few women on the island. Later research has given some support to this disparity: a sample of the skeletal remains show a difference of 14%.[37] This seems to be at the high end but, as women's fertility is key to reproduction figures, even a moderate disparity could be one more reason to assume low growth rates.

Table 8.1 Estimates of Easter Island's population in eighteenth-century accounts.

Author	Number of Inhabitants	Observations
Roggeveen 1722 Bouman Behrens	Mention no (total) numbers 'The inhabitants were swimming around in their thousands'[38]	'remarkable that we saw no more than two or three old women'; 'are young women hide away by men?'
Dalrymple (González?) 1770 Francisco Agüera Hervé	About 3,000 of both sexes[39] More than 800 people on the coast[40] One day [there were] more than 400 in the frigate[41] 900–1,000[42]	Estimated from the sloop; 'divided in batches'; 'the women were much fewer in number than the men' 'Of these very few are women – I do not believe they amount to 70 – and but a few boys'
Cook 1774 Georg Forster Johann Forster Clerke Wales Sparrman	600–700 in total[43] No more than 700[44] 300 or 400 people on our side. consequently not above 8 or 900 in the whole Isle[45] Not exceeding 500 Souls[46] Several hundreds[47] 'Round the beach at least 500 men[48] 600–700[49]	Two-thirds men 'Of whom 350 are Men' 'Gathered on the shore' 'Not more than 6 or 8 women' 'scarcely thirty of the other sex'
La Pérouse 1786 M. de Langle	Four or five hundred on the shore[50] 1,200 gathered around the bay 2,000 in total[51] 2,000[52]	'Of whom 300 are women' 'Without exaggeration' 'Two times more men than women'[53]
James Baker	1,500 to 2,000[54]	'The natives seem numerous"

Calculations remain calculations, and they do not entirely exclude the high population numbers (5,000 and up). But there are no plausible arguments for these enormous numbers, given the current assumptions about the colonising population.

Carrying capacity, water and food

Water and food are essential in order to keep a population alive and healthy. On Easter Island there are no 'living' sources of fresh water, brooks or rivers. There are three crater lakes, of which in any event the largest two have never been dry since the island has been inhabited. The pre-European population also use cisterns, natural hollows and caves in which rainwater was present or stored.[38] For household use they stored water in empty gourds and hollowed-out stone basins.[39] The French write that they are offered water in gourds.[40]

The Easter Islanders have never experienced serious water shortage; the quantity was sufficient. The European visitors are, however, less enthusiastic. They find it brackish.[41] The English in particular complain about its bad taste, but that was partly because they were in a fairly poor state when they arrived.[42] The findings of these visitors do not relate exclusively to the cisterns close to the coast. Cook noted what Pickersgill and Wales, who were trekking with a group into the hinterlands, had related to him:

> 'Towards the eastern end of the Island, they met with a well whose water was perfectly fresh, being considerably above the level of the Sea, but it was very dirty owing to filthyness, or cleanliness (call it which you will) of the Natives, who never go to drink without washing themselves all over'.[43]

Probably this relates to the crater lake Rano Raraku.

It is striking that the islanders also appear to gain moisture from certain foodstuffs. When the visitors make clear by using signs that they would like something to drink, the inhabitants arrive with sugar cane. It 'contained a very sweet juice, which the inhabitants presented to us frequently, and particularly whenever we asked for something to drink' writes Georg Foster.[44] Some researchers have made it plausible that the core of the trunk of the Easter Island *Jubaea* like-palm contained potable sap and that this could have been one of the reasons for cutting down the trees.[45]

As regards food, we must be careful both about what is reported on foodstuffs and about the information relating to the collection and production of food. The European visitors write extensively about the food available. What kinds of things do we find?

In Roggeveen's journal we read of 'tree-fruit, crops from the earth and chickens' as general categories.[46] Further on he mentions bananas, sugar cane, 'ubaswortelen' (yam?), 'bataat' (sweet potatoes) and he sees the opportunity of bartering 60 chickens and 30 bunches of bananas for linen.[47] The Dutch were offered well prepared chickens that tasted 'very good'. In itself a transaction that does not really fit in with the collapse story.

Bouman refers to what he knows of Dutch Suriname and calls the bananas in Surinamese 'backovens'. The sugar cane is thick, long and heavier than in Suriname. On his trek over the island he also sees a few small coconut palms and in the small gardens in addition to 'jannes' also some other unknown tuberous plants.[48]

The Spanish see no domestic animals apart from chickens. They also see a few rats and in the gardens 'yuca, yams, sweet potatoes, bottle gourd and several plantations of plantains and sugar cane'. They also mention several 'fruit bearing trees' with 'very small figs'.[49] Hervé sees on the coast 'sea urchins and small crabs, eggs of a sea-gulls and their fledglings'.[50] There will have been some coastal seafood although without seaworthy canoes no fish like tuna could have been caught, something that certainly had been done previously. Hervé also records that his men, just as the Dutch, are offered 'fruits and hens'. He also notices that the islanders 'do altogether without liquor of any kind'.[51] No alcohol, which certainly surprised the sailors.

Solid foodstuffs are reported in the English accounts, but they also add new ones. They see that rats are caught for consumption.[52] In two places we read that the men are given fish to eat, but that is a scarce item and the crew members are themselves not capable of catching a fish on the coast.[53]

The French expedition saw and was provided with not only Easter Island food, they also imported it. Apart from having seeds and plants, they also have livestock on board, a few pigs and goats in the hope that these will get the chance to multiply. We do not know whether that actually happened. The French themselves are unsure whether in the light of the poor quality of the water the pigs will manage to survive. They are more optimistic about the goats 'who drink but a little and like salt'.[54] Visitors who, 15 years later, came onto the island reported nothing about this.

The European visitors all write about the opportunities for growing food. At the end of his account of Easter Island, Roggeveen comes to the conclusion 'that the island is very fruitful, and could be made an Earthly Paradise if the inhabitants were to do something about it. Now they only cultivate what they need'.[55] He will certainly have thought about the industrious Dutch farmers in Zeeland, the province from which he came. Remarkably enough, the French come to precisely the same conclusion more than sixty years later:

> 'Hardly a tenth of their land is under cultivation, and I am sure that 3 days of labour are enough to provide a year's subsistence for each of them'.[56]

We also read positive reports as to the way in which the Easter Islanders grow their crops. For example, Bouman writes that the little square garden's look cared for and well set out.[57] All visitors write that the bananas are grown in well-arranged plantations. Cook writes:

> 'Their Plantations are prettily laid out', by which he probably also meant the small gardens where the tuberous crops were grown.[58]

Georg Forster had also noticed this: 'they were in excellent order, considering the stony quality of the ground'.[59] He sees that the islanders use grass to cover the soil in order to prevent it drying out, coming to the following cautious compliment:

'It should seem from these circumstances that the natives are not altogether ignorant of rural economy, and till the ground at a great expense of time and labour'.[60]

From later studies it is apparent that the islanders continued these agricultural practices all over the island until late in the 19th century.[61] The island's productivity was always great enough. Calculations indicate that even an (unlikely) population size of ten thousand inhabitants could have been well fed.[62] The island's capacity was greater than its people consumed for their own use. In the first half of the 19th century, Easter Island became a place where whalers and other passing vessels could obtain considerable amounts of potatoes in exchange for whale blubber or clothing.[63]

Discussion

How can the collapse theory be understood as supported by the European visitors' journals? My impression is that the English-language collapse authors predominantly based their arguments on the accounts of the journey of James Cook. They read these accounts from a present-day's perspective and through spectacles tinted by modern environmentalism, handed to them by the pessimistic literature of authors such as Paul Ehrlich and the Report to the Club of Rome. Cook and his fellow travellers compared the situation on Easter Island with what they knew from other islands in the Pacific. They were searching for a stopping off point for the British Empire where that nation's ships could berth in order to gain fresh supplies. But luck was against them. They did not find the fresh fruit that would immediately relieve their scurvy, the water was considered undrinkable (or in any event by the English), and the inhabitants were scantily clad, giving as a whole a penurious impression. The houses looked dilapidated: 'Its construction was such as evinced the poverty and wretched condition of its owners'.[64] It appeared that several statues had either fallen down or been pulled down deliberately. They found the population numbers to be small. But Easter Island is no Hawaii or Tahiti. It was no (sub)tropical paradise with palm trees but a bare and lean island where the inhabitants had to make do with the very basics. But even after the deforestation this appeared sufficient for a simple but sustainable society. The islanders were able to produce enough food, and despite its very limited variety it nevertheless appeared to be sufficiently well balanced in terms of minerals and nutrients. No maimed, crooked or bow-legged people were seen by the Spaniards. They managed to remain an exceptional healthy people. The Easter Islanders underwent a possibly unwished-for transition from their spectacular statue culture to an equally fascinating Birdman Cult, each of which in the beginning was sustainable, but were certainly different in quality. The ecological abundance and diversity gradually became impoverished, but the society displayed resilience and adaptability, fully in line with the ideas about the human condition expressed by Lapérouse the leader of the French expedition, in his journal.[65] All 18th century accounts support that story.

Conclusion

The theory claiming that deforestation on Rapa Nui caused hunger, armed conflict and collapse is clearly untenable. The conclusion of the rereading of the 18th-century travel accounts must be that they do not provide any support for the collapse theory as Ponting, Diamond and many others would have us believe.

Acknowledgements

This Chapter is a revised version of Boersema (2015a). I am grateful to the Belgium Royal Academy for Overseas Sciences (KAOW) for granting permission to republish. I'm also grateful to the editors of this book for their valuable comments.

Notes

1 An overview of the accounts is to be found before the bibliography.
2 Clive Ponting does not go so far as to give a description, but Joseph Tainter and Jared Diamond do. Tainter defines collapse as a *"rapid, significant loss of an established level of sociopolitical complexity"* Joseph A. Tainter (1988) *The Collapse of Complex Societies*. Cambridge: Cambridge University Press, p. 4. Diamond speaks of *"a drastic decrease in human population size and/or political/economic/social complexity, over a considerable area, for an extended time"* (Jared Diamond 2005: 3). In Diamond's view, the *"decrease"* proceeds quickly and the effects are long-lasting.
3 Jean Paul Barbier (2001) *Vanished Civilizations: From the Ancients to Easter Island*. Paris: Editions Assouline.
4 Bahn and Flenley (1992), p. 215 Reprinted in the 3rd edition 2011, p. 321.
5 Not all accounts that have been written during the 18th century are 'officially' published. Some, that we know of their existence, are lost, others that we didn't know of, show up. While working on his biography of Jacob Roggeveen, Roelof van Gelder came across in the library of Regensburg a copy of an account of Carl Friedrich Behrens, that was printed in 1728 and ever since non-existent in the Easter Island literature (Behrens 1728; Gelder 2012). Recently Zuzanna Jakubowska reported an even more spectacular finding of a completely unknown manuscript found in the Jagiellonian Library in Cracow, and composed by the Forsters, naturalist that traveled with James Cook. (Jakubowska 2014a, 2014b).
6 Like William Wales' *Remarks on Mr. Forster's account*.' published in 1778.
7 Translations could also be unreliable, see: (Jakubowska 2012).
8 'M. Hodges, peintre, qui avait accompagné le capitain Cook dans son second voyage, a fort mal rendu leur physionomie' La Pérouse (1987: 59, 60). And 'Mr Hodges's drawings of the statues is a very poor rendering of what we have seen' John Dunmore, volume 1, p. 61.
9 Georg Forster wrote in his account: 'This description also exactly corresponds with the Dutch account of Roggewein's voyage, printed at Dort in 1728' (Thomas

and Berghof 2000: 301). He appears to have (read) a copy of the *Tweejaarige Reyze*.
10 "Zoo dat wy gemakkelyk (wie zal zich niet verwonderen) zonder het hooft te buygen, tusschen de beenen van deze Goliats kinderen zouden hebben konnen doorgaan." Tweejaarige Reyze, 1728.
11 Bahn and Flenley (1992: 139).
12 Jacob Roggeveen's journal was confiscated in Batavia by the VOC (Dutch East India Company). A transcript turned up in 1836 in the archive of the WIC (Dutch West India Company) in Middelburg and is now in the National Archives of the Netherlands in The Hague. It was published in print in 1838 and republished and edited by F.E. baron Mulert in 1911. The journal of Cornelis Bouman was also lost. Part of it was found in 1910 in the estate of a Rotterdam harbour baron D. Hudig. That part (original?) is now to be found in the Rotterdam city archive. It was edited by F.E. baron Mulert and published in 1911 by the Royal Zeeland Society of Arts and Sciences.
13 See Mills (2009).
14 '. . . zy quamen aan boort sonder de minste wapenen, gelijk ons volk ook getuygde, die met de vaartuygen aan strant waren geweest, dat sy daar geen eenigh man met eenige wapenen hadden gesien' Bouman (Mulert 1911a: 86, 87).
15 Roggeveen in Mulert (1911: 118).
16 Roggeveen reports '10 à 12' (Mulert 1911: 119) while Bouman has '9 à 10' (Mulert 1911a: 88).
17 Behrens (1728: 10).
18 'Wie es schien, besaßen die Leute keine Waffen' Behrens 1923, p. 69. In the French edition of 1739: 'Les habitans de cette Ille ne portent point d'armes, du moins n'en avons-nous vû aucune' Behrens 1739, p. 134.
19 Corney (1903: 99). 'No se conoce género de armas entre ellos' (Foerster 2012: 130).
20 Corney (1903: 91). 'todos desarmados' Foerster (2012: 118).
21 Also noted by the Dutch: 'Zy hadden geen kennis van yzer, staal, nogh wapenen..' Bouman (Mulert 1911a: 91).
22 Corney (1903: 99). Most likely this relates to obsidian. Bouman already noted the use of obsidian to separate a banana from the stalk.
23 Beaglehole (1961: 339).
24 Thomas and Berghof (2000), Volume I, p. 303.
25 Sparrman (1953: 117).
26 Hoare (1982: 475).
27 Beaglehole (1961: 355).
28 Hunt and Lipo (2011: 93–107); Flas (2015). Lipo et al. (2015).
29 Beaglehole (1961: 342).
30 Dunmore (1994: 60).
31 Thomas and Berghof (2000), Volume I, p. 323.
32 Beaglehole (1961: 351).
33 Corney (1903: 96).
34 'gelijck wy sagen het geraamte van een nieuwe timmering' Roggeveen (Mulert 1911: 123).
35 See (Pollock 1993; Polet 2016; Stefan and Gill 2016).
36 Here I have used a simple growth function: $P = p.e^{rt}$, r being the growth rate, P the population, p the number of colonists and t the time.
37 Stefan (2000: 69)
38 The 'wells' in some accounts are most likely cisterns or underground ponds, filled with rainwater
39 'callebassen, daar zy water in hadden, 't welk ik proefde en bevond seer brak te zijn.' Bouman (Mulert 1911a: 91).

40 Dunmore (1994: 65). This probably relates to the same fruit that the Dutch called 'callebas', and the Spanish 'calabaza'.
41 'a well very close to the sea . . . full of impurities. When our people had cleared it, they found the water in it brackish, but the natives drank of it with much seeming satisfaction' Thomas and Berghof (2000: 308). 'There was little brackish water in holes by the shore' Dunmore (1994: 65).
42 'this was so strongly impregnated with Iron ore that it made sick who drank of it' writes Cook in his journal: Beaglehole (1961: 350).
43 Beaglehole (1961: 346).
44 Thomas and Berghof (2000: 308).
45 Mieth and Bork (2012: 75).
46 Roggeveen (Mulert 1911: 120).
47 'gestreept lijnwaet' Roggeveen (Mulert 1911: 120).
48 'kleyne kokosnootenboomen sagen wy weynigh' . . . 'jannes en ander soort van aardvrughten, die ik niet en kon' Bouman (Mulert 1911a: 90, 91). This relates to sweet potato, yam and taro.
49 Corney (1908: 101). This could be the Malay apple (*Syzygium malaccense*).
50 Corney (1908: 122).
51 Corney (1908: 127).
52 'The produce is Potatoes, Yams, Taro or the Eddy root, Plantains and Sugar Cane, all excellent in its kind, the Potatoes are the best of the sort I ever tasted' . . . 'rats which I believe they eat' Corney (1908: 349).
53 Beaglehole (1961: 350). On the contribution of marine food see Polet and Bocherens (2015).
54 Dunmore (1994: 65).
55 'de wyle wy het selve niet alleen niet zandig, maar integendeel uytnemend vrugtbaar bevonden hebben. . .Sulx dit land tot een aardsch Paradijs te maaken is, indien hetselve behoorlijck weird gecultiveerd en bearbeyd, 't geen nu alleen gedaan werd, nae de mate dat de Inwoonders benodigd sijn tot onderhoud des levens.' Roggeveen (Mulert 1911: 125, 126).
56 Dunmore (1994: 63).
57 'de inwoonders hadden kroonen kostgronden, vierkantigh met voren in goede ordre afgedeelt' Bouman (Mulert 1911a: 90).
58 Beaglehole (1961: 357).
59 Thomas and Berghof (2000: 307).
60 Thomas and Berghof (2000: 311).
61 Mulrooney (2013).
62 Boersema (2011).
63 See Richards (2016) and Chapter 9 in this volume.
64 Thomas and Berghof (2000: 307).
65 'but since Man is a being who, above all others, can adapt to every situation, these people seemed to me less unfortunate than they did to Captain Cook and Mr. Forster'. Dunmore (1994: 59).

Easter Island, early accounts

General accounts

Dumont D'Urville, M. 1834–1835. *Voyage pittoresque Autour du Monde. Resume général des voyages de découvertes de Magellan, Tasman, Dampier, Anson, Byron, Wallis, Carteret, Bougainville, Cook, Lapérouse . . . etc.* 2 Tomes. Paris: Tenré.

An earthly paradise? 173

Foerster, R. 2012. *Rapa Nui, primeras expeditiones europeas.* Rapa Nui: Rapa Nui Press.

Kerr, R. 1811–1824. *General History and Collection of Voyages and Travels, Arranged in Systematic Order: Forming a Complete History of the Origin and Progress of Navigation, Discovery, and Commerce, by Sea and Land, from the Earliest Ages to the Present Time.* 14 vols. Edinburgh: William Blackwood & London: T. Cadell. (Included in the Gutenberg project).

Vol. X Early Circumnavigations, or Voyages round the World, 1824. www.gutenberg.org/files/13130/13130-h/13130-h.htm

Vol. XI Chapter XIII Voyage round the World, by Commodore Roggewein, in 1721–1723, 1824: www.gutenberg.org/files/15376/15376-h/15376-h.htm

Lee, G, A. M. Altman, and F. Morin, eds. 2004. *Early Visitors to Easter Island 1864–1877. The Reports of Eugène Eyraud, Hippolyte Roussel, Pierre Loti and Alphonse Pinart.* Translated by Ann M. Altman. Los Osos, CA: Easter Island Foundation.

Major, R. H., ed. 1859. *Early Voyages to Terra Australis, Now Called Australia: A Collection of Documents, and Extracts from early Manuscript Maps, Illustrative of the History of Discovery on the Coasts of that Vast Island, from the Beginning of the Sixteenth Century to the Time of Captain Cook*, edited with an Introduction by R. H. Major. First Series Part I, no 25. London: Hakluyt Society. Reprinted in 2007 by Kessinger Publishing's Legacy Reprints, Whitefish, MT.

Nederlandsche reizen, tot bevordering van den koophandel, na de meest afgelegene gewesten des aardkloots. Doormengd met vreemde Lotgevallen, en menigvuldige Gevaaren, die de Nederlandsche reizigers hebben doorstaan. Met Plaaten, 14 delen 1784–1787, Te Amsterdam by Petrus Conradi Te Harlingen by V. van der Plaats. (Volume 13, 1787, has the story of the *Tweejaarige Reyze Rondom de Wereld*).

Richards, R. 2008. *Easter Island 1793–1861: Observations by Early Visitors: Before the Slave Raids.* Los Osos, CA: Easter Island Foundation.

Valentijn, F. 1724–1726. *Oud en Nieuw Oost-Indiën, vervattende Een Naaukeurige en Uitvoerige Verhandelinge van Nederlands Mogentheyd In die Gewesten, benevens Eene wydluftige Beschryvinge der Moluccos, Amboina, Banda, Timor, en Solor, Java, Bantam, Batavia.* Te Dordrecht, by Joannes van Braam andTe Amsterdam, Gerard onder de Linden (Reprint Franeker: Van Wijnen, 2002–2004). (Volume 3, 1726, has a short account of Roggeveen's Journey).

Expedition of Jacob Roggeveen 1721–1722

Behrens, C. F. 1728. *Reise nach den unbekandten Süd-Ländern und rund um die Welt/Nebst vielen von ihm angemerckten Seltenheiten und zugestoßenen wunderlichen Begebenheiten. Unbey eine wahrhaffte Nachricht von der Insul und Historie des Robinson Crusoe. In einem Send-Schreiben an einem guten Freund mit Poetischer Feder entworffen.* Frankfurt und Leipzig. www.regensburger-katalog.de/InfoGuideClient.ubrsis/singleHit.do?methodToCall=showHit&curPos=2&identifier=-1_FT_172312802&tab=showAvailabilityActive

Behrens, C. F. 1732. *Nader onderzoek door Karel Fredrik Behrens. En bericht van zyne reyze naar de Zuid-Landen gedaan, in dienst van de E: WEST-INDISCHE,*

COMPAGNIE, *in den Jare 1721 enz. Thans volgens eigen ondervinding, ten beste opgedragen aan de E: OOST-INDISCHE COMPAGNIE van Hollandt.* t'Amsterdam: gedrukt voor den Autheur.

Behrens, C. F. 1737. *Reise durch die Süd-Länder und um die Welt/worinnen enthalten die Beschreibung von der Canarischen und Saltz-Insuln, Brasilien, der Straß Magellanus und Lamer-Küste, Chili, und neuentdeckten Insuln gegen Süden ic. Dergleichen, von den Moluckischen Insuln und verschiedenen Plätzen in Asia und Africa, Als auch von ihren Einwohnern, Lebens-Art, Policey, Handel, Wandel und Gottesdienst ic. gehandelt wird. Nebst einer accuraten Charte der ganßen Welt und andern kupffern.* Frankfurt und Leipzig.

A second print: Behrens, C. F. 1739. *Der wohlversuchte Süd-Länder, das ist: ausführliche Reise-Beschreibung um die Welt, Worinnen von denen Kanarischen und Saltz-Insuln, Brasilien, der StraßMagellanus und Lamer- Küste, Chili, und neuentdeckten Insuln gegen Süden, ic. Deßgleichen von den Moluckischen Insuln und verschiedenen Plätzen in Asia und Africa, als auch ihren Inwohnern, Lebens-Art, Policey, Handel Wandel und Gottesdienst gehandelt wird. Nebst einer accuraten Charte der ganßen Welt, und andern Kupffern entworffen von Carl Friederich Behrens.* Leipzig: auf Kosten des Autoris, zu finden bey Joh. Georg Monath.

Translation in French: *Histoire de l'Expédition des Trois Vaisseaux, envoyés par la Compagnie des Indes Occidentales des Provinces Unies aux Terres Australes en MDCCXXI.* Par Monsieur de B. 2 tom. Aux dépens de la Compagnie. La Haye, 1739.

Translations into Nederduitsch (Amsterdam, 1759. and into English). London: Hakluyt Society, 1903.

Behrens, C. F. 1923. *Der wohlversuchte Südländer. Reise um die Welt 1721/22.* Nach den Originalausgaben bearbeitet von Dr. Hans Plischke. Leipzig: F. A. Brockhaus. (2 Auflage 1925).

Mulert, F. E. B. 1911. *De reis van Mr. Jacob Roggeveen ter ontdekking van het Zuidland 1721-1722.* Werken uitgegeven door de Linschoten Vereeniging IV. 's-Gravenhage: Martinus Nijhoff.

Mulert, F. E. B. 1911a. *Scheepsjournaal, gehouden op het schip Tienhoven tijdens de ontdekkingsreis van Mr. Jacob Roggeveen, 1721-1722.* Archief, uitgegeven door het Zeeuwsch genootschap der wetenschappen. Middelburg: J. C. & W. Altorffer. (Journal of Cornelis Bouman).

Roggeveen, J. 1838. *Dagverhaal der ontdekkings-reis van Mr. Jacob Roggeveen met de schepen Den Arend, Thienhoven en De Afrikaansche Galei in de jaren 1721 en 1722.* Met toestemming van zijne excellentie den minister van koloniën uitgegeven door het Zeeuwsch genootschap der wetenschappen. Middelburg: De gebroeders Abrahams.

T.d.H. 1727. *Kort en nauwkeurig verhaal van de reize, door drie Schepen in 't Jaar 1721 gedaan.* Te Amsterdam, bij weduwe Jacob van Egmont, boekdrukster en verkoopster op de Reguliersbreestraat in de nieuwe drukkerij.

T.d.H. 1727. *Kort en nauwkeurig verhaal van de reize, door drie Schepen in 't Jaar 1721. gedaan, op ordre van de Ed. Heeren Bewindhebberen van de West-Indische Compagnie in Holland, om eenige tot nog toe onbekende Landen, omtrent de ZUID-ZEE gelegen, op te zoeken. Waar in alles wat haar op de Reize, van haar uitgaan tot haar terugkomste toe, is wedervaren, wordt aangetoont; alsmede veele wonderlyke manieren, gewoontens, en zeden der ontdekte volken, etc.* Tweede Druk, verbetert. Te Amsterdam, By Johannes van Septeren, Boekverkooper op de Leydsestraat, tusschen de Heere- en Keysersgragt.

An earthly paradise? 175

T.d.H. 1727. *Het Waare en Nauwkeurige Journael der Reize, gedaan door drie Schepen, op ordre van de Ed. Heeren Bewindhebberen van de West-Indische Compagnie, om eenige tot nog toe onbekende Landen, omtrent de ZUID-ZEE geleegen, op te soeken. Waar in alles wat haar op de Reize is wedervaren, wert verhaalt en aangetoont; als ook de wonderlyke manieren, gewoontens, en zeden der ontdekte volkeren, en hoe dese Reizigers op eene wonderlyke wyze te Batavia zyn aangekomen etc.* Den Derden Druk, van veele Drukfeilen verbetert, op nieuws nagesien door een ooggetuyge van dese Reize, en met nodige Aantekeningen vermeerdert. Te Amsterdam, by Johannes van Septeren, Boekverkooper op de Leydsestraat, tusschen de Heere en Keysersgragt.

Tweejaarige Reyze Rondom de Wereld, Ter nader Ontdekkinge der Onbekende Zuydlanden. Met drie schepen, in het Jaar 1721 ondernomen, door last van de Nederlandsche Westindische Maatschappy, Waar in het wedervaaren en de Rampen op de Reyze verhaald, en de bezeilde en nieuw ontdekte Landen en Eylanden, met der zelver Bewoonders, beschreven worden. Nevens de Reyze van het Oostindisch SCHIP BARNEVELD, Uyt Holland tot aan de Kaap der Goede Hoope, in 't jaar 1719. BEHELZENDE Een verhaal van de langduurige tegenspoeden en zonderlinge voorvallen op het Eyland Madagascar, by de Woeste Souklaven, Met een Naauwkeurige Beschrijving van de vreemde Gewoontens, Godsdienst en Zeden dier Volkeren. Verçiert met een Nette Reyskaart en Prentverbeeldingen. Te Dordrecht, Gedrukt by Joannes van Braam, Boekverkooper, 1728.

Other editions: Dordrecht: Van Braam, 1758; Dordrecht: H. de Koning, 1764; and in: *Nederlandsche Reizen*, 1787.

Expedition of Capitán D. Felipe González 1770

Mellén Blanco, F. 1986. *Manuscritos y documentos españoles para la historia de la isla de Pascua*. Madrid: Biblioteca Centro de Estudios Históricos de Obras Públicas y Urbanismo (CEHOPU).

Corney, B. G., ed. 1903. *The Voyage of Captain Don Felipe Gonzalez in the Ship of the Line San Lorenzo with the Frigate Santa Rosalia in Company to Easter Island in 1770–1771*, Second Series. No XIII. Transcribed, Translated, and edited by Bolton Glanvill Corney. London: Hakluyt Society.

Expedition of Captain James Cook 1774

Beaglehole, J. C., ed. 1961. *The Journals of Captain James Cook on His Voyages of Discovery. II: Voyage of the Resolution and Adventure 1772–1775*. Cambridge: Published for the Hakluyt Society at the University Press. (Has also Accounts of William Wales and other members of the Crew: Furneaux, Burney, Clerke and Pickersgill).

Forster, G. 1777. *A Voyage round the World, in His Britannic Majesty's Sloop, Resolution, commanded by Capt: James Cook, during the Years 1772, 3, 4, and 5: By Georg Forster, F.R.S. Member of the Royal Academy of Madrid, and of the Society for Promoting Natural Knowledge at Berlin.* Volume I, London: Printed for B. White, J. Robson and P. Elmsly.

Forster, G. 1979. *Entdeckungsreise in die Südsee 1772–1775*. Neu herausgegeben von Hermann Homann. Stuttgart: K. Thienemanns Verlag.

Forster, G. 1983. *Reise um die Welt*. Herausgegeben und mit einem Nachwort von Gerhard Steiner, Frankfurt am Main, Insel Verlag.

Hoare, M. E., ed. 1982. *The Resolution Journal of Johann Reinhold Forster 1772–1775*. 4 vols. London: The Hackluyt Society.

Holmes, C., ed. 1984. *Captains Cook's Second Voyage: The Journals of Lieutenants Elliot and Pickersgill*. London: Caliban Books.

Jakubowska, Z. 2014b. *Still More to Discover: Easter Island in an Unknown Manuscript by the Forsters from the 18th Century*. Warszawa/Warsaw: Bibliotheka Iberijska.

Sparrman, A. 1785–1786. *A Voyage to the Cape of Good Hope towards the Antarctic Polar Circle Round the World and to the Country of the Hottentots and the Caffres from the Year 1772–1776*. Translated from the Swedish Original. With Plates. 2 Vols. London: G. G. J. Robinson and J. Robinson, Pater-Noster-Row.

Sparrman, A. 1975. *A Voyage to the Cape of Good Hope towards the Antarctic Polar Circle Round the World and to the Country of the Hottentots and the Caffres from the Year 1772–1776*. Based on the English Editions of 1785–1786 published by Robinson, London. Edited by Prof. V.S. Forbes. Translation from the Swedish revised by J. & I. Rudner. 2 Vols. Cape Town: Van Riebeeck Society. (Volume I has a few lines on Easter Island pages 115/116).

Sparrman, A. 1953. *A Voyage Round the World with Captain James Cook in H. M. S. Resolution*. Translated by Huldine Beamish and Averil Mackenzie-Grieve. Introduction and Notes by Owen Rutter. Illustrated by C. W. Bacon. London: Robert Hale Limited.

Thomas, N, H. Guest, and M. Dettelbach, eds. 1996. *Observation Made uring a Voyage Round the World: Johann Reinhold Forster*. Honolulu: University of Hawai'i Press.

Thomas, N. and O. Berghof, eds. 2000. *A Voyage Round the World: George Forster*. 2 vols. After the narrative published by George Forster in 1777, Honolulu: University of Hawai'i Press.

Wales, W. 1778. *Remarks on Mr. Forster's account of Captain Cook's Last Voyage Round the World, in the Years 1772, 1773, 1774, and 1775*. London: Printed for J. Nourse, opposite Catherine-Street, Strand.

Expedition Comte Lapérouse 1786

Dunmore, J., ed. 1994–1995. *The Journal of Jean-François de Galaup de La Pérouse 1785–1788*. 2 Vols. Translated and edited by John Dunmore. London: The Hakluyt Society.

Lapérouse, J.-F. de Galaup comte de. 1797. *Voyage autour du monde 1785–1788. sur L'Austrolabe et la Boussole*. Paris: De l'Imprimerie de la République. (Paris: Éditions La Découverte 1987).

Lapérouse, J.-F. de. *Voyage autour du monde sur l'Astrolabe et la Boussole (1785–1788)*. Choix des textes, introduction et notes de Hélène Patris. Edition 2008 actualisée, Paris: La Decouverte/Poche.

References

Bahn, P. and J. Flenley. 1992. *Easter Island, Earth Island*. London: Thames and Hudson.

Bahn, P. and J. Flenley. 2011. *Easter Island, Earth Island*. Third Edition. Rapa Nui: Rapa Nui Press.
Boersema, J. J. 2002. *Hoe groen is het goede leven? Over vooruitgang en het natuurlijk milieu in onze westerse cultuur*. Rede uitgesproken bij de aanvaarding van het ambt van hoogleraar in de *Culturele en levensbeschouwelijke dimensies van de relatie mens en natuur* bij de Faculteit der Aard- en Levenswetenschappen van de Vrije Universiteit op 3 oktober 2002, Vrije Universiteit Amsterdam.
Boersema, J. J. 2011. *Beelden van Paaseiland. Over de duurzaamheid van een cultuur*. Amsterdam: Atlas.
Boersema, J. J. 2015a. "Revisiting the Collapse of Rapa Nui (Easter Island) through a Voyage of 18th-Century Journals." In Easter Island: Collapse or Transformation? A State of the Art, edited by N. Cauwe and M. De Dapper, 153–175. Proceedings International Conference, Brussels, November 9–10, 2012, Brussels: Royal Academy for Overseas Sciences.
Boersema, J. J. 2015b. *The Survival of Easter Island: Dwindling Resources and Cultural Resilience*. Cambridge: Cambridge University Press.
Diamond, J. 1995. "Easter's End." *Discover Magazine* 9: 62–69. http://208.245.156.153/archive/output.cfm?ID=536.
Diamond, J. 1997. *Guns, Germs and Steel: The Fates of Human Societies*. London: Vintage Books.
Diamond, J. 2000. "Ecological Collapses of Pre-Industrial Societies." *The Tanner Lectures on Human Values*, Stanford University. May 22–24, 391–406.
Diamond, J. 2004. "Twilight at Easter." *The New York Review of Books* 51(5), March 25: 6–10.
Diamond, J. 2005. *Collapse How Societies Choose to Fail or Survive*. London: Allen Lane, Penguin Books.
Diamond, J. 2007. "Easter Island Revisited." *Science* 317: 1692–1694.
Ehrlich, P. R. 1968. *The Population Bomb*. New York: Ballantine Books.
Flas, D. 2015. "The Mata'a Typology, Technology and Function." In *Easter Island: Collapse or Transformation? A State of the Art*, edited by N. Cauwe and M. De Dapper, 59–73. Proceedings International Conference, Brussels, November 9–10, 2012. Brussels: Royal Academy for Overseas Sciences.
Gelder, R. van. 2012. *Naar het aards paradijs. Het rusteloze leven van Jacob Roggeveen, ontdekker van Paaseiland (1659-1729)*. Amsterdam: Uitgeverij Balans.
Hunt, T. L. and C. P. Lippo. 2011. *The Statues That Walked: Unraveling the Mystery of Easter Island*. New York: Free Press.
Jakubowska, Z. 2012. "Behrens' Narrative of the Discovery of Easter Island: Two Editions, Two Personalities, Two Realities." *Rapa Nui Journal* 26(1): 21–30.
Jakubowska, Z. 2014a. "The Forsters Back in the Spotlight: Unknown Manuscript on Easter Island Discovered in Poland." *Rapa Nui Journal* 28(1): 68–76.
Jakubowska, Z. 2014b. *Still More to Discover: Easter Island in an Unknown Manuscript by the Forsters from the 18th Century*. Warszawa/Warsaw: Bibliotheka Iberijska.
Lipo, C. P., T. L. Hunt, R. Horneman, and V. Bonhomme. 2015. "Weapons of War? Rapa Nui *Mata'a* Morphometric Analyses." *Antiquity* 90 349: 1–17. doi: 10.15184/aqy.2015.189.
Lipo, C. P. and T. L. Hunt. 2016. "Chronology and Easter Island Prehistory." In *Skeletal Biology of the Ancient Rapanui (Easter Islanders)*, edited by V. H. Stefan and G. W. Gill, 39–65. Cambridge: Cambridge University Press.

Meadows, D. L., D. H. Meadows, J. Randers, and W. W. Behrens III. 1972. *The Limits to Growth: A Report for the Club of Rome's Project on the Predicament of Mankind*. New York: Universe Books.

Mieth, A. and H.-R. Bork. 2012. *Die Osterinsel. Auf Tour*. Berlin: Springer Spektrum.

Mieth, A. and H.-R. Bork. 2015. "Degradation of Resources and Successful Land-Use Management on Prehistoric Rapa Nui." In *Easter Island: Collapse or Transformation? A State of the Art*, edited by N. Cauwe and M. De Dapper, 91–113. Proceedings International Conference, Brussels, November 9–10, 2012. Brussels: Royal Academy for Overseas Sciences.

Mills, A. 2009. "Violent Encounters: Historical Notes on the Curatorial Representation of Polynesian Weapons." *Journal of Museum Ethnography* 21: 186–201.

Mulloy, W. 1974. "Contemplate the Navel of the World (Sobre el Ombligo del Mundo)." *Américas* 26(4): 25–33.

Mulrooney, M. A. 2013. "An Island-Wide Assessment of the Chronology of Settlement and Land Use on Rapa Nui (Easter Island) Based on Radiocarbon Data." *Journal of Archaeological Science* 40: 4377–4399.

Polet, C. 2015. "Starvation and Cannibalism on Easter Island? The Contribution of the Analysis of Rapanui Human Remains." In *Easter Island: Collapse or Transformation? A State of the Art*, edited by N. Cauwe and M. De Dapper, 115–133. Proceedings International Conference, Brussels, November 9–10, 2012. Brussels: Royal Academy for Overseas Sciences.

Polet, C. and H. Bocherens. 2016. "New Insights into the Marine Contribution to Ancient Easter Islanders' Diet." *Journal of Archaeological Science* 6: 709–719.

Pollock, N. J. 1993. "Traditional Foods of Rapanui." In *Easter Island Studies: Contributions to the History of Rapanui in Memory of William T. Mulloy*, edited by S. R. Fischer, 153–157. Oxford: Oxbow Books.

Ponting, C. 1991. *A Green History of the World*. London: Sinclair-Stevenson, London: Nederlandse vertaling uit 1992: *Een groene geschiedenis van de wereld*. Amsterdam: De Boekerij.

Ponting, C. 2007. *A New Green History of the World: The Environment and the Collapse of Great Civilisations*. London: Vintage Books.

Richards, R. 2016. "Foreign Visitors to Easter Island 1772–1862: Isolation Proved a High Price to Pay." *Rapa Nui Journal* 30(1): 11–12.

Stefan, V. H. 2000. *Craniometric Variation and Biological Affinity of the Prehistoric Rapanui (Easter Islanders): Their Origin, Evolution, and Place in Polynesian Prehistory*. Ph.D. Dissertation, University of New Mexico.

Stefan, V. H. and G. W. Gill, eds. 2016. *Skeletal Biology of the Ancient Rapanui (Easter Islanders)*. Cambridge: Cambridge University Press.

9 The impact of the whalers and other foreign visitors before 1862

Rhys Richards

Introduction

Now that all the accounts of the less well known early visits to Easter Island have been brought together in a single language (Richards 2008), the impact of foreign visitors is much clearer. Some 79 visits can currently be identified that involved contact with the Easter Island people ashore before the slave raids in 1862. Seven were by explorers (from Roggeveen in 1722 to du Petit-Thouars in 1838), three by fur traders en route to the North West Coast of America, three by sealers, four by men-o-war and seven by trans-Pacific traders. All the remaining 55 visits were by whaleships – four British whalers before 1823, and 51 American whaleships between 1822 and 1862. It is noted that the Easter Islanders adopted trading practices that limited the impact of these visits ashore, but this may have helped to shelter them from the malign influences of foreign diseases until 1862. There is no evidence of a shortage of food to trade, but the Easter Islanders paid a high price for the method they chose which minimized their contact with the foreigners.

Whaling in the Pacific

In 1789, American whaleships began entering the Pacific, rounding Cape Horn to cruise off the Pacific coast of South America. Their immediate success prompted such a gold rush that within three years 40 whaleships were taking sperm whales off the coast of Chile and Peru. Their cruising grounds were from 30 to 8 degrees South latitude. Of these 40 whaleships, London had sent 21, Dunkirk nine, and Nantucket eight, but almost all of these whaleships were captained and crewed by Americans. Whaling in the Pacific boomed until the disturbances of the Napoleonic wars in Europe extended to the Pacific, with some British and French whaleships carrying "letters of marque" to allow them to prey like pirates on enemy merchant shipping. In retaliation, local authorities in several Spanish ports seized British whaleships, including 15 in 1798 (Richards 1996: 45). Thereafter, the whalemen avoided the larger ports and spread further north towards Peru and the Galapagos Islands.

Whaling in the southeast Pacific resumed slowly but worse disruption followed with the War of 1812 between the Americans and the British:

> American vessels in the Atlantic ran for home, but few succeeded as the devastation wrought by the British cruisers was thorough and virtually complete. In the Pacific, armed British whaleships brought tidings of the conflict and scattered the American fleet, some to seek refuge in Talcahuano, others to go further out to sea including to the Galapagos. To the Americans' rescue came the US frigate *Essex* which captured twelve British whaleships. This delivered a setback that prevented a resumption of British whaling in the Pacific until the 1820s, and thereafter for the most part based on Port Jackson not on the eastern grounds . . .
>
> With the conclusion of the War, American enterprise expanded . . . In 1818, only four years after the war had ended, 120 American ships were whaling in the Pacific, almost all on the On-Shore Ground [off Peru and Ecuador]. Throughout the history of Pacific whaling, the route round Cape Horn was favoured over that round the Cape of Good Hope by a ratio close to three-to-one.
>
> (Kugler 1971: 23)

Starbuck lists no less than 151 American whaleships whose principal whaling was in the Pacific Ocean before 1812, while there were perhaps almost as many again from London and French ports combined (Starbuck 1878; Jones 1986; du Pasquier 1990). At least nine American whaling journals and logbooks survive for cruises in the vicinity of the Galapagos Islands before the end of 1812, but only one for Easter Island (Langdon 1984). By comparison, there are four for visits by American whaleships to Juan Fernandez, and five for Masafuera, and many more for American sealing voyages (Kirker 1970). Consequently, it seems rather odd that so far no American whaleships have been identified that visited, or even sighted, Easter Island before 1812, and only two from London, namely *Adventure* in 1806, and in 1807 the *Thames*, Captain Charles Gardner, 1805–1808 (N.B. *Thames* not *Thomas*) (PMB 779). Apparently, at this early stage, the American whaleships were cruising closer to the coasts of Chile and Peru rather than following the outer route passed Easter Island.

Given the scale of the Pacific whale fishery after the peace of 1814, the number of whaleships that are known to have visited Easter Island before 1830, also seems uncharacteristically small: two in 1821, the *Thomas* of London, Captain John Brown (PMB 385); and *Coquette* of London, Captain James H. Wild (PMB 375); plus only three more American whaleships, *George and Susan* of New Bedford in 1823, (PMB 258); *Lydia* of Nantucket in 1827 (PMB 392), and *Eagle* of Nantucket in 1828 (also PMB 392). However, all of these were just sightings of Easter Island, with no contact with the islanders except in the case of the *Lydia*, where her terse logbook notes only "27 February 1827. One boat went out trading with the natives scraps for potatoes and yams" (PMB 392). Between 1832 and 1840, there were a further 23 visits by 17 whaleships, all Americans, with eight from New Bedford, six from Nantucket and one each from Plymouth, Fairhaven, and Salem (Starbuck 1878; Sherman 1986; Lund 2001). Of these 17, only 12 had contact with the Rapa Nui islanders.

Contact with Rapa Nui

Perhaps with further searching, and with various logbooks and journals added to library collections since 1976, some more useful accounts may be added to this meager total, but whaling logbooks were essentially records of navigation, weather, and whale sightings, and seldom contain much of wider relevance.

The visitors found the islanders keen to trade, but exuberant, excited and unruly, and without any chiefly authorities to take control when misunderstandings and disruptions occurred. The islanders soon earned a reputation for skillful petty thieving. On several occasions initially amicable exchanges deteriorated into hostilities, with the visitors pelted with stones thrown with Polynesian accuracy. Distrust grew on both sides, with islanders killed in 1806, 1822, and 1838, and at least one whaleman killed, in 1856. In the later years, the visitors believed some islanders made most friendly gestures to them to go ashore, but only in order to steal their clothes. Generally, however, the islanders discouraged visitors from going ashore even very briefly.

The practice of discouraging foreigners from landing on shore was a conscious decision by "the King" as early as 1805. That year, Captain Page in the London whaleship *Adventure* touched at Easter Island "to refresh his crew, they having the scurvy." When they departed "King Crang-a-low was supposed to be 125 years old, scarcely able to walk, and his hair as white as milk, and the father of twenty-three children, all of whom were alive." Captain Page brought away "the youngest son, a handsome man aged about 22," whom they called Henry Easter. He later told Captain Page that

> about a year previous to their departure, an American ship [now known to have been the sealing schooner *Nancy* of New London,] had visited them for the same purpose as the *Adventure*, but after receiving the different fruits which the natives were able to furnish them with, took seven of them away; which was likely to be attended with serious consequences to the next visitors [in the *Adventure*]; they, not knowing what had happened, approached the shore unguarded, when they were attacked with showers of stones from slings, with which the islanders are very dexterous, and struck the Captain [Page] on the breast with such violence as to nearly kill him. *Through the above affair, King Crangalow will not let any boat communicate with the shore.*
> (*Sydney Gazette* 8 December 1812, italics added; Richards 2016: 11–12. See Note on Sources preceding the References.)

The infamous behavior of the captain of the American ship *Nancy* was recorded more explicitly by the explorer von Kotzebue 12 years later while he was at Honolulu in 1816. He noted that while sealing at Masafuera, the captain of the *Nancy* of New London [sic] resolved to kidnap men and women from Easter Island to supplement his sealing gangs: "This cruel project was attempted in 1800 [sic 1804], landing in Cook's Bay . . . The battle is said to have been bloody, the islanders defending themselves with great bravery. However they were obliged to submit to European arms, and 12 men and 10 women" were taken alive. After three days below in irons, the captives were brought on deck, whereupon the men dived overboard, preferring to drown rather than be enslaved. The women were taken to Masafuera (von Kotzebue 1821: 19–28).

The name of this monstrous captain can now be established. On December 20, 1804, the 230 ton ship *Nancy* of Boston, Captain J. Crocker, while on a passage from Europe to Canton, sighted a high island which he named "Strong's Island" after the Governor of Massachusetts (*Monitor (Boston)* February 1, 1806; Ward 1966–67: vol. III: 534–538). At 5 degrees 11 minutes North, and 162 degrees 58 minutes East, this island was probably Kosrae in Micronesia. Later, Duperry named the discoverer as "Captain Crozer," but the spelling in the Boston newspaper was definitely "Crocker." The records of the Dutch traders at Canton include the arrival there on January 10, 1805, of the 230 ton ship *Nancy* of Boston under Captain Croker (Richards 1994: 48). Though Salem traders to China normally went via the Cape of Good Hope, traders to China from Boston normally took the route round Cape Horn.

So, from as early as 1805, the Easter Islanders required the visiting whalemen to adopt a form of trading that minimized the contacts and the danger. Most whaleships lay well off shore and sent two or more whaleboats close in shore, to lie or anchor just outside the surf. Islanders of both sexes then carried their baskets of produce into the water and swam them to the boats where the visitors took in the baskets and returned them with their trade items inside. On some occasions, near naked women got into the boats with great coquetry in order to obtain gifts and, if possible, to distract the crew so that other islanders could steal whatever small items they could. Generally, however, wise boatmen allowed them to trade only one by one, and to keep all others away least they combine and upset the boats. A considerable quantity of goods could be exchanged this way, with minimal personal contact between the visitors and the islanders.

Like those of the explorers, the ships of the whalemen were well provisioned for voyages of up to three years. Their main need was for water less stale than the water in the barrels brought from home. It was soon evident that Easter Island was not well equipped to supply fresh water. To prevent scurvy, many whaling captains would also trade for vegetables and fruit if these could be readily obtained without risks to their voyages and to their crews. Thus sweet potatoes, yams, bananas, plantains, and sugar cane were bartered for knives, nails, hoop iron and ironware, pins and needles for making fish hooks, and whatever trinkets the islanders fancied. Later many Islanders gave priority to taking toasted scraps from the whale-pots, which they devoured with great eagerness. These scraps became a standard trade item: in 1841, the *Columbus* of Nantucket obtained eight barrels of potatoes and 12 barrels of yams for three and a half barrels of scraps. Some ships, like the *Navigator* of Nantucket, took 50 barrels of potatoes in 1842 (Richards 2008: 77; PMB 674,675 and 795; PMB 380).

The local people ashore were not so impoverished, nor so hungry, that they would not barter valuable food, often playfully and in quite large quantities, for the "curiosities" offered by the visiting foreigners. Also, the islanders' willingness to trade their own "curiosities," such a *moko kava kava* statuettes and *moai moko* lizard figures, began vigorously at a very early date.

A young British seaman, Thomas W. Smith, was on his eleventh voyage when he shipped from London in October 1821 on the whaleship *Spring Grove* on a voyage round Cape Horn to Chile, Peru and the Galapagos Islands. Later, in mid-1823,

> We touched at Easter Island to obtain some refreshment for the crew. Two boats were sent in to trade with the natives while the ship lay off and on. The bartering articles consisted of bent needles and pins, buttons, beads and other trinkets, for which we received in return potatoes and sugar cane. The pins and needles were used by them to catch fish, being superior to native fish hooks which are made of hard wood or stone.
>
> Easter Island is about sixty miles in circumference and densely populated; the general appearance of the soil along the sea coast is of a dark red, and the soil appears to be good. They raise sugar cane, yams and potatoes in abundance. These productions of the islands, together with all kinds of shellfish, which they procure plentifully, constitute their subsistence.
>
> The natives are of a light colour; tall and handsome. Their chiefs are handsomely tattooed on their faces, necks, lips, tongues and arms. But they are in a most savage state, in consequence of which we did not venture to land, but were under the necessity of laying off in our boats at a distance from the shore while the natives swam to us with their goods. In this manner we obtained a sufficient quantity of potatoes and sugar cane to refresh the crew and thus prevent the scurvy which frequently visits whaleships while performing their long and perilous voyages.
>
> (Smith 1844: 168)

The *Spring Grove* then returned to Peru and the Galapagos before returning home via Valpaiso in October 1823 and on to London in March 1824 (Jones 1986: 73).

Also during 1823, the *Paragon* of Nantucket, Captain Henry Bunker, touched at Easter Island for supplies. Bunker reported that they "obtained sweet potatoes, yams, bananas, plantains, sugar cane etc., all of which were brought off by the natives of both sexes who swam to the boat lying at the back of the surf, and even for their produce they took nothing but whale scraps which they devoured with great eagerness" (Stackpole 1953: 238, citing *Nantucket Inquirer*, July 27, 1835). The *Paragon* was reported at Honolulu in April 1823 (Richards 2000: 42), and probably visited Easter Island later that year.

This standard method of trading was described explicitly by a young seaman on the third voyage of the Canadian whaleship *Margaret Rait* of St. John, New Brunswick, on December 26, 1843. After noting the island

> was teeming with inhabitants. . . . And the produce consists of sweet potatoes, yams, bananas and sugar cane,' he wrote that 'in exchange for these, they take the [crispy, deep fried] scraps which remain from whale blubber when it is dried out, small pieces of wood, and fish bones [perhaps whalebones?] The manner of exchanging articles with them is as follows: take your articles of trade – scraps etc – in your boat, and pull to within a cable length of the shore, which is pretty rough, and upon which the surf breaks heavily. The natives with a basket containing about half a peck of potatoes [tied] fast to their backs or round the waist, plunge into the breakers, swim off to the boats, pass their baskets in. We rifle their contents, put in the scrap, hand the basket to its owner, and away he goes to the shore . . . they were exceedingly animated and cheerful, almost continually laughing, and appeared to possess nothing savage or ferocious.
>
> (Robertson 1984: 69–72)

Evidently fragile items, including some that could not survive a wetting, could also be exchanged: in the New Brunswick Museum in St. John, there are two bark-cloth artifacts including a model fish (*pataki*) and a Janus-faced head with facial designs that may copy tattoo patterns (Richards 2008: 79–80).

Conclusions

The fascinating conclusion to draw from the records is the very high price that the Easter Islanders paid, indirectly, for their mode of trading just offshore and for their reluctance to allow any foreigners to remain on shore (Richards 2016: 12). Put in a wider Pacific context, it is extraordinary that as late as 1862 Easter Island still had had no resident foreign "beach combers," and no other foreigners living ashore. The first resident foreigners had been living in New Zealand, Fiji, and Tahiti by 1799, and in Hawaii and in the Marquesas Islands a little earlier, and foreign setters had been arriving

The impact of whalers, foreign visitors 185

in increasing numbers there ever since. Indeed, after 1858, there were more foreigners in New Zealand than Maori; and in Hawaii and elsewhere there were modern ports and thriving settlements with local born populations, often of mixed blood. By 1853, the Hawaiian Islands for example had nearly 1,000 part Hawaiians. And by contrast, Easter Island apparently had none.

But "civilization," including even the ubiquitous foreign and "native" missionaries, had passed by Easter Island, leaving only a few items of foreign manufacture, but little else, and certainly not the contribution to the human gene pool so prolific elsewhere in the Pacific. Thus by 1862, the Easter Islanders had not received the immunities that other indigenous peoples of the Pacific had acquired much earlier through close contact and interbreeding (McArthur 1967). So the smallpox and other diseases that were brought home to Easter Island by the pitiful handful of slaves that were released from Peru, were doubly devastating and doubly fatal.

The Easter Islanders had paid a very high price for their geographical isolation, and for the cultural isolation that followed when they chose to limit their trade with the foreigners to encounters offshore, outside the surf, as that distanced them from both the malign and the benign influences of foreign contact.

Note on sources

Several newspapers carried identical reports announcing that Henry Easter, "the youngest son of Crang-a-low, King of Easter Island," had been baptized at Rotherhithe, near London, in October 1811 (*The Morning Post* and *The Morning Chronicle*, both of London, both on November 6, 1811; *The Times*, London, on November 7; *Caledonian Mercury*, Edinburgh, November 9; *Hampshire Telegraph*, Portsmouth, November 11; *Lancaster Gazette*, Lancaster, December 21; and the *Massachusetts Spy* of January 8, 1811). However, what has not been found is an original, the slightly longer version, "dated London 31 October 1811," and carried to Sydney by Henry Easter, which the *Sydney Gazette* copied and published on August 8, 1812. This version alone notes King Crang-a-low's prohibition of shore visits, as quoted above in italics. Other information added to this Sydney report was that "this Native Prince . . . had been to school in England, spoke very tolerable English, and has manners more like those of a European than the native of a South-sea island. . . . The young man was handsome, very healthy, well cloathed and had every appearance of a satisfied mind." Henry Easter was then a crew member, "in what capacity we know not," on the London whaleship *Phoenix*, Captain William Parker, which had visited Sydney for a month from 29 June 29 to July 29, 1812 (Cumpston 1964: 81).

"Whether Captain Parker's idea was to return him [Henry Easter] to the place of his nativity [Easter Island], or not, we had not the opportunity to enquire; but from the benevolence of that gentleman's disposition, we cannot doubt this to have been his view" (*Sydney Gazette*, December 8, 1812).

Captain Parker took the *Phoenix* to New Zealand and the sperm whale fishery, returning to Sydney for two months, from June 22 to August 22, 1813. The *Phoenix* departed for Rio de Janeiro and London, and arrived home on May 24, 1814. On her next voyage, the *Phoenix* went first to the right whale fishery at the Derwent, and then to New Zealand for sperm whales, but called at Sydney from July 23 to August 3, 1815, and again in September, when she left for New Zealand and London (Cumpston 1964: 87, 97, 99). There is, alas, no evidence whether Captain Parker visited Easter Island again, and whether he ever returned Henry Easter there on either of these two voyages home, presumably both via Cape Horn, or on any of his subsequent whaling voyages.

References

Cumpston, J.S. 1964. Shipping Arrivals and Departures, Sydney 1788–1825. Roebuck Society Publication 22. Canberra: Roebuck Society.

Du Pasquier, T. 1982. *Les Baleiniers Francais au XIXe Siecle (1814–1868)*. Grenoble: Terre et Mer 4 Seigneurs.

Du Pasquier, T. 1990. *Les Baleiniers francais de Louis XVI a Napoleon*. Paris: Kronos, Henri Veyrier.

Jones, A. G. E. 1986. *Ships Employed in the South Seas Trade 1775–1861*. Canberra: Roebuck Society.

Kirker, J. 1970. *Adventures to China: Americans in the Southern Oceans 1792–1812*. New York: Oxford University Press.

Kugler, R. C. 1971. "The Penetration of the Pacific by American Whalemen in the 19th Century." In *Maritime Monographs and Reports No. 2*, pp. 20–27. Greenwich: National Maritime Museum.

Langdon, R., ed. 1984. *Where the Whalers Went: An Index to the Pacific Ports and Islands Visited by American Whalers (and Some Other Ships) in the 19th Century*. Pacific Manuscripts Bureau. Canberra: Australian National University.

Lund, J. N. 2001. *Whaling Masters and Whaling Voyages Sailing from American Ports*. Ten Pound Book Co.

McArthur, N. 1967. *Island Populations of the Pacific*. Canberra: Australian National University Press.

PMB. n.d. Pacific Manuscripts Bureau Microfilming Project. See Langdon. (The Numbers refer to the Microfilm Reels held at the PMB in Canberra).

Richards, R. 1994. *United States Trade with China, 1784–1814*. Special Supplement to Vol. 54 of *The American Neptune*. Salem, MA: Essex Peabody Museum.

Richards, R. 1996. *Jorgen Jorgenson's Observations of Pacific Trade: And Sealing and Whaling in Australian and New Zealand Waters before 1805*. With a translation by Lene Knight. Wellington: Paremata Press and Te Taa Haeretahi.

Richards, R. 2008. *Easter Island 1793 to 1861: Observations by Early Visitors Before the Slave Raids*. Los Osos, CA: Easter Island Foundation.

Richards, R. 2016. "Foreign Visitors to Easter Island 1772 to 1862: Isolation Proved a High Price to Pay." *Rapa Nui Journal* 30(1): 11–12.

Robertson, M. 1984. *Journal of the Margaret Rait 1840–1844, Captain James Doane Coffin*. Hantsport, Nova Scotia: Lancelot Press.

Sherman, S., J. Downey, V. Adams, and H. Pasternak. 1986. *Whaling Logbooks and Journals: 1613–1927: An Inventory of Manuscript Records in Public Collections.* New York: Garland Publishing Inc.

Smith, T. W. 1844. *A Narrative of the Life and Times of T. W. Smith.* New Bedford: Wm. C. Hill.

Stackpole, E. 1953. *The Sea Hunters: The Great Age of Whaling.* New York: Lippencott.

Starbuck, A. 1878. *History of the American Whale Fishery.* Washington, DC. (reprint by Castle Books, Secaucus, NJ. 1989).

Von Kotzebue, O. 1821. *A Voyage of Discovery, into the South Seas and Bering Straits.* . . . 3 vols. Translated from the Russian by H. E. Lloyd. London: Longman.

Ward, R. G., ed. 1966–67. *American Activities in the Central Pacific 1790–1870.* 8 vols. NJ: The Gregg Press.

10 Healing a culture's reputation
Challenging the cultural labeling and libeling of the Rapanui

Kathleen B. Ingersoll, Daniel W. Ingersoll and Andrew Bove

Introduction

Western explorers, anthropologists, archeologists, historians, novelists, and filmmakers create captivating and enduring stereotypes of other cultures. Once established, some of the stereotypes emerge as conceptually dominant and especially resistant to modification. We argue that the pre-European contact Rapanui (Easter Islanders) have been mislabeled and libeled since the initial encounters. Some of the prevalent stereotypes we will examine follow: the *moai* were built, not by the Rapanui, but by people from North or South America who arrived first but were later replaced by the Rapanui; the late period pre-European contact Rapanui became a society immersed in civil discord ruled by bloodthirsty warriors and cannibals; a massive cultural collapse occurred on Easter Island after the palms were harvested to extinction; Rapanui cultural practices led to ecocide. This paper challenges the dominant Western cultural characterizations of the Rapanui and attempts to redress the situation.

What the tourists think about Easter Island

One of us (Bove, n.d.), on a research trip to Rapa Nui in 2010, conducted a survey of what impressions visitors had about Rapa Nui before travelling there. At the top of the list were the theories of two writers: Thor Heyerdahl and Jared Diamond. Indirectly and/or directly, through Heyerdahl's work, especially Kon-Tiki and *Aku-Aku* (1959) (also see Heyerdahl 1989) and the volume by Diamond, *Collapse* (2005; and also see 2007), tourists to Easter Island, and many others worldwide, have had their consciousness of what Easter Island was and is constructed by Heyerdahl's and Diamond's ideas. From Heyerdahl derives the concept that Easter Island's monumental works – most notably, *moai* and *ahu* – were created not by people of Polynesian derivation, but by earlier colonists who sailed not from the west but from the east, most likely Peru. Later, the Polynesians arrived and displaced the North or South Americans, who had done the heavy lifting, replaced the symbol system with a new one, and led the island into a period of decadence.

From Diamond, though he is by no means the first to have made such claims, comes the latest prevailing notion that the Easter Islanders committed ecocide, in large part as a result of cutting down all the palm trees, thus exposing the soils to erosion, disrupting agriculture, and inducing population crash and cultural collapse.

O wad some power the giftie gie us: cultural labeling

Stereotypes exhibit a life of their own. They resist review, analysis, and replacement, and can function similarly to status markers (Becker 1973). Stereotypes do not confine themselves to inward thought processes – they also insert themselves into social interaction. In the discipline of sociology, an approach called labeling theory attempts to account for deviance: sociologists taking this approach claim "that most deviance results from some persons having been identified, or labeled, as deviants" (Stark 1989: 199). According to Liska's reporting on labeling theory (1981), once a person is labeled, the person's economic, occupational, and social chances may be altered. Even a person's own self-conception can be impacted. Sociologically, with the individual as the social unit of analysis, labeling theory makes sense. Perhaps you have been labeled at some point in your life, and then felt the limitations or the challenge of coping with the label – geek, nerd, wonk, dork, ivory tower intellectual, introvert, wallflower, prima donna, narcissist. . . But this paper is not all about us or you or about *persons* or individuals, but about culture. Here, we wish to transform an interaction-oriented sociological approach into a culture-oriented anthropological one. In labeling theory at the cultural level, stereotypes about cultures gain a foothold, and become part of that "given" cultural knowledge. And cultures interact with each other somewhat like persons within a society.

Westerners refer to Easter Island and its people using a Christian calendrical designation, a label attached by the Dutch expedition headed by Jacob Roggeveen in 1722, because his expedition "discovered" it at that time of the year: Easter, hence *Paasch Eiland*. In European languages, the names come out *Paasch Eiland, L'Île de Pâques, Isla de Pascua, Osterinsel*, or Easter Island. *Capitán de navio* Felipe González de Haedo, in November of 1770, visited Easter Island, planted three crosses on the Poike, claimed the land for Spain, and named it *San Carlos* (Fischer 2005: 60–62). Rapa Nui is what its residents now call it, and there are other names such as *kāinga* (territory) and *Te Pito 'o te Henua* (End of Land) (Fischer 2005: 91). Scholars writing about the island refer to it as Rapa Nui, two words, and the people, Rapanui, one word. Fischer (2005: 91) glosses Rapa Nui as "Greater Extremity." You can think of a name as one kind of cultural labeling, or in post-modern lingo, appropriation. A counter-labeling, counter-hegemonic move: use your own local name to refer to yourself or your place or your culture.

Early labeling: savages and cannibals

Polynesians, including Easter Islanders, have frequently been labeled "savages" and "cannibals." A major character in Melville's *Moby-Dick*, Queequeg, from the fictive island of Kokovoko, gives Ishmael a shrunken head. Ishmael, though shocked at first meeting, befriends Queequeg even though he comes from a culture thought to practice cannibalism. Melville mentions cannibalism numerous times in *Moby-Dick* (but please note that Melville in all his writings is actually very much an advocate of Polynesians and their culture). While expounding on the power of whales, he cites the attack of the whaleship *Essex* out of Nantucket (1967 [1851]: 178–179). In November 20, 1820, a whale rammed and sank the *Essex*. Philbrick tells the tale in his *In the Heart of the Sea* (2000). The Essex lay about 1500 nautical miles west of the Galapagos and about 40 miles south of the equator (Philbrick 2000: 79). The crew now in three whale-boats salvaged materials from the wrecked but still floating Essex hull. Captain Pollard recounted the decision about which way to sail:

> We now consulted about the course which it might be best to take – westward to India, eastward to South America, or southwestward to the Society Isles. We knew we were at no great distance from Tahiti, but were so ignorant of the state and temper of the inhabitants that we feared we should be devoured by cannibals, if we cast ourselves on their mercy. It was determined, therefore, to make for South America, which we computed to be more than two thousand miles distant.
> (Philbrick and Philbrick 2000: 197)

Stitched into Melville's copy of 1st Officer Owen Chase's published *Narrative of the Most Extraordinary and Distressing Shipwreck of the Whale-Ship Essex* were these notes:

> All the sufferings of these miserable men of the Essex might, in all human probability, have been avoided had they, immediately after leaving the wreck, steered straight for Tahiti, from which they were not very distant at the time, & to which, there was a fair Trade wind. But they dreaded cannibals, & strange to tell knew not that for more than 20 years, the English [25] [missionaries?] had been resident in Tahiti; and that in the same year of the shipwreck – 1820 – it was entirely safe for the [illegible] to touch at Tahiti.
> (Philbrick and Philbrick 2000: 78–79)

For all that the *Essex* crew feared landing on an island inhabited by cannibals, the survivors from two of the whaleboats lived by consuming the flesh of those who had perished, and on one of the whale-boats, actually agreed to draw lots to shoot one of their crew to be eaten, and so chose and did the deed. Three crew members, who had opted to stay on uninhabited Henderson Island instead of sailing on, managed to survive without consuming their fellows. They were later rescued. The fate of the third whaleboat is unknown.

The paragraphs below summarize the 18th and first half of the 19th century European encounters with the savages and cannibals of Easter Island. After boarding Roggeveen's ships anchored offshore (April 9, 1722), islanders somewhat boisterously snatched hats, caps, wood, and other items from the crew and ship and jumped overboard. The next day, the first and only day ashore, 134 fleet crewmen in five sloops landed, and started to march inland. About 20 stayed to guard the sloops on the shore; one shot, then many were fired. About 10 or 12 Rapanui lay dead, plus several wounded. The Rapanui were unarmed and no Europeans were harmed. Officer Cornelius Mens of the *Thienhoven*, who fired the first shot, "maintained that he had been assaulted, but all the other officers were of the opinion that he had acted out of cowardice" (Sayer 1990/1991: 51; also 1990, 1994). This is how European contact with the Rapanui began.

The visit of González in 1770 was mostly peaceful. During Cook's stop at Rapa Nui (1774), one islander was shot, perhaps only wounded, while trying to take a plant specimen bag from a sailor. During Lapérouse's visit (1786), French marines while in pursuit of an islander who took a boat grapnel were pelted with stones; they fired into the air but the islanders continued to throw stones. The marines then fired small shot at the stone throwers, but did not apprehend the assailant (Fischer 2005: 71). One version states blanks were fired (Richards 2008: 18). No deaths were reported. The 18th-century score: the Europeans lost lots of hats, caps, cloth, pieces of wood, and an anchor but no lives. The Rapanui lost a dozen or more lives, with an unknown number wounded.

During the first half of the 19th century, the situation worsened. In 1804, 1805, 1806, or 1808 (the accounts differ on the dates), the sealer *Nancy* of Boston stopped at Rapa Nui, seeking to capture hands to hunt seals on Más Afuera (now Alejandro Selkirk Island, one of the Juan Fernández Islands). A bloody battle took place as the crew sought prisoners, and 12 men and 10 women were captured and put in irons in the ship's hold. Three days sail later, the irons were removed, but the Rapanui jumped overboard and the men would not let themselves be recaptured (Richards 2008: 24). It is presumed that the men all drowned but one account claims that one managed to swim back to Rapa Nui. The recaptured women were taken to Más Afuera. Possibly the *Nancy* made more than one raid on Rapa Nui. The *Nancy's* was the first of a possible three massacres described by Richards (2008: 23, 37,75; 1822, ca. 1840) occurring before the slave raids in 1862. Two additional Rapanui were kidnapped during the first half of the century. Following the *Nancy*, many contacts and much of the trade occurred without landings, with Rapanui swimming or canoeing out to the ships. Stone peltings accompanied some European attempts at shore landings. When the

HMS *Blossom* visited in 1825, islanders made off with some caps, a clasp knife, and a musket ramrod. The ship's boats seemed to interest them the most. A disturbance about the time of the departure of the boats led to a hail of stone injuring several of a galley's crew. Several islanders were killed by gunfire. One of the boats contained several hundred stones of about a pound each (Richards 2008: 51–52).

One of the three journals from the whale-ship *Maria* out of Nantucket, 1833, stated: "The inhabitants I am informed are of a ferocious and savage nature and are cannibals which renders it very unsafe for the ship to stop there" (Richards 2008: 64). The *Maria's* captain, Alexander Macy, "talked hard about stopping to get some potatoes [probably sweet potatoes], but I believe he got frightened, and should like very well to stop there to have seen the monuments of those strange people" (Richards 2008: 64).

Not until 1856 does the death of a Westerner enter into the record. The bark *Prudent*, out of Greenport, New York, sent boats almost to shore, with the captain's warning "not to land as I thought they looked too savage, so we will trade from boats" (Richards 2008: 86–89). But the islanders took over the oars of a boat and capsized it, tearing the clothing off the crew members. The "boatsteerer" was captured and taken to shore where he, a man named Pease, stabbed and killed one of the islanders with a knife. The crew member Robert Weeks is thought to have been killed by means of a stone or paddle, but the event was not viewed by the crew – only the body. The boatsteerer (Pease) was forcibly rescued by 32 of his comrades. The islanders declined to return the boat.

Most of the visits from whalers sought refreshments (resupply) and exchange tended to take place peacefully, sometimes inshore. Richards estimates that between 1841 and 1851, whalers averaged about 8 visits per year with 24 known at this point (2008: 77). The existing ship logs report taking on impressive volumes – barrels and boatloads – of sweet potatoes, yams, bananas, and sugarcane, often bartered for whale scraps (Richards 2008: 77–85). Richards documents 8 visits in-shore between 1852–1862 (2008: 89–90).

Ship journals through the first half of the 19th century indicate healthy Rapanui populations; the volumes of produce bartered with the ships suggest that the economy of this small island was vigorous enough to produce a substantial surplus to barter with ships. Were the Rapanui savage? Look at the violence statistics from 1722 to 1862: 1 Westerner dead, several bruised by stones; several dozen Rapanui killed, 2 kidnapped, and an unknown number wounded. If statistics be the guide, who are the savages?

They couldn't have built the moai

We would now like to consider additional sorts of labeling in respect to Rapa Nui. The first of the labels concerns competency. The *moai* as a monumental class of objects totally fascinate Westerners. Just Google "Images of

Healing a culture's reputation 193

Moai" and you will find hundreds of examples. Who built the *moai*? How were they moved and erected? As with the impressive earthen mounds of North America, many Westerners could not imagine that the people who lived there – or their ancestors – possessed the wherewithal to fashion them, and therefore postulated other more likely candidates such as one of the Ten Lost Tribes of Israel, Siberians, Brazilians, Toltecs, Hindu, Tartars, or at least some extinct advanced race (Williams 1991: 41, 73–74, 168, 184). For Rapa Nui, the prevailing theory was that someone must have gotten there *before* the Polynesians.

Thor Heyerdahl's *Aku-Aku* (his spirit) says: "Where do you think the red-haired strain on Easter Island came from?" it asked. (Heyerdahl 1958: 356). In Peru, Pizarro asked:

> who the white-skinned redheads were. The Inca Indians replied that they were the last descendants of the *viracochas*." . . . According to their principal legend, before the reign of the first Inca, the sun-god Con-Ticci Viracocha had taken leave of his kingdom in Peru and sailed off into the Pacific with all his subjects.
> (Heyerdahl 1958: 357)

> When the Spaniards came to Lake Titicaca, up in the Andes, they found the mightiest ruins in South America – Tiahuanaco. They saw a hill reshaped by man into a stepped pyramid, classical masonry of enormous blocks beautifully dressed and fitted together, and numerous large stone statues in human form. They asked the Indians to tell them who had left these enormous ruins. The well-known chronicler Cieza de Leon was told in reply that these things had been made long before the Incas came to power. They were made by white and bearded men like the Spaniards themselves. The white men finally had abandoned their statues and gone with their leader, Con-Ticci Viracocha, first up to Cusco, and then down to the Pacific.
> (Heyerdahl 1958: 357; see Heyerdahl 1952: 224–268 for the legends he discusses)

> And I found what I hoped for.
> (Heyerdahl 1950: 18)

The legend continues, saying that the Con-Ticci Virachocha had long ears, which Heyerdahl then identifies with the Easter Island legends of the long and the short ears. The Kon-Tiki balsa raft voyage, of course, demonstrated that east to west travel through the Pacific was possible. Very few anthropologists or archaeologists subscribe to Heyerdahl's theory, but the everyday folk who have read and read Heyerdahl's books do. The book *Kon-Tiki*, alone, according to one source, has been translated into 70 languages and has sold more than 50 million copies (www.imdb.com/media).

If you buy into Heyerdahl's views, the contemporary Rapanui are descendants of invaders who, like the Vandals, overran and brought down a majestic culture. If you go with the majority of anthropologists, linguists, and archaeologists, they see the arrow pointing the opposite direction. Polynesians populated the Polynesian triangle from west to east (Kirch 2000). Polynesians excelled not only in navigation but also in all sorts of stonework. Contacts with South America and North America very likely took place, but the contacts involved *Polynesians* doing the sailing and distributing the sweet potatoes, etc., through the Pacific. Looking at it this way, the Polynesians regain credit for building those impressive *moai* and *ahu*.

Although we do not agree with Heyerdahl on many points, we do recognize the enormous contribution he and his team have made to Rapa Nui and Polynesian studies and to experimental navigation. His projects have generated a massive literature – volumes on archaeological excavations and anthropological observations and catalogs of art. The Kon-Tiki voyage helped to inspire the development of experimental studies in navigation and to open up new ways of thinking about migration and colonization. Today an exciting Polynesia cultural revival is unfolding, with a focus on Polynesian navigation. The navigation experiments of anthropologists Ben Finney (1994) and Sanford Low and others like Nainoa Thompson and David Lewis (1994 [1972]) and organizations like the Okeanos Foundation and the Polynesian Voyaging Society have offered alternatives to the theories of Heyerdahl. Last but not least, the presence of Heyerdahl and his team on Rapa Nui contributed to the growth of a tourist industry there, which otherwise might never have occurred – for example, the restoration of many *moai* to their *ahu* by William Mulloy (1997) and others, and the recording of diverse art forms (Heyerdahl 1975). Tourism, love it or hate it, with some 60,000 visitors per year is clearly the foundation of the Rapa Nui economy (Sanger 2011: 23; Campbell 2008: 48). And it is the *moai* and *ahu* that are the main draw, for this is heritage tourism, not tropical lay-out-on-the-beach-tourism.

Bottom line: the island of Rapa Nui is Polynesian from start to finish. The language, culture, and technology are thoroughly Polynesian. They navigated the Polynesian triangle and beyond in impressive craft. They built the *ahu* and raised the *moai*. Then their symbol system changed but that did not represent a collapse anymore than the shift from Feudalism to Capitalism indicated Western collapse. Rapanui culture remained and remains inspiring and impressive to this day. Rx for healing: grant the authors of the island monuments and their descendants their proper royalties.

The society committed ecocide

Diamond dismisses Heyerdahl's South American or Egyptian precursors and opts for Polynesians (2005: 82), but Diamond's Polynesians were pretty hard on the island's resources. The mantra now in the public realm via Diamond is as follows:

> The overall picture for Easter is the most extreme example of forest destruction in the Pacific, and among the most extreme in the world: the whole forest gone, and all of its trees extinct. Immediate consequences for the islanders were losses of raw materials, losses of wild-caught foods, and decreased crop yields.
>
> (2005: 107)
>
> Raw materials lost or else available only in decreased amounts consisted of everything made from native plants and birds, including wood, rope, bark to manufacture bark cloth, and feathers. Lack of large timber and rope brought an end to the transport and erection of statues, and also to the construction of seagoing canoes.
>
> (2005: 107)
>
> Easter's isolation makes it the clearest example of a society that destroyed itself by overexploiting its own resources.
>
> (2005: 118)

Now, Diamond was not the first to come up with this Easter Island narrative: as Peiser (2005: 514) points out, the ideas have been around since the early 1980s. Diamond published on the eco-disaster theme of Easter Island as early 1995, Flenley and Bahn in 1992, and Ponting, who made it a popular Green issue in 1992. But Diamond's publications, especially the journal, *Science*, for the research community, and *Collapse* (200,000 first copy printing) for laypersons turned Easter Island's ecocide into a household concept. Easter Island emerges as the metaphor for the World Island. By no means have Diamond's Easter Island ecocide claims gone unchallenged. For example Hunter-Anderson (1998); Rainbird (2002); Peiser (2005), Mulrooney et al 2010, and Lipo and Hunt (2010) have provided powerful counter-arguments, but their messages have not reached as broad an audience as Diamond. And perhaps their counter-messages lack the zing of unfolding apocalyptic drama.

Whereas in the case of Heyerdahl, few anthropologists and archaeologists – including a number of Heyerdahl's own team members – do not buy into the non-Polynesian source theory, so trying to dissuade anthropologists and archaeologists would be like preaching to the choir. Conversely, the Diamond ecocide theory represents the orthodox model (Peiser 2005: 514), one supported by many scientists and social scientists, including anthropologists and archaeologists, as well as laypersons. We believe the evidence supports a paradigm shift. We outline the major counters to the collapse school below:

They cut down all the trees. One of the most frequently mentioned causes for extinction is the over-harvest of the *Jubaea*-like palm and possibly other trees to supply rollers to move the *moai*. But as Hunter-Anderson (1998) and Ingersoll and Ingersoll (2012) point out, on average, only one to three *moai* per year were moved, hardly requiring a major draw. Additional potential palm uses would include fuel, for food (sugar, nuts, and hearts of palm), for fiber, and for wood. Published alternative explanations for extinction of the palms include climate change (too cold and/or too dry) and the introduction of the Polynesian rat (*Rattus exulans*) (Hunt and Lipo 2011). Our research on palms in general, points out many other possible variables such as nematodes, fungi, bacteria, viruses, insect infestations, birds, and combinations of these. All of these biological forms afflict palms elsewhere, but the Rapa Nui literature to date does not mention these possible causes of palm extinctions, although there is evidence for palm diseases which obliterated palms on other Pacific islands (Maude 1981: 6, Martienssen 2013; see Chapter 3 this volume). In a general cultural sense, the loss of palms due to human agency is somewhat perplexing as Polynesians tend to be exceedingly proficient at arboriculture throughout the Polynesian triangle.

Because they destroyed the palm forests, they could no longer make seagoing canoes. The dicot tree species used in most of Polynesia (*Alphitonia, Elaeocarpus, Acacia* [koa]) to make seagoing canoes were very rare to non-existent on Rapa Nui. In the pollen record, tiny numbers of pollen grains of these genera have been documented; in the archaeological record, a very small number of charcoal samples of these genera have been identified (Orliac 2000). The rare pollen grains might be ambient (wind-blown) and the charcoal might be derived from driftwood or derelict canoes made elsewhere in the Pacific. Could the palms have been harvested to make voyaging canoes? One review of the Pacific navigation literature by Hunter-Anderson (1998: 97, fn 2) found only a single of example of canoe hulls constructed from palm strips sewn together (Alexander 1902: 797), and these were relatively small, about 22 feet in length. We found one other instance in South America, canoes from hollowed out trunks used in fresh water, and generally only one use per hull before discard (Johnson and Mejía 1998).

The characteristics of palm – unlike trees such as oaks, pines, *Alphitonia, Elaeocarpus* and *koa* – render it a poor choice for marine use (Hunter-Anderson 1998). Palms, which are monocots, possess a relatively thin outer rind or epidermis and cortex, surrounding a soft, spongy interior composed of living, moisture- and nutrient-transporting vascular bundles. Drinking straw-like tubules constitute most of the interior, so different from trees in which only the thin active outer phloem, cambium, and xylem (from out to in) is alive, encasing the greater volume of inert wood, the annual rings. Palms lack those tough, supportive interior annular rings and are in general not as attractive for marine use. The greater mass of palm interiors consists of flexible vascular bundles which do not make strong boards, as is possible with the much more solid inner cores of trees. And for whatever reasons – fewer large trees, climate cooling, wind pattern changes – long distance travel slowed in almost all of Polynesia after the exploration and colonization phase.

Removal of the palms led to massive erosion and thus contributed to collapse. Soil erosion indeed occurred and the archaeological record documents it, but the period of increased erosion was followed by *increases* in

Figure 10.1 Boulder gardens at Hanga Oteo, the northern Rapa Nui coast. Virtually every stone you see has been mined, shaped, and placed by human agency

horticultural productivity due to new developments in technology. Extensive use of quarried rock for wind barriers, mulching, and surrounds, along with water diversion structures, successfully countered the wind and desiccation and erosional challenges. Soil amendments, especially those adding carbonized and other organic material to rock-mulched gardens and planting pits led to a sustainable horticulture (Figure 10.1). Now that more and more is being learned through archaeology about water control on Rapa Nui, we would venture that it is even possible that during the transition period horticulture – moving away from cultivating among palms to rock gardening – the Rapa Nui engineered a deliberately induced and controlled erosion to reconfigure some garden zones. That is, erosion itself potentially was a tool.

Following the disappearance of the palms, increased and sustainable productivity based on ingenious technology supported a larger population. There was no ecocide. Take a long, hard look at that "barren" landscape, as it is so often described, and see it in a new way: as a productive island garden, nearly every rock humanly shaped and rearranged, as much as in a Capability Brown park, and so also perceive the underlying anthrosoils, still fertile today. In your mind's eye, the slopes should no longer appear barren;

rather, predictable settlement patterns begin to emerge that tell a very different domestic story about the Rapanui people.

The population crashed

The Rapa Nui palm declined, perhaps gradually, then experienced total extinction, but the Rapanui population continued to grow until just before European contact. Because no census data existed until after European contact, the best data available on the Rapa Nui population are by proxy: the index for population reconstruction is by extensive site survey and site dating. The basic pre-European contact data look like this (Figure 10.2). If technological designations are added, the graph looks like this. Notice that in the second graph, the line approaches zero (Figure 10.3). But we just argued that ecocide never happened. It looks like the Rapanui almost became extinct some 500 years after deforestation.

The Rapanui did nearly become extinct in 1877, perhaps as few as 111 out of previous thousands inhabited Rapa Nui (Métraux 1971 [1940]: 23, citing Pinart 1878). But *not* because they had destroyed their environment. A first cause of population loss may have been diseases introduced by each successive European exploratory visits, beginning in the 18th century with Roggeveen (1722); González (1770); Cook (1774); La Pérouse (1786). Hunt and Lipo (2011) suggest a series of epidemics followed by population rebound after each. By way of comparison, thousands were lost to epidemics in the Austral Islands during the 1820s (Richards 2012). During the late

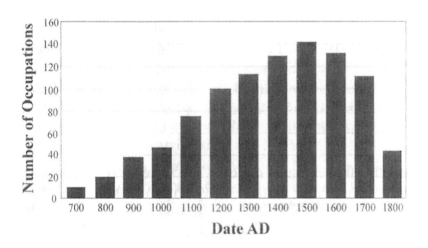

Figure 10.2 A population proxy: the number of dated occupation sites in the south central coastal region of Rapa Nui, through time, based on obsidian hydration dates. Source: Stevenson and Cardinali 2008: 8, Figure 8.1–8.5, redrawn and used with permission of the authors

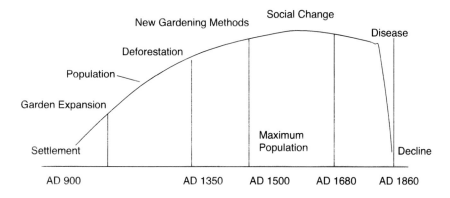

Figure 10.3 The relations of population and technology
Redrawn from a presentation given by C. M. Stevenson 2008, at St. Mary's College of Maryland, with permission.

18th century and first half of the 19th century, dozens of ships stopped at Rapa Nui: scientific expeditions, state visitors, whalers, and sealers (Richards 2008). This multiplied opportunities for exposure to disease.

But the worst happened in December 1862 when slavers landed, captured as many as 1500 Rapanui and took them to Peru to be sold as domestics and plantation workers (Fischer 2005: 89); a small number went to the Chincha Islands to mine guano. In Peru and the Chinchas, massive numbers of blackbirded (capture by ruse or forceful kidnapping of Pacific peoples for labor purposes) Polynesians from Rapa Nui, the Marquesas, Tuamotus, and the Australs succumbed to diseases like tuberculosis, dysentery, and smallpox. Bishop Jaussen of Tahiti and others took action that led to an international protest and repatriation of survivors. A horrendous smallpox epidemic brought in by the American whaleship *Ellen Snow* at Callao, took away most of the Polynesians grouped for repatriation (the Peruvians were vaccinated, but not the Polynesians) (Fischer 2005: 90–91). About a dozen Rapanui were repatriated, but one or more carrying smallpox brought a devastating epidemic to the island. Altogether, an estimated 6000 black-birded Polynesians perished. Maude in his study *Slavers in Paradise* (1981: 182) wrote: "For Polynesia the Peruvian slave trade thus constituted genocide of an order never seen before or since in her history."

Conditions on Rapa Nui worsened. Diseases like smallpox and tuberculosis took their toll. In 1869, Maison Brander and their agent Detrou-Bornier began "buying" up Rapa Nui land for a sheep ranch. In 1871, with less than 700 remaining, the "Exodus" occurred: Bishop Jaussen had arranged with Maison Brander to transport nearly 300 Rapanui to Mangareva, then of those some to Tahiti, to become indentured servants or laborers. Additional removals to Tahiti followed. While most such departures from Rapa Nui were willful, few or none would ever have left if disease and blackbirding had not destroyed the social and cultural fabric. Still, some declined to leave: in 1878, Pinart reported 111 souls. Imagine you live in a world once of 5000 folks. Take away 1500 who never return. Bring on disease. End up with 700. Then an exodus. You are one of the 111 remaining on home turf. How do you feel? Ecocide? Genocide?

Bottom line: Rapa Nui ecocide is a convenient untruth promoted by environmentalists looking for an apocalyptic *Lorax* tale that appeals to the popular press. The Rapanui were enslaved, extradited, battered by disease, suffered rendition, relieved of their land, and then, we have not mentioned this yet, effectively interned in the village of Hanga Roa until the 1960s. Scholars and Western nations: stop blaming the victim and take responsibility for what really happened. Credit the Rapanui for unparalleled resilience in the face of adversity. Today, Rapanui culture is alive, well, and vibrant, against all odds.

And yes, there are trees and palms on Rapa Nui.

References

Alexander, A. B. 1902. "Notes on the Boats, Apparatus, and Fishing Methods Employed by the Natives of the South Sea Islands, and Results of Fishing Trials by the Albatross." In *Report of the Commissioner for the Year Ending June 30, 1901*, U.S. Commission of Fish and Fisheries, George M. Bowers, Commissioner, 741–829. Washington, DC: Government Printing Office.

Bahn, P. and J. Flenley. 1992. *Easter Island Earth Island*. London: Thames and Hudson, Ltd.

Becker, H. S. 1973. *Outsiders: Studies in the Sociology of Deviance*. New York: Free Press.

Bove, A. n.d. In Preparation. "Easter Island as a World Heritage Site."

Campbell, P. 2008. "Easter Island: A Pathway to Sustainable Development." *Rapa Nui Journal* 22(1): 48–53.

Diamond, J. 1995. "Easter Island's End." *Discover Magazine* 16(8): 63–69.

Diamond, J. 2005. "Twilight at Easter." In *Collapse: How Societies Choose to Fail or Succeed*, 79–119. New York: Viking.

Diamond, J. 2007. "Easter Island Revisited." *Science* 317: 1692–1694.

Finney, B. 2009. "Ocean Sailing Canoes." In *Vaka Moana Voyages of the Ancestors: The Discovery and Settlement of the Pacific*, edited by K. R. Howe, 100–153. Honolulu: University of Hawai'i Press.

Finney, B., M. Among, C. Baybayan, T. Crouch, P. Frost, B. Kilonsky, R. Rhodes, T. Schroeder, D. Stroup, N. Thompson, R. Worthington, and E. Yadao. 1994. *Voyage of Rediscovery: A Cultural Odyssey through Polynesia*. Berkeley: University of California Press.

Fischer, S. R. 2005. *Island at the End of the World: The Turbulent History of Easter Island*. London: Reaktion Books.

Heyerdahl, T. 1952. *American Indians in the Pacific: The Theory Behind the Kon-Tiki Expedition*. Chicago: Rand McNally and Company.

Heyerdahl, T. 1959. *Aku-Aku, the Secret of Easter Island*. New York: Pocket Books [and Chicago: Rand McNally].
Heyerdahl, T. 1975. *The Art of Easter Island*. Garden City, NY: Doubleday.
Heyerdahl, T. 1984 [1950]. *Kon-Tiki: Across the Pacific by Raft*. New York: Pocket Books.
Heyerdahl, T. 1989. *Easter Island: The Mystery Solved*. New York: Random House.
Hunt, T. L. and C. P. Lipo. 2010. "Ecological Catastrophe, Collapse, and the Myth of 'Ecocide' on Rapa Nui (Easter Island)." In *Questioning Collapse: Human Resilience, Ecological Vulnerability, and the Aftermath of Empire*, edited by P. A. McAnany and N. Yoffee, 21–44. Cambridge: Cambridge University Press.
Hunt, T. L. and C. P. Lipo. 2011. *The Statues That Walked: Unraveling the Mystery of Easter Island*. New York: Free Press.
Hunter-Anderson, R. L. 1998. "Human vs Climatic Impacts at Rapa Nui: Did the People Really Cut Down All Those Trees?" In *Easter Island in Pacific Context South Seas Symposium: Proceedings of the Fourth International: Conference on Easter Island and East Polynesia*, edited by C. M. Stevenson, G. Lee, and F. J. Morin, 85–99. Los Osos, CA: Easter Island Foundation.
Johnson, D. V. and K. Mejía. 1998. "The Making of a Dugout Canoe from the Trunk of the Palm Iriartea Deltoidea." *Principes* 42(4): 201–205, 208.
Kirch, P. V. 2000. *On the Road of the Winds*. Berkeley: University of California Press.
Lewis, D. 1994 [1972]. *We, the Navigators: The Ancient Art of Landfinding in the Pacific*. Second Edition. Honolulu: University of Hawaii Press.
Liska, A. E. 1981. *Perspectives in Deviance*. Englewood Cliffs, NJ: Prentice-Hall.
Martienssen, T. 2013. "Palmerston: The Island at the End of the Earth." *BBC News*, Palmerston, Cook Islands. December 29, 2013. www.bbc.co.uk/news/magazine-25430383.
Maude, H. E. 1981. *Slavers in Paradise: The Peruvian Labour Trade in Polynesia, 1862–1864*. Canberra: Australia National University Press.
McCall, G. 1994. *Rapanui: Tradition and Survival on Easter Island*. Second Edition. Honolulu: University of Hawaii Press.
Melville, H. 1967 [1851]. *Moby-Dick*. Harrison Hayford and Hershel Parker, editors. New York: W. W. Norton & Company.
Mulloy, W. 1997. *The Easter Island Bulletins of William Mulloy*. Los Osos, CA: The Easter Island Foundation.
Mulrooney, M. A., T. N. Ladefoged, C. Stevenson, and S. Haoa. 2010. "Empirical Assessment of a Pre-European societal Collapse on Rapa Nui (Easter Island)." In *The Gotland Papers: Selected Papers from the VII International Conference on Easter Island and the Pacific: Migration, Identity, and Cultural Heritage*, edited by P. Wallin and H. Martinsson-Wallin, 141–153. Visby: Gotland University Press.
Orliac, C. 2000. "The Woody Vegetation of Easter Island between the Early 14th and the Mid-17th Centuries AD." In *Easter Island Archaeology and Research on Early Rapanui Culture*, edited by C. M. Stevenson and W. S. Ayres, 211–220. Los Osos, CA: Easter Island Foundation.
Peiser, B. 2005. "From Genocide to Ecocide: The Rape of Rapa Nui." *Energy and Environment* 16(3/4): 513–539.
Philbrick, N. 2000. *In the Heart of the Sea: The Tragedy of the Whaleship Essex*. New York. Viking.
Philbrick, N., and T. Philbrick, eds. 2000. *The Loss of the Ship Essex, Sunk by a Whale: Thomas Nickerson, Owen Chase, and Others*. New York: Penguin Books.

Ponting, C. 1992. *The Green History of the World*. London: Penguin.

Rainbird, P. 2002. "A Message for the Future? The Rapa Nui (Easter Island) Ecodisaster and Pacific Island Environments." *World Archaeology* 33(3): 436–451.

Richards, R. 2008. *Easter Island 1793 to 1861: Observations before the Slave Raids*. Los Osos: Easter Island Foundation.

Richards, R. 2012. *The Austral Islands: History, Art, and Art History*. Paramata, New Zealand: Paremata Press.

Sanger, K. K. 2011. *Easter Island: The Essential Guide*. Los Osos, CA: The Easter Island Foundation.

Sayer, H. von. 1990. "Some Details of the Journal of Jacob Roggeveen." *Rapa Nui Journal* 4(3): 33–35, 45.

Sayer, H. von. 1991 [1990]. "Some Details from the Journal of Captain Bouman on the Discovery of Easter Island." *Rapa Nui Journal* 4(4): 49–52.

Sayer, H. von. 1994. "The Complete Journal of Cornelius Bouman, Master of the Ship Theinhoven, Forming Part of the Fleet of Jacob Roggeveen, from 31 March to 13 April 1772 During Their Stay around Easter Island." *Rapa Nui Journal* 8(4): 95–100.

Stark, R. 1989. *Sociology*. Third Edition. Belmont, CA: Wadsworth Publishing Company.

Stevenson, C. M. 2008. Sustainability Lessons for Easter Island: Re-Thinking Rapa Nui's Ancient Agriculture. PowerPoint Presentation, Slide 49.Lecture delivered at St. Mary's College of Maryland, Department of Anthropology, March 6, 2008.

Stevenson, C. M. and S. Haoa Cardinali. 2008. "The Rapa Nui Context." In *Prehistoric Rapa Nui: Landscape and Settlement Archaeology at Hanga Ho'onu*, 1–14, edited by C. M. Stevenson and S. Haoa Cardinali. Los Osos, CA: The Easter Island Foundation.

Williams, S. 1991. *Fantastic Archaeology: The Wild Side of North American Prehistory*. Philadelphia: The University of Pennsylvania Press.

11 Reflections

You may have noticed from your reading in this volume, as in nearly all realms of life, a typhoon of controversies has enveloped Rapa Nui – even in what to have called the island. Our contributors have discussed a few of these disputed themes and show that our understanding of the island environment, the human impacts to that environment, and the social/technological response to an evolving context have changed profoundly over the decades. Nevertheless, who now advances the latest solution to the unresolved quandaries of Rapa Nui environmental and social change? Who ventures to question the logic of the former solutions? Whose data now evoke criticism? Who can resolve the differences?

Let us begin with a basic question, ever controversial: when did everything happen on Rapa Nui, such as with the matter of first colonization? Tools such as radiocarbon dating, stratigraphic excavations and pollen core analysis, and radiocarbon isotope and obsidian hydration dating provide the means to build chronologies, but each tool offers advantages and suffers disadvantages. Researchers formerly advocated first colonization dates for Rapa Nui as early as AD 300–400 (Bahn and Flenley 1992; Flenley and Bahn 2003). More recently, with the systematic evaluation of archaeological and linguistic evidence the pattern of human dispersal across the Pacific has come into sharper focus (Kirch 2000). This has been augmented by a re-evaluation of the radiocarbon dates on Rapa Nui (Mulrooney 2013), and has supported the assertion that first colonization might not have occurred until as late as AD 1100–1300 (Wilmhurst et al. 2013). Here, the work of Stevenson et al. (Chapter 1), indirectly supports the revised chronology with colonization beginning around AD 1100; authors Mieth and Bork (Chapter 2) feel that reliable evidence suggests valid dates as early as AD 700–900, which chronological framework they feel allows adequate time for population growth and cultural development before what is observed between AD 1100 and AD 1300 in the form of a much more developed culture. One thing we can expect: different models of cultural and environmental processes will continue to be advanced according to differing and competing chronologies. Even within the framework of a single scholar's research through time, we may encounter variation accompanied by revised inferences and conclusions as fresh, new data become available. The study by Flenley and Butler, reported in Chapter 4 offers a case in point – their most recent pollen and charcoal analysis suggests the possibility of a human presence on Rapa Nui sites as early as AD 100. Charcoal particles within lake sediments are a proxy for human modification of the landscape and a convincing alternate interpretation has been hard to come by.

Considering tiny Rapa Nui lifts only around 170 square kilometers (less than 66 square miles) above the sea, a disproportionately massive literature – books, conference tomes, newspaper and journal articles, travel logs, and internet sites await the curious reader. Perhaps the *moai* win first place in gaining the attention of both professionals and the public (e.g. Hunt and Lipo 2011): how were the *moai* built and by whom, how were they moved, why were they allowed to fall down, and why did the *ahu* that once supported them come to be reworked into new configurations? Pick a question. If you want to investigate how *moai* made it from quarry to *ahu* many theories, often accompanied by experiments, invite your perusal. These multi-ton images could be dragged on wooden rollers, slid on small rocks like roller bearings, pulled on wooden sledges prone, on wooden sledges supine, by walking (like when we modern folk move refrigerators), by rolling huge cylindrical discs containing the future interior *moai* to be birthed at the end site. These efforts may have been conducted on special roads and ramps, with or without sweet potatoes for lubricant . . . or even exploded from a volcano. All of these theories are fascinating, of course, but we the editors, want you the reader to stop and look around, and think about the perspective of the *moai* (assuming they were conscious beings present from the very beginning) once situated on *ahu*, and who gazed inland. What was the world they looked upon and how did it change over time?

Another lingering question revolves around the uncertainty of interchiefdom conflict in the 17th century and was there an accompanying population crash? This question has generated a substantial controversy, with the promoters and supporters of collapse and ecocide theory gaining international attention. Drawing upon the oral history (Routledge 1919; Métraux 1940) and its synthesis by Mulloy (1975), Bahn and Flenley (Bahn and Flenley 1992; Bahn and Flenley 2011 Flenley and Bahn 2003) have supported the collapse model in their books but not directly in their contributions to this volume (Flenley and Butler, Chapter 4, and Bahn as one of the coauthors of Chapter 7). Several chapters in this volume offer alternatives to the collapse position. Boersema (Chapter 8) tests the question through examination of the observations recorded in the journals of the first European visitors and models of population growth, and concludes "the theory claiming that deforestation on Rapa Nui caused hunger, armed conflict and collapse is clearly untenable." Ingersoll and Ingersoll (Chapter 11) argue, rather than a collapse, that cultural resilience was expressed in the archaeological record. The loss of the palms did not lead to societal chaos but rather to an ingenious and sustainable horticultural system (Wozniak, Chapter 5), and that no major population crash occurred until Europeans came onto the scene in the AD 1860s. Although not directly dealing with the concept of collapse, Richards (Chapter 9), picking up where Boersema left off, in surveying the whalers' and other accounts from the late 18th century until AD 1862, sees the Rapanui of that time period, not as impoverished but as sufficiently prosperous to supply a generous range of provisions to their visitors. As he states: "There is no evidence of a shortage of food to trade." While not a focal point of their chapter (Chapter 6), Vogt and Kühlem identify the collapse theory as advanced in Diamond (2005) as "rejected by the majority of scholars." We would amend that statement just a bit to "the majority of scholars engaged in Rapa Nui research." Editors Ingersoll and Ingersoll have observed that anthropologists *not* engaged in Rapa Nui studies in general still support the collapse theories.

Despite these statements, detailed alternate models for socio-political development have not emerged. The expression "continuity" has been used to describe the last 150 years of Rapa Nui prehistory (Rainbird 2002), a period that includes the European post-contact period (AD 1722–1867). Despite the appearance of a host of new archaeological signatures that include changes in burial practice from traditional cremation to extended burial, large-scale stone and earthen replicas of European ships (perhaps 60 to 70 meters in length), and the construction of subterranean rooms, alternate hypotheses for the interpretation of archaeological features are lacking. We are in many ways still reliant upon the collapse scenario in our interpretation of the archaeological record. For example, the houses at Orongo are still seen as a 16th century development even though the radiocarbon dates are on bulk samples and untrustworthy (Mulrooney 2013, Pollard et al. 2010); subterranean rooms (*ana kionga*) with tunnel entrances are interpreted as "refuge caves" based upon a single informant questioned by Metraux (1940) in the 20th century; obsidian "spear points" (*mata'a*) continue (until recently) to be interpreted as weapons of war even though such evidence of their use in that context is lacking (Church 1998; Church and Rigney 1994; Church and Ellis 1996; Lipo et al. 2016).

Equally surprising is the fact that few explicit research designs have emerged to examine the regional prehistoric demography of Rapa Nui. The early contact literature has been considered, and re-considered, with informative outcomes, but a step forward from this point on would now seem to be the responsibility of archaeology. A vast archaeological record has been documented by regional pedestrian surveys conducted by McCoy (1976); Cristino et al. (1981); Vargas et al. (2006); Stevenson and Haoa (2008), and it would seem time for innovative methodologies that could find material residues indicative of habitation size, number of occupants, duration of site activities, and changes in social and economic activities. The analysis of radiocarbon dates (Mulrooney 2013) and obsidian hydration dating (Stevenson et al. 2015) has provided some general regional data about the trends in island landscape use identified by these proxy measures but they do not directly document at high temporal resolution changes in architecture, subsistence, social organization, and ritual events that we need to clarify the late prehistory/protohistory of Rapa Nui. There appears to be a great need for an intensive focus on household archaeology that can detail the past. Such an approach was initiated many decades ago within the context of the Norwegian Archaeological Expedition (Heyerdahl and Ferdon 1961) but has only continued on sporadically (e.g. McCoy 1976; Ayres et al. 2000; Stevenson and Haoa 2008). With over 15,000 archaeological features to choose from there should be no shortage of suitable sites for excavation.

In contrast to the above, there has been no shortage of alternate hypotheses about the process of deforestation on Rapa Nui. What happened to the palms; were they cleared by swidden agriculture, overharvested for their sap, destroyed by climate change, inhibited in their regeneration by seed destruction from rats, or decimated by disease? The answer may lie in one or more of these reasons and it is up to researchers to find evidence within the archaeological record. Material remains to date includes burned palm stumps which supports the preferred explanation for the destruction of the 16 million palm trees. This is in keeping with observations about human destructive capacity on other Pacific islands and continental settings. Yet, not all forested islands were denuded (Kirch 2000) and other possibilities external to human activity should be explored. Finding convincing evidence may be difficult especially if that evidence is at the micro or molecular level.

The modern research into Rapa Nui's past has been ongoing now for a little over fifty years, and that research has become much more expansive, exploring well beyond the monumental and the arts, to develop new understandings of culture, society, and the landscape. For example, not until the 1990s did archaeologists begin to realize how much the landscape had been transformed from a natural volcanic landscape to an anthropogenic one, above and below ground, and one supporting a novel kind of sustainable horticulture. This major perspective change facilitates a whole new way of seeing Rapa Nui: the landscape emerges potentially and dramatically transformed in your mind's eye. The chapters by Stevenson et al. (Chapter 1), Wozniak (Chapter 5), and Vogt and Kühlem (Chapter 6) illustrate the incredible evolution of the landscape, impacting horticulture, architecture, water management, and ritual.

Another intriguing outcome of expanded horizons can be identified in the recognition of previously underestimated symbolic expression, the case with ship and canoe symbols, variously located in material culture such as house configurations, ornaments, petroglyphs on rocks, *moai*, and *pukao* (topknots), and in large scale stone and earthen replicas of ships. Reading across the chapters by Lee et al.(Chapter 7), Boersema (Chapter 8), and Richards (Chapter 9), one can appreciate the presence of this powerful and extensive ship and canoe symbolism, a symbolism perhaps rivaling that of the *ahu*, *moai*, and birdmen.

If you wished to encounter mysteries solved, we hope this book, which finds more questions than answers, did not disappoint you. There is still much to learn about Rapa Nui and the Rapanui, past and present. It is the voyage that makes life exciting rather than crossing the finish line.

References

Ayres, W., R. L. Spear, and F. R. Beardsley. 2000. "Easter Island Obsidian Artefacts: Typology and Use-Wear." In *Easter Island Archaeology: Research on Early Rapa Nui Culture*, edited by C. M. Stevenson and W. S. Ayers, 173–190. Los Osos, CA: Easter Island Foundation.

Bahn, P. and J. Flenley. 1992. *Easter Island Earth Island*. London: Thames and Hudson, Ltd.

Bahn, P. and J. Flenley. 2011. *Easter Island, Earth Island*. Third Edition. Rapa Nui: Rapa Nui Press.

Church, F. and J. Rigney. 1994. "A Microwear Analysis of Tools from Site 10-241 Easter Island- An Inland Processing Site." *Rapa Nui Journal* 8(4): 101–105.

Church, F. and G. Ellis. 1996. "A Use-Wear Analysis of Obsidian Tools from an *Ana Kionga*." *Rapa Nui Journal* 10(4): 81–88.

Church, F. 1998. "Upland, Lowland, Citizen, Chief: Patterns of Use-Wear from Five Easter Island Sites." In *Easter Island in Pacific Context South Seas Symposium: Proceedings of the Fourth International Conference on Easter Island and East Polynesia* (University of New Mexico, Albuquerque, 5–10 August 1997), edited by C. M. Stevenson, G. Lee, and F. J. Morin, 312–315. Los Osos, CA: Easter Island Foundation.

Cristino, C., P. Vargas, and R. Izaurieta. 1981. *Atlas Arqueologica de Isla de Pascua*. Santiago, Chile: Universidad de Chile, Centro de Estudios Isla de Pascua.

Diamond, J. 2005. "Twilight at Easter." In *Collapse: How Societies Choose to Fail or Succeed*, 79–119. New York: Viking.

Flenley, J. and P. Bahn. 2003 [2002 New York]. *Enigmas of Easter Island: Island on the Edge*. Oxford: Oxford University Press.

Hunt, T. L. and C. P. Lipo. 2011. *The Statues That Walked: Unraveling the Mystery of Easter Island*. New York: Free Press.

Kirch, P. V. 2000. *On the Road of the Winds*. Berkeley: University of California Press.

Lipo, C. P., T. L. Hunt, R. Horneman, and V. Bonhomme. 2016. "Weapons of War? Rapa Nui Mata'a Morphometric Analyses." *Antiquity* 90(349): 172–187.

McCoy, P. 1976. *Easter Island Settlement Patterns in the Late Prehistoric and Protohistoric Periods*. New York: Bulletin 5, Easter Island Committee, International Funds for Monuments, Inc.

Métraux, A. 1940. *Ethnology of Easter Island*. Bernice P. Bishop Museum Bulletin 160. Honolulu: Bishop Museum Press.

Mulloy, W. 1975. "Preliminary Cultural Historical Research Model for Easter Island." In *Las Islas Oceanicas de Chile*, edited by G. E. Duco and P. A. Espina. Vol. 1, 105–151. Santiago: Instituto de Estudios Internacionales de la Universidad de Chile.

Mulrooney, M. A. 2013. "An Island-Wide Assessment of the Chronology of Settlement and Land Use on Rapa Nui (Easter Island) Based on Radiocarbon Data." *Journal of Archaeological Science* 40: 4377–4399.

Pollard, J., A. Paterson, and K. Welham. 2010. "Te Miro O'one: The Archaeology of Contact on Rapa Nui (Easter Island)." *World Archaeology*, 42(4): 562–580. doi: 10.1080/00438243.2010.517670.

Rainbird, P. 2002. "A Message for the Future? The Rapa Nui (Easter Island) Ecodisaster and Pacific Island Environments." *World Archaeology* 33(3): 436–451.

Routledge Mrs, S. (Katherine). 1919. *The Mystery of Easter Island: The Story of an Expedition.* London: Sifton, Praed, and Co. Ltd.

Stevenson, C. M. and S. Haoa. 2008. *Prehistoric Rapa Nui.* Los Osos, CA: Easter Island Foundation and Bearsville Press.

Stevenson, C. M., C. Puleston, P. M. Vitousek, O. A. Chadwick, S. Haoa, and T. N. Ladefoged. 2015. "Variation in Rapa Nui (Easter Island) Land Use Indicates Production and Population Peaks Prior to European Contact." *Proceedings of the National Academy of Sciences* 112: 1025–1030.

Vargas, P., C. Cristino, and R. Izaurieta. 2006. *1000 Años en Rapa Nui: Arquelogía de asentamiento.* Santiago: Editorial Universitaria, S.A.

Wilmhurst, J. M., T. L. Hunt, C. P. Lipo, and A. J. Anderson. 2013. "High Precision Radiocarbon Dating Shows Recent and Rapid Colonization of East Polynesia." *Proceedings of the National Academy of Sciences* 108(5): 1815–1820.

Index

agricultural impact: deforestation, 32–56, 195–7; European explorer observations, 166–9; Hiva Hiva lava flow settlements, 9–11, 20, 22, 26–9; *see also* rock gardens
ahu, 106–7; Ahu Hanua Nua Mea, 114, 124–6; allure, 1–3; Ava Ranga Uka A Toroke Hau, 53, 114, 124–6, 129; Hiva Hiva lava flow settlements, 15; *pukao*, 133–52
Ahu Akahanga, 141–2, 148
Ahu Hanga Poukura, 147
Ahu Hanga Te'e, 141–2
Ahu Hanua Nua Mea, 114, 124–6
Ahu Heki'i, 142–3, 147, 149
Anakena, 35, 62
anthropogenic, 12; environmental changes, 32–56
Ap soil, 92, 94, 96, 107; *see also* rock gardens
Ava Ranga Uka A Toroke Hau, 53; Ahu Hanua Nua Mea, 114, 124–6; archeological artifacts, 116, 118–20, 122–30; water management, 114–18, 120–4, 125–8, 129–30

Bahn, Paul, 157, 158, 204
bananas, 99, 103, 105
Bayoud disease, 64–5
Behrens, Carl, 161, 166
birdman cult, 133, 141–2, 144, 146–7, 148, 150
Bouman, Cornelius, 99, 160–1, 166, 167
Bursaphelenchus cocophilus, 65–6

collapse theories, 2–3, 157–9, 188–200
Cook, James, 99, 137, 160, 162, 163, 167, 169

deforestation, 32–56, 88–9; environment, civilization, 34–6, 42–56, 195–7; environment, pre-civilization, 9, 33, 37–41; Poike peninsula, 40, 47–8, 51–2; pollen analysis of, 36–8, 46; radiocarbon dating, 44–6; societal effects, 54–6; soil nutrient analysis, 50–2; *see also* pollen analysis
Diamond, Jared, 1–2, 6, 157, 158, 189, 194–5

Easter Island *see* Rapa Nui
Easter Islanders *see* Rapanui
Easter Island Petroglyph Documentation Project, 138–40
environment, civilization, 88–91; deforestation effects, 34–6, 42–56, 195–7; pollen analysis, 74–84, 75, 77
environment, pre-civilization, 9, 33, 37–41, 78–81; pollen analysis, 74–84, 75, 77
European contact, 6–7, 156–70, 179–86, 190–2; Behrens, Carl, 161, 166; Bouman, Cornelius, 99, 160–1, 166; Cook, James, 99, 137, 160, 162, 163, 167, 169; explorer accounts, 159–70, 166; Forster, Georg, 149–50, 162, 163, 166, 168–9; Forster, Johann, 162–3, 166; La Pérouse, 99, 114, 149, 151, 152; Pickersgill, Richard, 163, 167; Roggeveen, Jacob, 156, 159–61, 166, 167, 168; whaler accounts, 179–86, 192
exchangeable Ca, 19, 21, 22, 23, 24
Explorer contact, 159–70, 166, 190–2; Behrens, Carl, 161, 166; Bouman, Cornelius, 99, 160–1, 166; Cook, James, 99, 137, 160, 162, 163, 167, 169; Forster, Georg, 149–50, 162,

163, *166*, 168–9; Forster, Johann, 162–3, *166*; La Pérouse, 99, 114, 149, 151, 152; Pickersgill, Richard, 163, 167; Roggeveen, Jacob, 156, 159–61, *166*, 167, 168

Flenley, John, 157, 158, 204
Forster, Georg, 149–50, 162, 163, *166*, 168–9
Forster, Johann, 162–3, *166*
fungi *see* Bayoud disease
Fusarium oxysporum forma specialis albedinis, 64–5

gardening *see manavai*; rock gardens; subsistence strategies

Hanga Roa, 62
hare moa, 15, 16, 98, 107
Heyerdahl, Thor, 1–2, 188–9, 193–4
HHGU2, 19–21
HHP01, 19–20, 22–5
Hiva Hiva lava flow settlements, 3, 9–29, *10*, *11*; agricultural impact, 9–11, 20, 22, 26–9; archaeological survey, 11–24, *11*, *12*, *13*, *14*, *17*, *18*, 26; chronological dating, 24–6; rock gardens, 10–12, 15–19, *17*, *18*, 26–9; soil nutrient analysis, 19–24, *20*, *21*, *22*, *23*, 27
horticulture *see manavai*; rock gardens; subsistence strategies

Jubaea, 36, 39–43, *39*, *41*, 62–5, 83; Ava Ranga Uka A Toroke Hau, 120, 124, 126; *see also* palm tree

La Pérouse (site), 95, 96–7, 99, 142
La Pérouse, Jean-François, 99, 114, 149, 151, 152
lithic mulch *see* rock gardens

mana, 134, 137, 148
manavai: Hiva Hiva lava flow settlements, 15, 17; subsistence strategies, 91, 97–8, 102–4, 107; yams, 102–3, *104*
Maunga Terevaka: deforestation, 40, 47; subsistence strategies, 94, 97, 106
moai: allure, 1–3; Ava Ranga Uka A Toroke Hau, 124; moving, 106–7; origins, 5, 7, 192–4, 204; *pukao*, 133–8, *136*, 148–50; *see also* Rapanui

Nancy, 181, 182, 191
nematodes *see Bursaphelenchus cocophilus*

obsidian hydration dating: Hiva Hiva lava flow settlements, 24–7, *25*, 29; population analysis, *198*, 203, 205
Oryctes rhinoceros, 66–7

Pacific rat, 46–7
paenga, 15, 16, 26, 107, 122, 133
Palmerston palm blight, 60–2
palm tree: Ava Ranga Uka A Toroke Hau, 120, 124, 126; Bayoud disease, 64–5; *Bursaphelenchus cocophilus*, 65–6; deforestation, 32–56, 195–7; disease-based extinction, 59–71; evidence of, 39–43, *39*, *40*, *41*; *Jubaea*, 36, 39–43, *39*, *41*, 62–5, 83; *Oryctes rhinoceros*, 66–7; Palmerston palm blight, 60–2; *Paschalococos disperta*, 36, 39, 59, 68, 81, 83; *Phytoplasma palmae*, 66; Rapa Nui virus, 62–3; *Rattus exulans*, 46–7; sap utilization, 48–50; Tongareva palm blight, 59–60, 61–2
palynology *see* pollen analysis
Paschalococos disperta, 36, 39, 59, 68, 81, 83; *see also* palm tree
petroglyphs, 133–152, *136*, *139*, *141*, *143*, *145*, *146*, *149*; Ahu Akahanga, 141–2, 148; Ahu Hanga Poukura, 147; Ahu Hanga Te'e, 141–2; Ahu Heki'i, 142–3, 147, 149; analysis, 147–52; birdman cult, 133, 141–2, 144, 146–7, 148, 150; documentation techniques, 138–41; Easter Island Petroglyph Documentation Project, 138–40; Puna Pau quarry, 144–7, 148, 151–2; Vinapu, 142–4, 149–51; *see also pukao*
phytoliths, 37
phytoplasma *see Phytoplasma palmae*
Phytoplasma palmae, 66
Pickersgill, Richard, 163, 167
Poike penisula: deforestation, 40, 47–8, 51–2; subsistence strategies, 94, 96–7
pollen analysis: comprehensive island survey, 74–84, *75*, *77*; coring results and interpretation, *75*, *77*, 78–81; in deforestation investigation, 36–8, 46
population analysis, 25–8, *55*, 82–4, 89, 157–8, 164–6, 198–200, 204–5

poro: Hiva Hiva lava flow settlements, 15, 24; *pukao,* 137, 138, 151
pre-civilization environment, 9
pukao, 133–52, *136, 139, 141, 143, 145, 146, 149*; Ahu Akahanga, 141–2, 148; Ahu Hanga Poukura, 147; Ahu Hanga Te'e, 141–2; Ahu Heki'i, 142–3, 147, 149; analysis, 147–52; characteristics, 133–8, *136*; documentation techniques, 138–41; Easter Island Petroglyph Documentation Project, 138–40; *mana,* 134, 137, 148; *poro,* 137, 138, 151; Puna Pau quarry, 144–7, 148, 151–2; Vinapu, 142–4, 149–51; *see also* petroglyphs
Puna Pau quarry, 144–7, 148, 151–2

Quebrada: archeological artifacts, 116, 118–20, 122–30; water management, 114–18, 120–4, 125–8, 129–30

radiocarbon dating: deforestation, 44–6; Hiva Hiva lava flow settlements, 24–6; pollen analysis, 75–7
Rano Aroi: pollen analysis, 36, 75; water management, 114
Rano Kau: pollen analysis, 36, 75–84, *75, 77*; water management, 114
Rano Raraku: pollen analysis, 36, 74–5, 79, 80; water management, 114, 126, 130
Rapanui: collapse theories, 2–3, 157–9, 188–200; counter-theories on societal collapse, 195–8; European contact, 6–7, 156–70, 179–86; petroglyphs, 133–152; population analysis, 25–8, *55*, 82–4, 89, 157–8, 164–6, 198–200, 204–5; rock garden utilization, 10–12, 15–19, 26–9; subsistence strategies, 87–108, *101, 102, 103, 104, 105*
Rapa Nui, 1; agricultural impact, 3–6, 9–11, 20, 22; Ahu Hanua Nua Mea, 114, 124–6; Ava Ranga Uka A Toroke Hau, 113–30; deforestation, 32–56, 88–9, 195–7; disease-based palm extinction, 59–71; European contact, 6–7, 156–70, 179–86; Hiva Hiva lava flow settlements, 3, 9–29, *10, 11*; petroglyphs, 133–52;

pollen analysis, 74–84, *75, 77*; pre-civilization environment, 9, 33, 37–41, 87–8; rock gardens, 10–12, 15–19, 26–9
Rapa Nui virus, 62–3
Rattus exulans, 46–7, 83
resin P, 19, 20, *21, 22, 23,* 24
rock gardens: categories, 94–5; Hiva Hiva lava flow settlements, 10–12, 15–19, *17, 18,* 26–9; subsistence strategies, 91–6, *93,* 100–2, 106–7; taro, 98–102, *101, 102*
Roggeveen, Jacob, 156, 159–61, *166, 167,* 168

settlements: Hiva Hiva lava flow, 3, 9–29, *10, 11*; Te Niu, 92, 97–9, 101, 106–7
slash-and-burn, 100, 107, 206
soil analysis: deforestation, 50–2; exchangeable Ca, 19, *21, 22, 23,* 24; HHGU2, 19–21; HHP01, 19–20, 22–5; Hiva Hiva lava flow settlements, 19–24, *20, 21, 22, 23*; resin P, 19, 20, *21, 22, 23,* 24; subsistence strategies, 92–9
Sophora toromiro, 70–1
stone mulch *see* rock gardens
subsistence strategies, 87–108, *101, 102, 103, 104, 105*; bananas, 99, 103, 105; *manavai,* 91, 97–8, 103–4, 107; rock gardens, 91–6, *93,* 100–2, 106–7; taro, 98–102, *101, 102*; yams, 98–9, 102–3, *103, 104; see also* rock gardens
swidden agriculture, 27, 100, 107, 206

taro, 98–102, *101, 102*
Te Niu, 92, 97–9, 101, 106–7
Tongareva palm blight, 59–60, 61–2
top knots *see pukao*

Vinapu, 142–4, 149–50, 149–51

water management, *49, 52, 53,* 113–14; Ava Ranga Uka A Toroke Hau, 114–18, 120–4, 125–8, 129–30; Quebrada, 114–18, 120–4, 125–8, 129–30
Whaler contact, 179–86, 192

yams, 98–9, 102–3, *103, 104*